SOCIAL INTELLIGENCE

A REALISTIC HANDBOOK FOR WORK AND LIFE

JONATHAN BALDIE

First edition published in 2019 by Subject Zero Ltd.

eBook ISBN: 978-1-9993098-2-4

Paperback ISBN: 978-1-9993098-3-1

Hardcover ISBN: 978-1-9993098-4-8

CONTENTS

To my faithful dog Poppy, for whom I need none of the following strategies.

SELECTED BIBLIOGRAPHY

The 33 Strategies of War by Robert Greene; Profile. Copyright © Robert Greene and Joost Elffers, 2006.

Abraham Trembley's Strategy of Generosity and the Scope of Celebrity in the Mid-Eighteenth Century by Marc J. Ratcliff; *Isis* 95. Copyright © Marc J. Ratcliff, 2004.

The Archetypes and the Collective Unconscious by C. G. Jung; Routledge. Copyright © Bollingen Foundation, Inc., 1959.

Battle Cry of Freedom: The Civil War Era by James McPherson; Oxford University Press. Copyright © Oxford University Press, 1988.

Benjamin Franklin: An American Life by Walter Isaacson; Simon & Schuster. Copyright © Walter Isaacson, 2003.

The Campaigns of Napoleon by David G. Chandler; Weidenfeld and Nicolson. Copyright © David G. Chandler, 1967.

China Watcher: Confessions of a Peking Tom by Richard Baum; University of Washington Press. Copyright © University of Washington Press, 2010.

The Confederate War by Gary W. Gallagher; Harvard

ACKNOWLEDGEMENTS

I will begin by thanking my parents, Deborah and Nicholas Baldie, for their encouragement in this project. Your feedback over our Sunday dinner time discussions provided me with excitement and validation for the project.

I must also thank Robert Greene for introducing me to the concept of Social Intelligence in his book *Mastery*. As Robert correctly points out in his master work, no long-lasting success can come without an understanding of human nature—his various other works have certainly instilled this timeless lesson for me.

I would also like to thank Becca Allen for copyediting the text, and Damonza for providing the cover design.

I must not fail to mention the encouragement from my partner Katie Preece, whose feedback on early drafts helped me to realise that this project could really mean something to people. Your suggestion for the title "How Not to Be a Dick at Work" was most welcome, and we'll keep it as the unofficial codename for the project.

There is no better way to conclude than to acknowledge

the colleagues who have provided me with countless examples of Social Intelligence (and its lack thereof) throughout
my career, inspiring me to start this project. Without the
fascinating drama and pain you supplied, this book would
not exist.

ABOUT THE AUTHOR

Jonathan Baldie is a writer and software developer. He has a degree in mathematics and lives in Stoke-on-Trent, England.

INTRODUCTION

The Oak and the Reeds

A very large oak was uprooted by the wind and thrown across a stream. It fell among some reeds, which it thus addressed: "I wonder how you, who are so light and weak, are not entirely crushed by these strong winds." The reeds replied, "You fight and contend with the wind, and consequently you are destroyed; while we on the contrary bend before the least breath of air, and therefore remain unbroken, and escape."

— AESOP

There is nothing more valuable than the ability to understand people. Whether we like it or not, we are bound to live our lives in the social realm, among others just like ourselves. Each of us acts in ways dictated by ageless and unconscious rules of human nature, directing us to feel envy, pressuring us to follow social norms. But often these behaviours are mysterious and we struggle to predict their effects.

We find ourselves hurt by people's critical words and inconsiderate actions; at work, we can't understand why people reject our ideas, no matter how logical they seem to us. On the new realm of the Internet, we feel an instinctive triggering of anger at a friend's social media post. Our inability to read people's motives, to see things from their perspective, and our resultant social blunders, makes us cause each other needless pain.

We have all heard one story or another of a person with great creative potential, held back and misunderstood both by their peers and greater society. Their ideas seem profound, yet they're only met with defensiveness and scorn. They fail to win support for their product or their cause not merely due to the quality of their work, but more often due to their inability to understand the people around them. This person's creative potential goes to waste, and if we fall into the same traps, not paying attention to our peers, then the same will happen to us. People working in all fields can make their professional lives much less stressful and much more profitable by embracing the realities of human nature rather than fighting them.

The most tragic cautionary tale of this phenomenon is that of Nikola Tesla (1856-1943). The Serbian scientist was perhaps the most prolific inventor of the modern age. But people who were far less creative than him, though far more skilled at dealing with people, constantly outwitted and outplayed him. Tesla's inventions included the alternating current (AC) system of transmitting electricity that is still used to this day; this revolutionary technology was subjected to a smear campaign by the tycoon Thomas Edison, who understood better than anyone the power of reputation and how to put talented people to his own use. Tesla is also the real father of radio, having filed a patent in 1897 that Guglielmo Marconi completely relied upon for his famous

broadcast across the English Channel in 1899; but Marconi
was much better at communicating his achievement to the
public and therefore gained the credit. And the great Pitts-
burgh magnate George Westinghouse persuaded Tesla to
accept a buyout of his AC electricity system patents for just
over $200,000—a princely sum for the time, no doubt, but a
mere shade of the boundless fortunes they were truly worth.
Tesla died alone, penniless, and bitterly resentful of the
people who had so easily exploited his mind and its creative
products. He received little credit for the true magnitude of
his impact on modern society until long after his death.

The sad story of Nikola Tesla's life may fill us with feelings of anger and injustice, and this is understandable. But
Tesla is not without blame. He repeatedly made the mistake
of believing that the quality of his ideas and work alone
would win people over—but he would always upset these
people in some way, offend them and make them feel defensive, or he would put his naïveté on display, making him a
ripe target for predatory entrepreneurs. Tesla felt disgust at
smooth talkers and what he perceived as their insincere,
empty talk. But rather than learn how to deal with such
types, he fell victim to their tricks repeatedly throughout his
career.

How often have we fallen into this trap? We believe—
against the evidence—that there is some meritocratic arc of
the universe that will recognise our good intentions and
anoint us at the end of the journey. When people demonstrate the poor results of our intentions, we close up and get
defensive, even though we're staring at the most literal feedback we can ask for. The truth is that humans often choose
warm, comforting ideals over cold reality, and we cannot
measure the sum of the pain caused by people making this
false choice across history. You must understand that the
most profitable realisation you can make in life is to see this

reliance on good intentions for the dangerous siren call that it is. Our inability to see past this illusion results in wasted time and needless anxiety. No matter how brilliant you are, you simply cannot succeed in this world unless you treat human nature as a legitimate force.

The only way to snap out of this illusion and break the cycle of social blunders is to develop a better understanding of the people around us. A sense, of sorts, that allows us to read people's behaviour and act in a way that will develop positive results for everyone involved. We will call this sense **Social Intelligence**. Developing such an understanding will not be an easy process, but it may be the most worthwhile journey we can ever embark upon. For some, it may involve unlearning decades-old destructive habits, and cringing as we recognise some past blunder of our younger gauche selves. But enduring all this pain will be worth the payoff: the ability to read and predict people's intentions from their actions or subtler cues; to identify what is really bothering someone and ease their anxiety, and to see how we have unintentionally rubbed someone the wrong way and then mend the relationship. Social Intelligence is the most real kind of superpower we can attain.

The quintessence of this Social Intelligence we seek is Jeanne-Antoinette Poisson (1721-1764), better known as Madame de Pompadour. As the royal mistress of King Louis XV of France, she was in a notoriously perilous position. Young ladies in the court of Versailles constantly vied for Louis' attention, and past kings of France had usually become bored with their string of mistresses as they inevitably aged and became unable to meet the king's demands in bed. Past royal mistresses, painfully aware of this position, would become greedy for royal largesse and bully their fellow courtiers while they could still hold the king's affections. Unfortunately, in doing so, they would bitterly alienate their court colleagues, who happily hastened her decline. Observing the futility of this cycle, Madame de Pompadour used a different strategy. She would organise hundreds of masked balls, fêtes, and theatre shows to entertain the famously fickle king and keep his focus away from the bedroom, keeping herself at the centre of his attention. On top of this, Madame de Pompadour would always treat her fellow courtiers with the utmost politeness and respect, earning her much love and affection from Louis' nobles and cabinet ministers. Although some courtiers did plot to get rid of Madame de Pompadour, the king defiantly kept her in the official role of royal mistress because of his love for her and the power she had gained within Versailles. She died of an illness at the age of 43, after an unprecedented twenty-year reign as the king's official mistress. This middle-class daughter of a bank clerk had risen to become the most powerful woman in France, gaining total control over the king himself.

Although we are long past the time of royal mistresses and scheming courtiers, do not make the mistake of thinking that the same dynamics of human nature are gone—they are more alive than ever. At your workplace or group, there are people trying to finagle the limelight, happy to do so at the expense of others. If you're not careful, these types will steal the credit for your hard work, or manoeuvre you into petty battles that distract you from your key projects. Fortunately, there is a way to defend yourself from this common dynamic, and your approach will be two-fold: you will not make grand, one-off displays, because these are only temporary and fleeting at best; instead, you will win support from your colleagues gradually, staying out of office politics and growing a positive reputation for your good work and respectful manner. In a similar fashion, it is better to grant your "king" small, regular favours, than to make large and clumsy gestures that make you seem like a suck-up to your colleagues. Gaining the support of your fellow "courtiers" is always more important than simply attaching yourself to the boss, since power most reliably sits upon a wide base. In times of emergency, when it seems like your job is on the line, your colleagues' support for you will pay off, and you can delight in the alarmed surprise of the more attention-seeking predators in your group. Understand that the person holding the strongest position in a group is rarely the loudest or most autocratic, but the one with the widest base of support.

The first step in acquiring Social Intelligence is to look back at your past social blunders: the unintended faux pas that upset your boss; the time your spouse blew up at you over the seemingly smallest thing, or your tense dealings with the jealous co-worker who marked you in their crosshairs from day one. You should identify where you might not have appreciated the other person's perspective, and how you could have made the situation more mutually beneficial. *But if they're rude to me, why shouldn't I be rude right back?* It is natural to sense feelings of resentment and injustice bubble up during this exercise, as we feel the temptation to hurl blame and demand more respect and better treatment. The key to analysing past mistakes is to stay calm and rational by treating it as an observational exercise—be like the entomologist observing the behaviour of unfamiliar creatures, taking notes. It would not make sense for the scientist to resent the beetle encroaching on the ant's territory—instead, she recognises it as part of the beetle's nature. Nor does the decent historian allow personal feelings to interfere with his job of getting at the truth of some past battle or political event. Observe these past blunders of yours without passion, and make the following oath to yourself: "I shall never repeat such a mistake again," and let the matter drop.

You are not your mistakes, and the only way to avoid making them is to learn the lesson and move on.

THE SEVEN SOCIAL BLUNDERS

In identifying your past blunders you may notice patterns emerging—common failings that seem to repeat themselves over time. This means you are making excellent progress, because you're identifying the traits deep within your personality that are evidently holding you back. It is easy to feel defensive or uneasy when reading about these blunders, but this work is critical to enhance your understanding of human nature and deal with people in a more positive manner. The following seven social blunders are common to all people across cultures and the ages.

Failing to validate others. Aside from food, water, and air, human beings have no greater need than to feel validated. We feel the signature of this basic need when we're passed over for a promotion at work, not listened to in a conversation, or our friends ignore our big news on social media. In each of these cases we don't feel recognised by other people, and it is a deeply hurtful pain—a pain that you have likely inflicted on someone else. Conversely, we love spending time with friends who take the time to understand us, the family member who always knows the right gift to give us, and the boss who rewards our efforts with public praise, assuring us that our intelligence and efficiency are not going unnoticed. These people reflect a mirror of consideration and love to everyone around them, and they deservedly receive the same love and respect right back. They are models of Social Intelligence, and you should follow their example.

Submitting to waves of emotion. We must not repress or deny our emotions, but recognise that most people live their lives in a daily torment, a chaotic whirlwind of unpredictable whims. These people rarely achieve any long-term success or satisfaction, because they can never see past the current moment. Not only that, but it is easy for others to control them—bullies at school and in the work world are adept at recognising emotional people and take a sadistic joy in twisting them in knots. If this has happened to you, then you'll know how irrational this makes you, as you blurt out incoherent comebacks that just make you look ridiculous, and the bully grins with delight. Understand that if a person can activate and engage your emotions, then you are their slave. When your boss intentionally makes a comment to wind you up, with an arrogant smirk on his face, refuse to give him the satisfaction of seeing your heart clench with anger. Ignore him, or pretend you misheard and make him repeat the immature comment for all around to hear—we will explore many such tactics later in this book. But above all, you must stay calm and assess what the emotional abuser is trying to do. A bully's only tactic is to make you feel just as anxious and unsafe as they constantly feel during every waking moment of their lives—if you successfully deny them this power, then you have severely blunted any danger they might pose to your sanity.

The need for certainty. Life constantly throws challenges at us, and they land hardest when we least need or expect them. From the aspiring novelist facing her tenth query rejection, to the software developer whose latest project is full of bugs and overrun deadlines, we must all deal with a daily tide of rising and falling setbacks. It is useless to deny this fact of life, and even worse to fight it. If we don't see the opportunities in these temporary setbacks, then we'll become consumed with doubt until we become its victim, shrinking into our shell and refusing to come out and deal properly with people. This is the primary pitfall that we need to avoid. The Chinese character for "crisis" is the character for "danger" in front of the character for "opportunity." All crises, no matter how hopeless they seem in the moment, are filled with hidden opportunities. That novelist's tenth query rejection might give her the clarity to see that there's something wrong with how she's approaching agents. She realises that this has actually helped her become a better writer than if she'd breezed through and won a six-figure contract on her first try. The software developer's bugs enable him to practise key coding skills and give him the chance to to develop his skills in dealing with conflict, perhaps from an angry customer or boss. He grows from the ordeal and has an incrementally stronger skill set. The poet John Keats coined the term "negative capability" to denote this ability to deal with constant setbacks for the sake of the greater campaign. Those who lack this ability are blown about by life's daily problems and ultimately fail; those who embrace it cannot help but grow their skills, becoming stronger with each issue that fate throws their way.

Often in the modern work environment, there is a strong emphasis on creating standard operating procedures for common scenarios. This is a powerful practice, because it allows us to use proven techniques and create predictable outcomes. But it is possible to take this approach too far. If we rely on methodologies that worked in the past, then we shut off our strategic capabilities and expose ourselves to danger. We must therefore accept that each situation will be different, offering subtle changes in the level of threat. Rather than seeing this constant change and variation as something to fear and control, we must embrace it. Learn fluid strategies and principles rather than rigid tactics, and always stay alert to changes in the situation. This fluid approach has been the source of power for great generals in history, such as Napoleon, Douglas MacArthur, and Sun-Tzu. Do not be so arrogant to assume that you can always predict reality or control it—instead, see the beauty in its fluidity, and use each new situation to sharpen your principles and strategies.

Waterloo syndrome. The myth of overnight success, and the undue focus on a situation's culminating point, is one of our society's greatest problems. Video games and addictive apps play on our dark need for instant gratification, eating up our attention span until we can barely focus on the most basic work. When looking at the history around the French emperor Napoleon, there's often an overemphasis on the Battle of Waterloo. Far more books have been written and published on this one culminating moment at the end of Napoleon's career than on any of the events that led up to it. This mistake ignores twenty years of fascinating build-up: his masterful victory at the Battle of Austerlitz, the exploitation of the rigid Prussians, and the disastrous invasion of Russia. We make this same mistake in goal-setting for ourselves and others, and the impatience that results from it hurts our chances of growing mutually beneficial relationships with people. We cannot force such relationships to grow—we have no choice but to leave this task to the gradual movement of time itself, and the consistency of small but considerate actions.

Seeing everything through the moral lens. We live in a time when great public figures are judged not for the results of their actions, but for the morality of the words they express in public. They all struggle to appear the most sympathetic to some minority group, hoping that the media will anoint them with a trend piece that puts their moral rectitude on display. Instant communications have made it easy for a person's words to get twisted and misunderstood, damaging their reputation. We have reached this situation because many people see events and actions around them with a moral lens, constantly judging, and feeling the need to express these judgements to anyone who'll listen. Social media encourages us to forget the principles of Social Intelligence, because it incentivises the sharing of "viral" anger-inducing content.

Allowing your vision of both past and present to be warped, distorted, and coloured by this moral lens is a great mistake because you won't see reality as it is. To whine about some perceived injustice is to deny a clear aspect of reality, all to no obvious utility. In truth, we all feel an instinctive dislike for such whiners, especially those possessed by ideology. These people may outwardly preach their moral judgements, and some may agree, but many more will respond negatively to their arrogance and lack of perspective. The study of history is particularly liable to the dangers of the moral lens. The moraliser looks at the past horrors of slavery, genocide, and inequality, and snorts with patronising derision at their ancestors' actions, as if they would have acted differently. Understand that history is the biography of the human race. It's *your* story as much as it is everyone else's. To think that you would have acted more virtuously in someone else's shoes is the height of arrogance. It is the same when viewing events in the past and present. Too many people use this as an excuse to dismiss and patronise others—this is no way to build positive relationships.

To determine whether you're seeing the world through the distorting view of the moral lens, try to notice whenever you feel a pang of dislike for some self-interested action a colleague makes. Instead of judging this person's actions, try to see things from their perspective—put yourself in their shoes and assess rationally whether you'd do the exact same thing. The essence of this enhanced liberal perspective lies in the phrase "Live and let live." Taking off the moral lens, and being more open to other people's perspectives can relieve years of misery and repression, making you much more productive and pleasant to be around for other people. Recognise how ideas have controlled your behaviour in the past, and make the decision to take this control back. The Swiss psychotherapist Carl Jung (1875-1961) was right when he said that "People don't have ideas; ideas have people."

In 399 BC, in the Athenian Agora, 500 citizens sentenced the philosopher Socrates to death. In modern times we often see Socrates's execution as an inhumane tragedy. But it reveals much about human nature, as well as the usual fate of moralisers. Despite growing to adulthood during the rise of Pericles—history's first liberal politician—and Greece's golden age of trade and democracy, Socrates developed a set of beliefs that set him at odds with his fellow Athenian citizens. He was not a democrat, nor did he believe in equality— in his view, the people were like a herd of sheep in need of direction from a wise shepherd. Writing in the third century AD, Diogenes Laertius described how Socrates "discussed moral questions in the workshops and the marketplace," and that his unpopular views, expressed with a condescending tone, caused his grumbling (and unwilling) audience to "set upon him with their fists or tear his hair out."

Socrates's main accuser, the poet Meletus, brought the trial against the great philosopher out of personal offence for his often scathing criticisms. While we associate Socrates with wisdom and virtue, his contemporary Athenians saw him as an irreverent bore, and the source of three tumultuous anti-democratic movements between 411 and 401 BC. Even during his trial Socrates moralised at the court, arguing that they were persecuting him because they didn't truly understand his views—an infuriating charge in any age. They *had* to get rid of him. We can admire Socrates for his steadfastness in the face of persecution—his death, after all, made him a martyr and proved a profound turning point in Western history. You should stand up for your beliefs when necessary, but in everyday dealings with your community and work colleagues, err on the side of keeping your views to yourself.

Rigidity in the face of contradiction. An uncooperative, inflexible attitude is conspicuously anti-seductive. People who show this attitude cannot build positive relationships, since they clearly display to others that they won't move an inch for anyone. Others may relent to their stiff demands, but then the relationship is marred by resentment lurking underneath the surface. Although we often talk about staying true to our principles and not engaging in activities that don't feel right, it is easy to take this too far and never cooperate with anyone. To become less rigid, it is not necessary to compromise our beliefs or repress the essence of what we truly think—it merely involves being flexible and letting people show you their world. If a friend excitedly tells you about some new diet they're trying out and encourages you to look into it, giving you research materials that they've found useful, then the worst thing you can do is dismiss them and flatly refuse to even look into it. *But I'm just being honest.* You can be honest without completely crushing someone's passionate spirit—that person now knows to stay clear of you, and to not involve you in something that might be of future benefit.

In a negotiating situation, it may sometimes work to your strategic advantage to refuse to budge, but it rarely works in day-to-day business. Your refusal to compromise on anything had better be backed up with a service or product that's known for its quality, or potential partners will avoid you like the plague. Recognise this lack of reasonable compliancy for what it is: a fear of failure, of opening yourself up to compromise, of leaving the safe status quo. It is most common among people with anxiety-filled childhoods, who tighten up and react like prey animals to any kind of threat, whether perceived or real. An inflexible attitude is also strategically weak, since it makes you hopelessly predictable to predatory types. Adopt a flexible, open attitude instead, and reap the countless benefits.

Taking things personally. At the root of our defensive reactions to people lies our refusal to deal with or acknowledge our dark side. There are parts of you that you've become skilled at hiding. These aspects to your personality make you flinch. If you see a post on social media or an article that expresses that aspect in some way, or if you come across someone who embodies that trait, you instinctively look away, sneer with derision, make a snarky comment. *That's not me*, you tell yourself, but the strong reaction you had towards it shows that the precise opposite is true. Modern society has trained people to present a rigid persona: the front we present to the world, whether that's being a hard worker, someone who's punctual, or someone who's a good Christian, anything we actively work to make people know about ourselves. We repress anything that directly contradicts this self-concept of ours, and these thoughts get buried deep into our unconscious.

These internalised issues get projected onto others, and we perceive the slightest comment as a personal slight, making us react defensively. Carl Jung called this bubbling cauldron of resentment and frustration the shadow. If we follow our instincts and further repress the shadow, this naturally distorts our perception of reality. If we identify with one political party and hear someone make an opposing comment, then we instantly recognise it and reject it without taking the viewpoint under calm consideration. Perhaps we even make a nasty comment right back at them—ruining any good future interaction we might have had with them. But there are certain people we meet who just seem comfortable with themselves. They never get defensive or offended, they're wonderful to be around—we can feel the energy radiating from them. These people have integrated their shadow. They've identified what sets off their insecurities and become okay with their limitations.

The most important part of this is to become aware of the parts of us we least want to show—only then can we achieve the calm, objective mental state necessary for true Social Intelligence. Shining light on these negative emotions and moving the rumblings of the unconscious into our conscious awareness can be one of the most freeing activities we can engage in, leaving us feeling like we've shed a heavy load off our shoulders. We no longer act defensively, or take every comment from our coworkers personally; we instead become relaxed, seductive, and pleasure-giving in our demeanour.

HOW TO USE THIS BOOK

This book will teach you a series of invaluable skills, strategies, and methods for surviving and thriving in the social realm. Each chapter contains a diverse range of historical examples that demonstrate its lessons, followed by detailed analyses that explain how you can put them to use yourself. Though each chapter is self-contained and can be read independently, a full start-to-end read-through is recommended for first timers. This will give you a broad overview of Social Intelligence and allow you to enjoy the full range of diverse stories across time and cultures.

In Part I you will learn five sets of strategies for attaining success in the social realm, with many practical examples to use in the modern workplace. These will form a strong foundation, allowing you to develop positive relationships and avoid the most common social blunders described in the previous section. Next, Part II will address the most common challenges facing leaders. You will learn how to build a loyal, hard-working, and happy team that constantly produces creative ideas and effective solutions. Stories of successful leaders in the business world and elsewhere are described in full, always followed by a detailed analysis of the lessons they provide. Lastly, Part III will equip you with a set of methods for defending yourself against the more malicious elements of the social realm. You will learn how to ward off aggressors, credit-stealers, and tyrannical bosses, all with a consummate smoothness and grace.

Heed the following warning before you begin: The advice given in this book comes from detailed research into the lives of masters of the social realm, and on first impression you might see them as overly pragmatic, even amoral. As explained previously, you must resist any instinct to read this book with a moral lens—if you find this too difficult, then it may be safer to turn back, lest you become seduced by the power that true Social Intelligence can bring. Understand that you have a right to seek a life with less anxiety and more insight, and also that there is no morality in being bullied or unknowingly offending others. You should seek to gain a deep understanding of the inner workings of the modern workplace, rather than becoming emotional and fighting useless battles against patterns that don't change. True virtue is not in banishing all the snakes from the Garden of Eden, but in becoming a better snake-handler. By learning more about people and how to deal with them, you'll become a better friend, colleague, and leader. Social Intelligence is an approach that develops very real positive outcomes, more so than any abstract sense of morality.

It is a mistake to think of this book as a how-to manual for manipulating or deceiving people. See it as a reliable sword and shield to protect yourself against the predatory vipers out there who are all bursting to exploit your naïveté. This book will give you the prudence required to survive and thrive in an unpredictable world full of hidden dangers and needless pitfalls. But reading alone will not do; you can only develop true Social Intelligence by practising it in the real world. Stop reacting emotionally to other people's actions and instead focus on observing and learning from their patterns of behaviour. By paying attention to people around you and better understanding their motives, you'll feel calmer and more objective, which itself speeds up the process. Instead of being blown about by unknowable forces, each encounter becomes a fascinating opportunity to practise your skills and learn something new about human nature.

I

SOCIAL INTELLIGENCE

A bad manner ruins everything, even justice and reason. A good manner makes up for everything: it gilds a "no," sweetens truth, and beautifies old age itself. How something is done plays a key role in all affairs, and a good manner is a winning trick. Graceful conduct is the chief ornament of life; it gets you out of any tight situation.

— BALTASAR GRACIÁN

In working towards our goals at work, the greatest distractions and resentments often come not from the work itself, but in the mutual misunderstandings we have with our peers. We can't understand why our hard work goes unnoticed, or why our best ideas either go ignored or get stolen by unscrupulous colleagues. Even worse, we may be causing a subordinate a great deal of pain without even realising it.

It is most often the case that you are being too self-absorbed, projecting your inner desires onto others. Self-absorption is a universal flaw—the question is not whether you are under its spell, but *how*, and to what degree. Everyone goes about their day inside their own perspective, and they may interpret reality in a completely different way from you. We misinterpret what they say, taking it personally; or we completely miss the constant cues they give off, which are filled with crucial details about their intentions.

You must aim to be one of the few who shrugs off this universal flaw, focusing on other peoples' perspectives. Yes, you have your own needs, but you'll feel surprised at how much more enjoyable and interesting life becomes when you get out of your own head and start paying attention to those around you. By watching others, noticing their subtle behavioural cues and shifts in body language or mood, you can better discern their motivations and act accordingly. Even better, you can build up a series of observations of people over time, picking up on the trends in their behaviour, any patterns that you need to be aware of when dealing with them.

The following five chapters will help you to develop these skills in applied scenarios, each chapter examining a particular strategy. By reading through and understanding them, you will learn how to grow your respect, prestige, and influence inside your group.

1

ABRAHAM TREMBLEY AND LUCULLUS

FOSTER STRONG ALLIANCES WITH CONSISTENT, LONG-TERM GENEROSITY

T*he strongest friendships are grown with small, helpful, and appreciative favours, consistently given over long stretches of time. Above all, they require a genuine desire to help the friend, without expectation of reward. Generosity is the key, and you must not hold back in your favours—cheapness always sends people a negative impression, for people attach assumptions of respect and love to the gifts they receive. The greatest leaders in history gained their prestige not through miserly stinginess, but by spreading a full table of rich food for their guests. Help people, genuinely help them and mean it, feel good when they feel good, and they will not forget your favours. They might pay you back, they might not—they most often will—it is not the point. To direct your focus outward will bring more positive results inward, bringing you both deep satisfaction and a team of reliable allies in times of need.*

STRATEGIC GENEROSITY

Abraham Trembley (1710-1784) was born in the Republic of Geneva in modern-day Switzerland, and from an early age he showed an abnormal curiosity for nature. He gained a degree in the relatively new mathematical field of calculus, which Isaac Newton had established in the prior century. But Trembley's interests did not lie in purely theoretical science; he needed to teach and carry out practical experiments. He became the tutor for a Dutch nobleman's sons, performing experiments for the boys and for himself in his leisure time. Trembley would take the boys fishing in the ponds surrounding their father's castle, showing them the variety of fish and other creatures that made their home there.

One creature they fished out of the water was more curious than the others: It was tiny, plain-coloured, and tube-shaped, with a set of writhing tentacles. Trembley could not see how this unique creature would fit into the animal kingdom—it seemed to lack a brain or any kind of reproductive organs. They cut it in two to determine its internal properties. To his and the boys' amazement, the two cut-apart halves grew into separate, independent copies before their eyes, both still alive. Trembley didn't know it at the time, but he had independently discovered freshwater polyps—creatures now known to belong to the *hydra* genus, classified for their unique regenerative abilities.

During his time as a tutor, Trembley had begun a correspondence with René-Antoine Ferchault de Réaumur, an established French naturalist who had made a name for himself studying insects and other small organisms. Réaumur complained to Trembley in his letters at the difficulty of transporting such organisms across Europe, ensuring they stayed alive and intact on the often long and arduous journeys. The Frenchman had set up quite an ingenious network of couriers—usually eager young scientists like Trembley—and he would teach them all how best to store these creatures, and impart some of his valuable scientific experience.

When Trembley excitedly told Réaumur about his

discovery in the ponds in 1740, this seemed to present a unique opportunity—aquatic samples were usually even more difficult to transport than other organisms, but these hardy creatures would surely survive long trips across Europe. He received a request from Réaumur to send some samples to Paris: "If you were to have enough of these small bodies to deprive you of several of them, it would perhaps not be impossible for you to enable me to see them, by sending them in a very small bottle filled with water, through the post."

Trembley obliged, but by the time the fifty samples reached Réaumur, they were all dead—Trembley had covered the water-filled bottles with wax, depriving the creatures of air. Réaumur suggested a second package, this time using larger bottles secured with cork, a porous material that would allow air to pass through. This next shipment of samples all survived the twenty-five-mile trip, and Réaumur got to work that very evening. Most considerately, Trembley had attached detailed notes and instructions on how to repeat the same experiment he had conducted, with sketched-out diagrams showing both the steps and material equipment required. Réaumur named these creatures "polyps," classifying them in the animal kingdom. Over the next few years they exchanged more samples, and Réaumur gave Trembley valuable feedback on how to improve his experiment. Both men made more discoveries about the incredible regenerative qualities of these creatures—they created a polyp with seven heads, induced one polyp to "eat" another, and even turned one inside out.

Réaumur decided to tour a series of universities in England, demonstrating his findings to the academic community. But to many scientists, the idea of self-replicating sea creatures seemed too much like fantasy—in Cambridge, academics rudely laughed and jeered at Réaumur. But

Martin Folkes, president of the Royal Society, heard about Réaumur's polyps and his curiosity was piqued. He wrote to Réaumur and Trembley, applying for confirmation that the reported phenomenon of polyp regeneration was indeed real. Trembley, still annoyed by how his mentor had been treated in England, gladly sent samples of his polyps to Folkes, complete again with detailed instructions and diagrams. Folkes appreciated the thought Trembley had put into the package and invited twenty of his Royal Society colleagues to his home to perform the experiment. Sure enough, the scientists were all astonished at the experiment's clear demonstration of polyp regeneration—on Folkes's request, the optician John Cuff had duly brought along one of his best microscopes to aid in viewing the results. All twenty of the Royal Society fellows present for Folkes's demonstration vouched for the regenerative properties of polyps. That same year, Trembley's young nephew Charles Bonnet, also a naturalist, published a book called *Philosophical Transactions*. This book detailed Bonnet's own experiments into "regenerating worms," and he had written it in such a clear and exciting manner that it could be read widely amongst the public, adding to the sense of wonder around these brilliant creatures.

Any scepticism or jokes directed at Trembley's polyps quickly ceased. Prominent scientists like Réaumur, Folkes, and the Royal Society fellows, all eagerly defended his findings by showing the same experiment to whomever they could persuade to watch. Folkes himself felt astonished by how quickly the experiment silenced the remaining disbelievers' protests, and Trembley gladly continued to send his experiment package to any remaining scholars who remained doubtful. Folkes and Réaumur continued their own correspondence on polyps, writing further notes that would give Trembley the credibility that came with the seal of

the scientific establishment. The discovery of polyp regeneration also spawned new discussions in the field of metaphysics,
as questions arose about whether the two regenerated halves
of a polyp were truly still the same creature. In November
1743, Folkes awarded Trembley the Copley Medal, praising
him for his ability to distribute shipments of perfectly
preserved polyp samples all across Europe, and for taking
the time to write the simple, easy-to-follow instructions that
always accompanied them:

> We are no less sensible of your great candour, and the
> Readiness you have shown not only to transmit to us
> faithful abstracts of your own experiments, but also to send
> us the Insects themselves, whereby we have been enabled
> to examine by our selves, and see with our own Eyes the
> Truth of the astonishing Facts, you had before made us
> acquainted with.

INTERPRETATION

Abraham Trembley is today considered one of the early
pioneers of experimental zoology, and by some historians as
the father of biology. While these scientific credits are rightly
justified, his greatest success was in the free and wide distribution of his experiment boxes across Europe. Not only did it
signify an advance in transporting live organisms across long
distances, but it also signifies an effective form of what the
historian Marc J. Ratcliff has described as Trembley's
"strategic generosity," the force that truly spread his ideas
and granted him such success and widespread respect.

After Trembley had discovered the marvellous regenerative properties of the polyp, it would have been easy for him
to want to keep his discovery all to himself. We often feel a
pang of this feeling when we find something uniquely amaz-

ing, as if we want all the glory and credit for ourselves. It traces back to our scavenger origins, as our long-distant ancestors were protective of their territory, food, and belongings. In the modern world, however, such over-protectiveness is rarely an effective strategy. Such instincts come from a scarcity mentality—the feeling that our space or resources are constantly under threat, and that we must act to defend them. This frame of mind can only be a self-fulfilling prophecy, because people who manifest it in their attitude become isolated and less likely to benefit from mutual relationships. You must spread your ideas as freely and enthusiastically as Trembley did to ensure they get the biggest traction—do not worry about the credit; it will come, because people will always remember their appreciation for your generosity. Yes, there will always be crooks and vultures out there, but see that Trembley overcame his doubters and remains duly recognised for his work centuries after his death.

Trembley's success shows that getting others to take part in your work is vital. The courtesy and attention to detail showed in the instructions he sent to Réaumur and Folkes encouraged the two eminent scientists to try the experiment themselves, making them both eager partners in his discovery. In return, both men sent helpful feedback to Trembley on how to improve the experiment, such as Réaumur's suggestion on safely packaging the samples, and Folkes's insistence on using a strong microscope to better observe the results. By including such well-respected scientists in his experiment, he made them invested in its success, and eager to show their colleagues. This gave Trembley a valuable seal of approval from the scientific establishment and created a kind of automated system to ensure the discovery of polyp regeneration reached as far as possible. Folkes's respected colleagues at the Royal Society gladly vouched for the experiment's results' veracity, which gave Trembley further credence, and the clarity with which it showed the results silenced the criticism of even the most unreasonable scientists. Trembley's willingness to distribute his experiment kits also encouraged the creation of new experimental labs at universities all across Europe, which earned him his status as an early pioneer of such experiments in biology. As Trembley wrote in 1744:

> I made it my duty to communicate my discoveries, in proportion as I carried them out. I gave polyps, as much as I could, to those who desired to repeat my experiments; and I explained to them how I managed to perform the experiments. It came hence that the polyps were generally known in a short time, and that, in several places, people were put in a condition to verify a part of my experiments.

Whatever field you work in, you must learn the following lesson from Trembley: Share your work freely with trusted colleagues, encourage them to participate, and then ask them for their feedback. In particular, take the time to explain your work in a detailed yet simple and easy-to-follow way. People will greatly appreciate your effort and they'll be more likely to engage with your work. By encouraging them to give feedback on your work, and then overtly putting their advice into practice, they'll feel that their skills and knowledge are valuable and recognised, making them form an emotional investment in your work's success. Never hoard your ideas, and do not be cynical about people being crooks and thieves—though they do exist, you'll be surprised at how quickly and vigorously your participants will rush to your defence, but only after you've included them and treated them as valued and respected colleagues. These prized friends will be all too glad to work on your behalf, defending your name against critics and vouching for the veracity of your results to all who will listen.

THE BENEFACTOR

During the winter between 89 and 88 BC, citizens of Rome completed a fresh round of elections. They had elected a military man named Lucullus to the post of Quaestor, responsible for taxation and auditing, and they elected his friend Sulla to the post of Consul, then the joint-highest post in the Roman Republic. In the autumn of 88 BC, Sulla sent Lucullus to reclaim Greece from the Kingdom of Pontus, in what would later become known as the First Mithridatic War. Lucullus dutifully succeeded in this, having minted most of the money required for the venture in the Peloponnese, a privilege allowed to him as Quaestor. Lucullus encouraged his soldiers to let this money circulate widely as they travelled through Greece—something they appreciated—earning him respect and love from the local Greeks.

Having later conquered Athens, and thus returning Greece to Roman rule, Sulla turned his friend's attention to the island of Crete. This island would act as a launching point for his army to cross into Cyrene, a colony of Greeks in modern-day Libya. The Pontic kingdom had a powerful navy under the command of the admiral Neoptolemus, and thus Sulla had ordered Lucullus to buy ships from Rome's colonies and neighbouring kingdoms to support their own naval strength. Although technically a Roman province, for seven years the Cyrenians had endured a bloody and exhausting civil war under the sway of a series of cruel tyrants. The Cyrenians were all too glad to welcome the liberating Roman army, and Lucullus settled the conflict and moulded a new government, to which they gratefully submitted. In return, Lucullus left the colony with the naval ships at the senate's request.

This first part of the campaign completed, Lucullus carried onto Egypt by sea, to request naval ships from King Ptolemy. Pirates on the journey harassed his fleet, and he only narrowly made it to Alexandria. The young king Ptolemy deferentially greeted Lucullus with his entire naval fleet in full array, a great compliment usually only given to royalty. Unlike any other foreign commander, Lucullus received grand lodging in Ptolemy's own palace. Although he had been offered, according to the great biographer Plutarch, "four times as much" as each of his soldiers in presents and luxurious food, Lucullus refused any excess. He also refused to go with Ptolemy to see the celebrated wonders of Egypt, because it would involve leaving his troops alone and exposed in Alexandria, and also because he was strictly on senate business—the Pontic kingdom's navy was still at large in the Mediterranean, and time was scarce. Although Ptolemy refused the senate's request for help, he hosted a grand parting ceremony for the Romans and offered Lucullus a precious emerald set in gold. Lucullus at first refused it, but once Ptolemy showed him that he had cut Lucullus's own likeness on it, he relented, feeling that to continue such a denial for a generous gift would be rude and endanger his long return journey to end the war the against Pontus.

Narrowly evading Neoptolemus's fleet, Lucullus made it to the island of Rhodes where he, in return for help from their strong navy, agreed to join the Rhodians on an expedition of their own. Together they drove Pontic armies off the Greek island of Chios and liberated the city of Colophon from the oppressive tyrant Epigonius. The Rhodians were most grateful to the Romans for their help in driving tyrannical kings and dictators off their neighbouring islands and thus agreed to join them in their war against Pontus. Lucullus and his fleet, now with the aid of the marine might of the Rhodians, could outmanoeuvre and destroy the fleet of the Pontic admiral Neoptolemus. Peace now achieved between Rome and Pontus, Sulla ordered Lucullus to levy a harsh tax on Pontus as punishment for daring to threaten Rome. Although Lucullus was forced to allow more lenient penalties, many Pontic provinces revolted against the tax. However, this only meant that Lucullus's strong army could defeat them militarily and plunder their riches themselves—in one such case with the Mitylenaeans, Lucullus defeated their forces in a brilliant ambush manoeuvre, riding away with "six thousand slaves and a very rich booty," according to Plutarch's account.

Returning to Rome in 80 BC with the great wealth he and his army had plundered, Lucullus and his brother Marcus were both elected to share the rank of Aedile, responsible for the distribution of grain and holding of public games. The two men used the money to pay for a celebratory series of games much appreciated by all classes of Rome's population, and Lucullus's popularity with the masses soon earned him the election to the praetorship—capping off a truly meteoric rise to the top of Roman society. However, after only a year he voluntarily gave up this powerful role to take up command of the armies in Roman Africa. Little is known about this period, but his contemporary Cicero wrote that Lucullus "ruled Africa with the highest degree of justice," paying particular note to his treatment of people who were neither Greek nor Roman. Sulla dedicated his memoirs to his dutiful subordinate and friend, choosing him to become guardian of his son, which Lucullus's contemporary Pompey greatly resented, and in 74 BC he was elected to Rome's highest office of Consul in Sulla's place, sharing rule with Marcus Aurelius Cotta, Julius Caesar's uncle.

After his year as consul, Lucullus once more set sail for Asia, where the Pontic king Mithridates was again at large. According to Plutarch, not only did the Asian cities receive Lucullus well, but they regarded him as "their salvation from the intolerable miseries which they were suffering from the Roman money-lenders, and revenue farmers," whom Lucullus banished and whose ill-gotten wealth he plundered. His senate colleague Cotta had eagerly attacked Mithridates' armies, only to find himself besieged in the city of Chalcedon, part of modern-day Istanbul. Diverting his mission, Lucullus left to save his friend. A former Pontic commander who had turned over to the Romans complained to the former consul that if he had not distracted his fight against Mithridates, he would own for himself all of Pontus. Plutarch reported Lucullus's response as saying that "it did not become him to be more cowardly than huntsmen, to leave the wild beasts abroad, and seek after sport in their deserted dens."

Lucullus eventually invaded Armenia, where Mithridates had fled to gain protection of King Tigranes. In an incredible battle the outnumbered Romans outwitted and crushed Tigranes's army. Never before had one Roman commander defeated two powerful kings in a single stroke, having beaten Tigranes militarily, and Mithridates through the steady advancement of time. The people of Armenia had long suffered under the oppressive tyrant Tigranes, and were most grateful to the liberating Romans, who had brought the notoriously bullying king to such destitution and humiliation. After seizing upon Tigranes's great accumulated wealth, Lucullus celebrated the victory by staging triumphant games, giving back 8,000 talents of gold and silver to the conquered kingdom's capital city, and 800 drachmas to each of his soldiers. Further liberating the Gordyenians, who had also long suffered under Tigranes, Lucullus's army plundered a large treasure of gold and silver and "three million measures of corn," as reported by Plutarch. Lucullus had completely defeated Mithridates once and for all, and ended the tyrannical rule of Tigranes—for which he took not one piece of gold for himself, instead resolving to use it for Rome's benefit.

This glory ended when his long-standing political rival, Pompey, summoned Lucullus back to Rome. Pompey had long been jealous of Lucullus's military achievements and wanted the same honour and glory for himself, and abruptly ordered the great general to retire. Lucullus, seemingly unfazed, happily agreed and submitted to the man who now wielded great power and influence in the senate, even giving him some of the gold his men had plundered across Asia to pay for his adventures. He immediately retreated from public life, and spent the rest of his time in Rome becoming a great benefactor, using his vast store of wealth to host lavish banquets, building temples and baths that still stand today, and furnishing a large library with a wide variety of manuscripts, freely opening up its vast shelves and reading rooms not only to all classes of Romans but also to all Greeks. Lucullus's generosity was given at a great distance from the murky political intrigues that Pompey and Crassus continued to get themselves into, keeping hold of his beloved and honoured reputation among the people. When Lucullus died some time between 57 and 56 BC, the Roman people gave his funeral procession full civic and military glory, and men of all ages eagerly volunteered to help carry his body to the same resting place where his old master Sulla had been buried years prior.

INTERPRETATION

Lucullus's long list of military achievements may create a grand, mythic image of a leader who had plundered boundless wealth. But the core of his success is something we can all use for our own benefit: his generous and just nature. In his early career, he dutifully accepted the orders from the senate, engaging in long, exhausting wars far from home. Even when his men reportedly became sick and tired of these campaigns, he stayed creative in his job as a military commander, and never appeared to feel sorry for himself. None of his numerous conquests across Greece and Asia seemed to go to his head—he was merely carrying out the role that the senate had given him, making sure to return all the various plunder his solders had won. As the turncoat Pontic commander had said to Lucullus himself, it would have been easy for him to have taken the throne of Pontus for himself, putting the vast wealth of gold coins and slaves to his own personal use. But he didn't—in each case documented by Plutarch, Cicero, and Sulla, he was generous with this booty, freely distributing it among his troops and conquered cities.

Lucullus's name is associated with material generosity, but he also gave freely of generosity in the arguably more moral form of his just and virtuous nature. He was renowned in his own time as a "philhellene," for both his admiration of Greek culture and his treatment of Greek people, from his conquests of Mithridates's armies, to the liberation of the Cyrenians, to the opening of his great library to the Greek people living in Rome. We can only assume that Lucullus saw this benefaction of both his immense store of wealth and his personal generosity as his *duty* to his country. His various commands prove that he was happy performing the everyday, unglamorous administration duties that come with a career in public service. This generosity and humility must stand in stark contrast to his contemporaries, particularly Cicero and Pompey. Cicero was never as dedicated to the less glamorous work of public administration, and Pompey constantly sought personal glory for himself, demanding great military posts despite the limited results he had achieved.

The examples here show that Pompey's approach, seeking the limelight for its own sake, attempting to thwart our colleagues, and burning with resentment and jealousy, are all counterproductive. It's ironic that Lucullus's approach of subsuming our egos, doing our duty, and giving generously of both favours and praise generate the *real* honour that Pompey would have happily killed for if given the chance. Plutarch reported that cities in Asia and Greece not only accepted Lucullus's liberation with open arms but also gladly spread the word to other neighbouring cities asking to be conquered and liberated from the oppressive tyrants controlling them. Bullying tyrants like Tigranes, cowards like Mithridates, and glory-hungry politicians like Pompey may have their day in the sun, but none of their legacies will last with as much love and respect as the dutiful Lucullus, who served his people and gave freely of his wealth. Such a benefactor who loves his fellow citizens and gives them appreciated favours will always get the greater glory. That is something the express glory-hunters will never understand.

KEYS TO SOCIAL INTELLIGENCE

Both of the historical examples with Abraham Trembley and Lucullus reveal the surprising yet time-tested power of strategic generosity. These men lived in different cultures and time periods, but both of their stories show the positive respect and love they received from their friends and colleagues, as well as the respective societies they lived in. Even now, when learning about these fairly obscure historical figures hundreds or even thousands of years after their deaths, we can't help but like them. One can only conclude that our positive response to genuine, appreciative generosity is a fundamental and universal part of the human psyche. In Norse mythology, the most universally liked god is Balder because he embodies the sun, radiating everyone with his warmth—in stark contrast, Loki is the least well liked, due to his sardonic, self-absorbed, and morose manner.

As well as receiving generosity in a positive way, we also feel better for openly giving it to others. In his book *Authentic Happiness*, Martin Seligman explains that happy adults are creative, tolerant, constructive, generous, undefensive, and lateral. Although generosity is explicitly part of Seligman's list of happiness traits, it really underpins all the others. Creative people are generous in expressing their spirit; constructive people are generous with their labours; undefensive people are generous with their egos, and lateral people are generous with their ideas and exhibit flexibility in their approaches to work. To direct your focus outward to others will yield disproportionately positive results inward, bringing you both deep satisfaction and reliable allies in times of need.

Becoming a generous person seems like a wonderful idea, but often it is easier said than done. Our busy, fast-paced modern lives throw daily challenges at us, and we become self-absorbed in what we're not getting from other people. We think, *Damnit, why didn't I get that pay rise?* or *Damnit, those people must be prejudiced!* and we become consumed with a resentment that, if taken to its fullest extent, can affect all aspects of our mental and physical health. But nothing positive can ever come from such jealousy and resentment—if we let it manifest by being rude to our boss or acting presumptuously with our spouse, they'll only reflect that same negativity back onto us, making them even less likely to give us the rewards we feel we deserve. Resentment is a self-fulfilling prophecy—when manifested on both the personal and greater societal level, it is an easily digested poison that justifies your worst presuppositions about yourself and others, destroying you from the inside. Avoid such ungenerous feelings like the plague, and try giving your time or money in small ways at first—when you see how good it makes others and yourself feel, you'll get hooked, and you'll feel much better. The clinical psychologist Lisa Firestone has observed that generosity and an outward-directed focus can even help cure symptoms of depression. In her work, Firestone has pointed out that generosity can be a "natural confidence builder" by crowding out neurotic thoughts, and that through its inevitably social aspect it "actively combats feelings of isolation and depression." There are no simple cure-alls for mental illness, but generosity is always worth a try.

It is reassuring to know that generosity will make us both well-liked within a group and also measurably happier. But what are the optimal ways to apply it in a work or personal setting? The following are five tips to apply strategic generosity and gain the happiness, respect, and success that you want.

Small, consistent favours are better than large ones with telegraphed motives. There's nothing more awkward than receiving the huge, dramatic bouquet sent to your office the day after a mediocre date. You feel torn by the social need to show gratitude, the smirking comments of your colleagues, and the panic you feel about your date's clear over-eagerness. The poor fellow was no doubt sincere and genuine in what he saw as a romantic gesture, but the effects of it are far from positive. The receiver feels pressured, socially humiliated, and almost resentful at his presumptuousness.

On the other hand, small favours given consistently over time sum up to a greater value than the single grand gesture of seemingly "equivalent" value. If the person doesn't know you well, or you don't have a track record of treating them well, then your large gift seems insincere, and it's met with more scepticism than gratitude. Consistent giving creates a pattern which earns you a reputation for generosity. If you have a friend who's trying to start a business, then regularly sharing her content and talking about how her products or services have helped you, will both go a long way. Don't go overboard with unmitigated praise or grand gestures, because it's an undignified way to act and only creates awkwardness. Take the time to work out the intersection between your friend's *wants* and *needs*—identify the things they ostensibly want and that would also be of real benefit to them. For the friend mentioned above, starting a new business can be a frightening, lonely endeavour. When she sees that you regularly talk about her business to others over several months, and that your positive recommendations are genuinely bringing in new customers, she will never forget the help you gave her and will be far more receptive when you ask her for a favour later on.

Embrace *Mitfreude*. Envy is an unfortunate fact of the human psyche, and it has long been understood for its destructive power. Even the original writers of Genesis understood it 2,000 years ago when they described Cain's murder of his brother Abel after God said he preferred the latter's produce. Though we express disgust at Cain's fratricide, his soul sits within all of us. We may never want to kill our siblings, but we've manifested our inner Cain whenever we've felt resentful at someone else's success, or worse: feeling a glint of happiness at that same person's pain. We call the latter schadenfreude, or "harm-joy," and it is a complex emotion. Though it outwardly manifests more in children than adults, we only get better at concealing it as we grow up. *No, that's not me, I would never be so cruel.* Yes you would, and you have already done so—think of the last time someone you dislike had a bad turn, even if it was only a fictional character in a movie. It is not productive to deny its existence within us, for we all carry the same spirit of Cain— but it only manifests if we let it.

The great philosopher Friedrich Nietzsche theorised that our personal resentment and envy aggregates up to the greater societal level—it is, after all, the driver behind revolutions and mass protests. As an alternative to schadenfreude, he proposed that we instead embrace *Mitfreude*, or "shared-joy," encouraging us to feel happy for others' successes, driving our friends and colleagues forward. How much better would it be for the human race if we were generous with our help, instead of acting like crabs in a bucket? Practise feeling a selfless joy when you help your friend with his project at work instead of railing at some abstract political figure on social media and see which one adds a net benefit to the harsh world we all must share. Generosity is the valuable coin that adds value to both its giver and receiver. It has an infinite supply.

Reflect people's best selves in the gifts you give to them. When giving gifts to people, choose items that best reflect the recipient's ego, not those that idly reflect his most well-known interests. Instead of showing a thoughtless ambivalence, you validate his deepest aspirations. There is nothing inherently wrong with giving idle gifts, but don't expect great bursts of enthusiasm or anything more than the basic levels of polite gratitude demanded by societal standards. If you want to make a true impact with your gifts, then instead work to identify what the recipient aspires to do. If they've talked about writing a novel in the past, but they have experienced some kind of social ridicule for that, then you'll stand apart by buying them books on writing and a progress journal. By giving this gift, you show them that you've not only seen this intent in them but also that you believe they can realistically achieve it. Used to receiving idle gifts, they will be completely shocked, humbled, and delighted at your thoughtfulness.

Don't be a lone wolf. Let others get involved in your work. The story of Abraham Trembley shows the benefits of opening your work up to others. The first benefit is that your colleagues will give you valuable feedback. They use their distinct perspective to suggest ideas that you hadn't thought of, or notice errors that you wouldn't have otherwise spotted. The second benefit is that your colleagues, having given you this feedback, become invested in your work's success, because your work's success proves their worth and yours. They will become staunch advocates of your work among others, defending it and yourself from criticism, which can be a source of great relief if your work is controversial or goes against the grain of some convention of your field. The third benefit is that your colleagues' support gives your work a veneer of social proof. A powerful form of this strategy is to gain the support of a respected person in your field, since it gains your work the seal of the establishment. Having many friends support you is great, but having an additional powerful figure vouch for your work provides a knockout punch to any scepticism or criticism. Like with Trembley and his polyp regeneration theory, your colleagues will act almost like an automated system, supporting and spreading your ideas on your behalf, exponentially growing its impact if your work is truly good enough.

Acting like a lone wolf, attempting to take on the world by yourself, is lonely and a bad strategy. Books worked on by a

single person tend not to be that valuable or entertaining—
the author must use the help of a professional editor and
cover designer to ensure that his work is the best quality.
Historically, this division of labour has worked out very well
for us as a species. This means having to recognise where
your skills are strongest and weakest. Lone wolves are bad at
this, usually because they can't accept that they have weaknesses. Their egos are fragile, and they operate under a
mentality of scarcity, utterly convinced that if they share their
work, it will be stolen or plagiarised. All this does is open
their work up to even further and more pointed criticism
than would otherwise be given. Your colleagues will also feel
snubbed and wonder why you didn't want to include them
on your project. This problem is often the case with political
leaders who don't get the opposition involved—it only gives
their opposition the ripe opportunity to play the victim and
judge the results of their work harshly, because they clearly had nothing to do with it. It is much easier to say "we were
wrong" than "I was wrong," and leaders who get others—
especially their staunchest critics—involved to cooperate
from the start are using the highest form of strategy and
Social Intelligence. If their critics refuse to cooperate, then
they look childish—ultimately it turns an enemy into a
friend. Getting others involved in your work is a win-win
strategy. Cooperation is humanity's greatest strength, so
use it.

**Understand that your time here is limited, and think
about your long-term reputation.** Miserly, ungenerous
people are generally not remembered well after they're
gone. Look at the examples of Trembley and Lucullus:
Though they're not particularly well known, their biogra-
phers heap universal praise on them for their generosity.
This is the long-term effect of earning a reputation for
generosity. It is better to accept the fact (and it is a fact) that

your time here is limited, and you need to consider that limited amount of time when attempting to plan out your future. Cooperation with others and gaining a mentor's guidance may hurt your fragile ego, but these steps will streamline your efforts and help you to avoid wasting your precious time.

By consistently giving generously of your time and material possessions over the long term, you build relationships that are as strong as iron. Your friends, colleagues, and allies will stand by you when times get tough, and offer their help when you least expect it. To build lifelong relationships of mutual benefit, bestselling author Timothy Ferriss has advised people to think of the relationship first and the transaction second. The brilliance in Ferriss's approach is in seeing relationships as long-term investments that must be cultivated at regular intervals. It won't do to give idle favours randomly—as we get older, it is frightening to see how quickly our old friends drift away, and this happens because we don't tend to these friendships as much as we should. By building lifelong friendships through generosity, we ensure that in the latter half of our lives we have trusted people around us. Don't end up alone —it is a failure in Social Intelligence, and a miserable way to live.

It's a great thing to earn people's admiration, but more so their affection. This is partly a matter of luck, but mostly of effort; it begins with the first and is pursued with the second. Outstanding talent is not enough, although people imagine that it's easy to win affection once respect has been won. For benevolence, beneficence is required. Do endless good; good words, better deeds; love, in order to be loved. Courtesy is the greatest, most politic spell the great can cast. Reach for great deeds first, then for the pen; go from the sword to sheets of paper, for the favour of writers, which exists, is eternal.

— BALTASAR GRACIÁN

REVERSAL

The danger with unmitigated generosity is that it can lead you into one-sided relationships. Just as there is no virtue in conscious stinginess, there is also little virtue in unconscious, unmitigated generosity. You must give judiciously to avoid becoming a naïve sucker. The crooks' and the charlatans' ears will prick up when they hear about your success and generosity, so stay on your guard for such types. Unable to create anything of value themselves, and unwilling to part with any item or wealth they possess, these types will reveal their vulture-like inclinations through brief flashes of selfish behaviour.

If you suspect that you are dealing with such a type, then test them by trying to divert the conversation to something other than your money or material possessions. Seeing you as an object to be won, and consumed with a need to possess what you have, they will betray their boredom or lack of engagement with this other topic, and try to bring it back to their pyramid scheme or other fraud. If they persist in trying to recruit you to their "membership scheme" or "joint invest-ment" where you provide the funds and do all the work, then there is no shame in politely yet firmly declining their requests. They have cynically tried to use whatever prior friendship you had to envelop you in their own toxic spiral, so don't fall for any of their moralising tactics. There is nothing polite or good in encouraging someone towards their financial ruin.

Understand that the most successful con men in history

did not always look for the richest mark, but the most insecure, whose desperation for instant wealth would lead them
down any treacherous path. You're better than that, and by
explicitly telling the crook that you know what they're up to
in your refusal, they will leave you alone.

2

BENJAMIN DISRAELI AND LOU ANDREAS-SALOMÉ

SOFTEN PEOPLE'S RESISTANCE BY ENTERING THEIR SPIRIT

I *n recent times, the term "seduction" has become conflated with deception and trickery, particularly in a romantic context. But seduction is really the softening of resistance in any kind of situation. This has endless power, for it allows you to earn people's kindness, love, and influence. When you politely greet the store clerk before buying your groceries, or respectfully address a superior at work, you are practising a form of seduction. The best seducers in history were not always the most flamboyant dandies, but those who were most able to enter another person's spirit and move with them. In all cases, they were a source of great pleasure to people. This is not mere insincerity —it involves seeing through the façade of a person's persona, deeply understanding their true motivations, and reacting accordingly. On the contrary, it is perhaps the most sincere we can ever be.*

THE CHARMER

In 1868 the Earl of Derby, prime minister of the United Kingdom, fell ill and informed his fellow ministers that he could not go on as the head of government. Derby chose his finance minister, Benjamin Disraeli, to take his place. Asked if ready to take on this monumental role, Disraeli responded, "Yes, I have climbed to the top of the greasy pole." His new government under the Conservative party did not even have a majority in parliament. Putting his role under further scrutiny was his ethnicity—Disraeli was a dark-skinned Jew, making him the victim of great prejudice in English high society. It seemed like everything was stacked against the new leader, and that his premiership would be brief.

Unfortunately for Disraeli, this became true, as William Gladstone's Liberal party resoundingly defeated his short-lived first government two years later. As Gladstone's government dominated parliament, Disraeli could do little more than protest, deciding to retreat and wait for Liberal mistakes. Out of government, he had time to write a novel called *Lothair* in 1870. Although Disraeli had lost the election, the public had felt some of his charm, and a novel written by a former prime minister was an unusual thing—it became an instant bestseller, and his notoriety and mystery only grew.

In 1873, Disraeli's premonitions of a Liberal mistake came to fruition. William Gladstone put forth legislation for a new Catholic university in Dublin, Ireland, bitterly dividing the Liberal members of parliament along sectarian lines. A series of further scandals led Gladstone to resign, and Queen Victoria sent for Disraeli, who unexpectedly refused. He would not take the reins of a government so wracked by impropriety. People could not fathom Disraeli's refusal to see the queen, but it only made his public notoriety grow. Some loved his roguish charm, and many—Gladstone included—could not stand what they saw as Disraeli's impudence and insincerity.

A year later, Gladstone finally relented and called a general election in which Disraeli's Conservative party won by a landslide. Even in Scotland, where the Conservatives were usually weak, they took an additional twelve parliamentary seats. Although Queen Victoria was impartial in all matters of politics, she too was pleased with Disraeli's victory. Victoria had disliked Gladstone and did not get along well with him. In their weekly meetings, Gladstone would flatly expound his views to her in the most patronising fashion. He did not try to charm people and was usually unaware of how intensely people disliked him. Disraeli, on the other hand, was a notorious smooth talker, sometimes shamelessly flattering the queen for her wisdom and beauty. Despite the reactions of her courtiers, Victoria often welcomed this—she appreciated being made to feel like a woman, not like some lifeless ornament.

Outside of politics, Disraeli and Victoria had much in common. Like Disraeli, Victoria had written books, among them *Leaves from the Journal of Our Life in the Highlands*, about her time with John Brown, her Scottish manservant. Victoria was no great writer and very few people read her books, which naturally disappointed her. But Disraeli would go to great lengths to compliment her writing, referring to himself and her in his letters as "We writers," which she greatly appreciated. In stark contrast to Gladstone's dull lecturing, Disraeli would often ask the queen for her opinion on matters, something his predecessor never did. He made her feel not just appreciated as a woman, but also a wise leader of a proud, august empire. Some years into Disraeli's premiership, he pressed parliament to add "Empress of India" to her long list of titles. This plan succeeded, and Victoria was abundant with joy at the news, later rewarding Disraeli with the title "Earl of Beaconsfield." Although Disraeli and his government succumbed once again to his long-standing Liberal rival, Victoria never forgot about him, even after his death in 1881.

As they lowered his coffin into the ground, all eyes were on a simple wreath of primrose flowers—Queen Victoria had sent it herself, with a note that read "His favourite flowers." This gesture's plain intimacy perfectly captured the appreciation Victoria had for her prime minister.

INTERPRETATION

Little has been written on Disraeli outside the context of his working relationship with Queen Victoria. Although he is a romantic figure, and whose compassion for Victoria was real and sincere, Disraeli was always conscious in how he dealt with her. Disraeli looked past the royal grandeur surrounding Victoria, and saw in her a woman whose life had become stale and grey since the death of her beloved husband Albert. Being preceded by William Gladstone played to his favour, because it showed a great contrast in the two men's characters. Victoria had become exhausted with Gladstone's blunt manner, his moralising, his assumption that, regardless of her rank, she was a woman that he needed to educate. When Gladstone was still prime minister, Victoria would sometimes take revenge by not permitting him to sit in her presence, shortening their weekly meetings—being an older man, Gladstone's legs would tire quickly.

That Victoria went to such lengths illustrates why you must avoid developing a personal manner similar to Gladstone's. If you feel any kind of sympathy for him, you must soon realise that people are perfectly capable of coming to their own conclusions, and that you should never assume that people know less than you simply because they disagree with your ideas. Though people may feign politeness in your presence, they are actually trying to get away from you, and deeply resent the arrogant, know-it-all manner that such an attitude displays. You will persuade no one and, if you make condescension a habit, you should count yourself lucky that you make it to an old age with your hide still intact.

A much easier path for all involved is to see inside people's desires and motives. Stop being obsessed with what you want and, like Disraeli, play to other people's soft points. Victoria had become accustomed to being treated as a mere ornament and found herself weak to even the most shameless flattery and male attention. Disraeli complimented her writing, a source of great insecurity to her, and he also praised her judgement in rule, something else she was sensitive to after Gladstone's weekly lectures. Though this may sound exploitative and insincere on Disraeli's part, it brought a welcome pleasure and satisfaction to Victoria, her courtiers noticing that her spirit was lifted whenever Disraeli's name was mentioned. She would even become jealous if overhearing of another lady interacting with her prime minister.

More people are like this than you think. We go about our daily lives, constantly rebuffed and reminded of our negligible importance in the grand scheme of things—particularly at work, where we feel treated like mere cogs in a machine. So when someone comes into our lives, paying genuine attention to the things we deeply care about but keep hidden due to our latent insecurities, we cannot help but feel recognised and validated. If we succumb to this pleasure, we give them everything they want. It is truly the height of Social Intelligence.

THE SIREN

Lou Andreas-Salomé was born in St Petersburg, Russia in 1861, the youngest of six children and the only daughter. The family, headed by a wealthy and decorated army general, encouraged her to attend her brother's school classes in mathematics and philosophy, and had all the children speak not only Russian in the home but also German and French. This well-cultured upbringing gave Salomé an exposure to a rich and varied education rare for young women of the time. At age seventeen she persuaded the Dutch priest and theologian Hendrick Gillot to teach her everything he knew about philosophy and literature. Salomé had a voracious hunger for knowledge and paid particular attention to Gillot himself. Uniquely as a priest, he was confident and good-looking, calm yet also passionate when he explained theological doctrines and German literature. The energy between them was intense, and it seemed like the feelings between them were mutual, until Gillot gave in and asked Salomé to marry him, even offering to divorce his wife. This unexpected turn shocked and disgusted her—Gillot was twenty-five years her senior, and the idea of marriage or any kind of conventional romantic commitment repulsed her. She broke off their teacher-student relationship and, after her father's death, moved with her mother to Zürich in 1880 to continue her studies.

Although Salomé enjoyed her year at the university in Zürich, one of a few institutions that accepted women, she was so intent in her studies that her health began to fail, and to her great dismay she was instructed to move to warmer climates. With great reluctance, she and her mother moved to Rome in 1882. Saddened to have left university and the chance to earn a degree, she visited Rome's literary salons, desperate to find some kind of intellectual stimulation. In one such salon, Salomé met a young German named Paul Rée. The two sparked a friendship quickly, and she relished the chance to help him formulate some of the philosophical theories Rée would later publish. A naturally quiet and reserved man, Rée was not used to such enthusiastic attention from any woman, let alone one as vivacious and enthusiastic for his knowledge as Salomé, and it was not long before he became hopelessly smitten with her. He proposed marriage to her, but she refused. Salomé offered to live with him, but only as "brother and sister," and only so long as he invited a fellow male academic to join them, forming a kind of intellectual commune. Upset by her rejection but still eager to continue the relationship, he offered to invite his friend Friedrich Nietzsche in the third role. Nietzsche was a philosopher of some repute by this time, and Salomé excitedly agreed.

Like Salomé, Nietzsche was a voracious student of philosophy, and had also needed an opportunity to move to warmer climates due to his failing health. Upon reading Rée's letter, curious to meet this young female philosopher his friend spoke of, he hurried to Rome. Much like his friend Rée, Nietzsche fell under Salomé's spell almost immediately. He too was seduced by the attention she gave him; never before had a woman been so interested in his philosophical theories and learning everything he had to share. Nietzsche learned much from Salomé too—she helped him develop his theories of morality, and he was so moved by her poem "Hymn to Life," that the experience influenced the concept that he later developed into his phrase *amor fati*—Latin for "love of fate," the attitude of embracing everything that happens in one's life, including pain and loss.

As the trio travelled around Italy and Switzerland over the next year, both Rée and Nietzsche made multiple romantic advances on her, all of which she refused. Nietzsche's obsession with Salomé became so enthralling that his sister Elisabeth wrote to him, warning him of what she described as "the immoral woman." To Nietzsche's despair, after a summer of travelling together, Salomé and Rée conspired to expel him from their group—secretly, Rée had wanted Salomé to himself all along. Heartbroken at this betrayal, Nietzsche went into a depression, pinning the blame of his failure on his sister and her intrigues. Driven by the pain and despair of being rejected by Salomé, Nietzsche wrote *Thus Spoke Zarathustra*, but really he was never the same man again. He lived his remaining years in his mother's care, having completely lost his sanity.

Salomé and Rée moved to Berlin where they would live together for a time, until she accepted a marriage proposal from Friedrich Carl Andreas. He too was an intellectual, the latest of many to fall under her spell. Salomé reluctantly agreed to the marriage, Andreas allegedly having threatened suicide if she refused. To Andreas's dismay, the couple never consummated their marriage, and she continued to carry on affairs with Rée and other scholarly men. Rée continued to suffer with his unrequited love until October 1901, when he died while hiking in the Swiss Alps—as he had fallen off a cliff, it was unclear whether it had been an accident or suicide, but either way it drove Salomé into an emotional crisis. She would only overcome this with the help of the Viennese doctor Friedrich Pineles. In her vulnerable state and once again under a mentor's influence, Salomé began a romantic affair with Pineles that led to her becoming pregnant—in a panic and still uncomfortable with any kind of commitment, she had a voluntary abortion.

At the age of fifty, just before the outbreak of the First World War, Salomé began a regular correspondence with the pioneering psychotherapist Sigmund Freud, whom she had met at a psychoanalytic conference in Weimar. At once, she had become his disciple, eager to learn all he had to teach about the young field of psychology, which she believed provided the best lens through which to address her problems in philosophy. Their letters contained a lively exchange of deep ideas, and their friendship grew—Salomé even sharing with Freud her poem that had inspired Nietzsche years before in Rome. Salomé embraced Freud's new field of psychoanalysis, and became the only female scholar in the Vienna Psychoanalytic Circle, herself becoming a practising psychoanalytic therapist. Through her clinical work with a variety of patients, particularly women, and her unique blend of psychoanalysis with the philosophical theories she'd learned from Nietzsche, she wrote much of the early work on narcissism and female sexuality that would help build the foundation for modern psychoanalytic theory.

INTERPRETATION

Although she practised it less consciously than Benjamin Disraeli, Lou Andreas-Salomé was devastating in her seduction of the many great men she met throughout her life. She had a rare upbringing for a woman of the time in a household full of books, lively philosophical discussions, and an education equal to her brothers. It all gave her a passion for knowledge that she kept throughout her entire life, and she always sought to learn from the best teachers she could find. Salomé gave her teachers complete attention, engaging in hours of dialogue with them on the topics that most fascinated her. She had such an intensity to her on these occasions that she and her teacher would form an instant rapport, almost unconsciously seeking his wavelength and then resonating with it.

The men she learned from did not stand a chance against such seductive encounters. All of her male teachers and contemporaries were scholarly, introverted types, and none of them were used to the attention they received from a woman as beautiful and intense as Salomé. Gillot, twenty-five years her senior and already married, asked to elope with her; Nietzsche, who had considered himself far from conventional, asked Salomé to marry him twice, and each time she showed scorn and derision that this brilliant philosopher could be so hopelessly and pathetically enamoured with her. Although she rejected these romantic advances, she kept the door open for friendship, which the men gratefully accepted. Salomé determined not to burn bridges with the brilliant minds she wanted in her intellectual commune.

The lesson from Salomé's encounters is that people crave attention and will gladly follow those who give it to them. Shy, introverted types are especially vulnerable to this, because it's so rare for them to feel their ideas validated and recognised by others. When a Salomé type enters their life, asking them to share the opinions and theories they hold deepest in their heart, and receiving them with warmth and gratitude, the introvert is helpless to resist. People of this type will frequently match the pattern word-for-word when describing their first ever romantic encounter.

Far from attracting people as Salomé did, we are often less skilled in conversation than we like to think. As the other person speaks, we burst waiting for them to finish so we can interject with our own anecdote or opinion on the matters being discussed. This means that we never truly pay attention to our conversation partner, and it goes both ways, leaving neither of you feeling recognised or validated. In your interactions with people, practise focusing more attention on your partner. Ask them to expand on their points, and express genuine admiration at the stories they tell you. Subsume any instinct you have to inject your own views into the conversation unless directly asked. Not only will this create an air of mystery around you, but most people are unprepared for such sincere attention and will enjoy your company immensely, happily paying you back with generous favours.

Beware, however, of enwrapping people to the extent that Salomé often did. Giving people such attention may create unintended consequences. Just as many people find such raw, unrestrained attention disturbing, and it's possible that you'll creep them out instead. Salomé's weakness was that she could not control her intensity because it was unconscious—it led sensitive men like Rée and Nietzsche to their doom. On the other hand, if this kind of conversational art is new to you, then you are at an advantage because the skills are instead conscious and you therefore have control over them. Learn to dial your conversational intensity up and down as the situation requires and you will make great friendships without adverse consequences.

KEYS TO SOCIAL INTELLIGENCE

Conversation offers a rich soil of opportunities that we often fail to till. In our meetings with others we remain self-absorbed, transfixed on our own resentments and desires. In conversation, we hardly think of what the other person might want from the interaction; in meetings, we couldn't be less bothered about the needs of the business or team, we just want to put forward our own agenda. We're not really engaged in any of these encounters, and it makes us eminently anti-seductive. Our one-sided demand for attention achieves the complete opposite: people avoid us and they don't give us what we want. It's not only out of sheer wilfulness or perversity that they react this way, but also because we have completely failed to recognise their needs, their point of view. Some may pride themselves on an approach of pure, unfiltered honesty. These types, going around bluntly saying whatever pops into their head without the slightest thought for those around them, will only cause anxiety. We either avoid them, for fear of what they'll say to us, or laugh at them, enjoying watching the same happen to others. Contrary to what its wielders may think, the blithe, disregarding approach has no great virtue—it is lazy and causes needless pain and misunderstanding.

If we close our eyes and think about the people we're most happy to do genuine favours for, every example is a person who, consistently, has proven their consideration for us somehow. This is no mere coincidence—it reflects our deep desire for validation and recognition. Far from today's image of slimy, dishonest tricksters, history's greatest seducers were the most skilled at wielding this validating mirror at people around them. Instead of bluntly demanding unearned respect and favours from people, master seducers would soften resistance with sweet words and heartfelt gestures. Do not think that such skills are useless in the practical world of work—they are as indispensable in the modern office as they were in the old aristocratic court. To masters, seducers are not merely flattering but also useful and pleasant to deal with; to subordinates, they give orders in the most subtle and oblique fashion, making employees feel like colleagues, valued for their work.

Do not make the mistake of thinking this approach involves lying or being insincere with people. Every workplace is a bubbling cauldron of resentments and conflicting desires. To navigate such a dangerous environment with grace and dexterity takes great skill, and it is also critical to our survival. If we say the wrong thing to the wrong person, the consequences could be dire. We may not realise that the person we are talking to holds an unexpectedly high influence over the boss, and that upsetting them with a blunt, dismissive remark could irreparably damage our reputation. It is far better to match our words to each situation, entering people's spirits as Disraeli would do with Queen Victoria and his colleagues in the British parliament.

Our goal is to gain a reputation for always being thoughtful, patient, and cooperative with friends and colleagues.

The modern world we live in does not make this easy, encouraging us to become self-absorbed, obsessed with our image on social media, activating our natural narcissism. It keeps us in a perpetual state of adolescence when we should turn outwards and learn more from others. We must actively work to suppress the urge to always talk about ourselves, always dominating the considerations of others with thoughts of our own needs, and instead turn our attention outwards. Be patient with your own needs, and take extra time to consider what might make people feel defensive in your office or family, and communicate to them that you understand completely. People will feel overcome with gratitude for your recognition of their fears and resentments, and much more open to your points of view and requests for favours.

No one practised this approach better than Lyndon B. Johnson (1908-1973). As a green Texas senator, he would attach himself to the service of older, more senior colleagues, and focus all his attention on them. Johnson had just won his first senatorial election by the slimmest of margins and was desperate to learn more and gain political influence. Being green and relatively low down the political ladder, the only way he could do this was to learn from mentors and hopefully gain some influence through them. But Johnson would never outright demand the committee memberships he so coveted; instead he would become useful to these older men, doing them small but consistent favours, such as helping persuade senators in marginal votes, and doing the legwork of recruiting new staffers. Johnson successfully courted Richard Russell, the senior Democrat senator from Georgia, and one of the most powerful men in the senate. Much as he had done with Speaker Sam Rayburn during his time in the House of Representatives, he courted Russell assiduously, visiting him in his office every day, calling him "the Old

Master." Johnson's wife Lady Bird would entertain Russell at their home with delicious Southern dishes, something he greatly appreciated as a Georgian. This affable, seductive attitude of Johnson's did not come naturally to him though— he was naturally quite an aggressive man, always going fiercely after his goals. Such a hard approach would not work for a green senator, particularly a Democrat from the South. Others would turn in, going on the defensive and feeling insecure around him. So instead, he focused on being patient and playing the long game: making alliances with key figures like Russell, who he made feel like a beloved father figure, himself a loyal son and disciple. Johnson learned from observing Russell that he loved baseball, felt passionately about waste in government expenditure, and prided himself on his strong work ethic, and so he embraced all of these qualities, pledging that he had simply "learned from the Old Master." Johnson repeated this strategic seduction with other senators, and over time he amassed enough power and influence to become a master of the political scene in Washington, eventually becoming president.

Rather than try to charm people with his great ideas, or bully them into accepting his demands, Johnson would subsume his ego to the person he was trying to win over. This is the opposite path that most people take when trying to get their way: They overtly attempt to *persuade* through argument, bashing them over the head with point after point, believing that endless logical cases are enough. Overt persuasion like this only puts people on the defensive. They tighten up as if reacting to a rehearsed sales pitch, far from having the good feelings we want them to have in our presence. We may eventually get them to do what we want, but by this time they're full of resentment and know to stay clear of you in the future. Persuasion rarely works, and when it does, it always leaves a bruise.

Softening the soil before asking for favours is a far more efficient and effective strategy. Assume a junior position to the person you're talking to—ask for their advice, their opinions on matters, and demonstrably put their advice into practice, telling them of the results. This will make them feel deeply validated. You must do this consistently over a long period of time, making it a pattern rather than a sudden one-off change of heart, otherwise it will seem insincere. By the time you ask for a favour, it will feel more like asking your neighbour to tend to your plants while you're away on holiday than the titanic obligation it may have seemed like at the beginning. In his political career, Benjamin Disraeli would initially act like he disagreed with the person he was trying to influence, only then to be "won over" by their arguments. This tactic is a brilliant application of Social Intelligence, because it creates a bond of friendship between the two people, while giving one a feeling of comfortable superiority over the other—intellectual ability being a very prickly part of the human ego.

The greatest hurdle you may have to cross when developing this social skill is your own ego. You may find it difficult to subsume yourself to others, when quieting yourself during conversation or asking for advice. Understand that you will never be a source of pleasure to people if you constantly put yourself first, and that they will instinctually put up barriers against you. It is a life full of stress and anxiety, since no one will completely allow your domineering nature to roam free and you will face constant battles. If you can't bear the thought of someone knowing more than you, and you constantly feel the need to impress your perceived greatness on others, one-upping their stories or rubbishing their accomplishments, then you are trapped in adolescence and enslaved to your ego.

The first step is to recognise how much this attitude is

holding you back, and the positive benefits you could enjoy from a less intoxicating experience of life. By paying people attention as Lou Andreas-Salomé did, asking for their knowledge, and considering their needs and motivations, your life will become much easier. People will open doors for you, appreciating your validation of their principles more than you can realise. It's perhaps one of the most counter-intuitive lessons we can learn in our lives, that subsuming your yourself to others will, if done with sincerity and consistency over time, pay you back with interest.

> The true spirit of conversation consists more in bringing out the cleverness of others than in showing a great deal of it yourself; he who goes away pleased with himself and his own wit is also greatly pleased with you. Most men would rather please than admire you; they seek less to be instructed, and even to be amused, than to be praised and applauded.
>
> — JEAN DE LA BRUYÈRE

REVERSAL

It is never good to neglect entering a person's spirit and fail to make even a small attempt to understand how they're feeling. It can, however, sometimes work well to act cold every so often. In contrast to your usually warm demeanour, this will make them feel alarmed, and they'll try to guess what they might have done wrong. When the time is right, do not feel afraid to ask what you want. The goal is not to be subversive at all times, but to till the soil so that when you do ask for what you want, you are almost guaranteed to receive it.

King Louis XIV of France would often use this tactic. If he wanted a favour from a courtier or noble, he would rarely ask them outright. Instead, the courtier would find that his son had been appointed to a well-paying job within the government, or he would be granted an artwork he had longed for. Then, after this series of small but appreciated favours, Louis would back off, ignoring him. When this courtier realised what was happening and panic about his waning relationship with the king, Louis would suddenly swoop in and ask him for the favour he had wanted all along —the tactic never failed.

This kind of reverse manoeuvre shows that seduction's reversal is only possible when it is conscious and temporary —and even then, you are practising a more subversive form of seduction. Balance your coldness sparingly, and be careful of going too far in either direction: too cold, and your target feels hurt, even betrayed; too hot, and you risk your target either falling madly in love or running very fast in the opposite direction.

3

CLOVIS AND THE ATHENIANS

ACCOMMODATE A GROUP'S MYTHOLOGY TO
GAIN THEIR TRUST AND SUPPORT

*M*uch of our stress in the workplace comes from new people joining our team. These people are eager to impress, and try to show off their best qualities, especially to the group's leader. We rarely see this, however, and instead feel threatened, as if this person's attempts to impress us are really a form of competition. Sometimes they attempt to change our existing processes, and certain types of narcissistic leader will revel in exploiting this new member's eagerness. We become defensive, unwilling to share our knowledge with the perceived usurper. You yourself might have triggered this same reaction without realising it, not realising the unnecessary friction and resentment that it causes. When joining a new group, see that it is counterproductive to shine brightly and impress, due to other people's latent insecurities. Instead, try to find the "vibe" of your new team and make a show of accommodating it in some way. You will find that your acceptance into the group comes much faster and with less friction, allowing you to show your best qualities when your position is more firmly established.

FLEXIBLE ACCOMMODATION

In 481, King Childeric of the Salian Franks died, allowing his son Clovis to ascend the throne. Clovis (466-511) now controlled a sizeable territory that spanned modern-day Belgium. The Salian Franks were one of many Germanic petty kingdoms allowed to settle in Roman Gaul, and the death of the able Roman general Flavius Aetius in 454 meant that imperial influence in the region had steadily declined. Aetius's death had left the region open to a series of bloody power struggles between the Germanic tribes, and the last remaining power in Roman control rested tenuously with a weak Gallic military commander named Syagrius.

Seeing the opportunity to expand his rule, Clovis allied himself with his relative Ragnachar, king of Cambrai in modern-day Hauts-de-France, and another Frankish king named Chalaric. The Roman general Syagrius reigned over the Belgica Secundus region that surrounded the Salian Franks, so to grow his small kingdom, Clovis would need to conquer the two largest settlements under Syagrius's control, Soissons and Reims. In 486, this triumvirate of Frankish kings marched their armies to Soissons, and won a decisive victory against Syagrius, who fled south-west to Visigoth Spain.

Having defeated this last cornerstone of Roman influence in the region, Clovis now controlled the Frankish kingdoms and the northern territories of Roman Gaul. This mix caused an unexpected challenge to his rule, because of the cultural differences between his new subjects—it would be difficult to consolidate his territorial gains if he could not unite these distinct peoples and form a single army. The Gauls had adopted the new Roman religion of Christianity, and other Germanic tribes surrounding the Franks had converted to Arianism, a sect of Christianity that asserted the status of Jesus Christ as the literal son of God. These latter tribes fell into constant disputes with the Gauls over their mutually differing interpretations of Christianity.

Clovis's northern Franks, on the other hand, had remained pagan throughout this time, and had upset many among the Gallic-Roman Christian clergy by raiding churches in his conquest of Soissons. The cities of Verdun and Paris stubbornly resisted Clovis's rule, only yielding after long and hard-fought sieges. Clovis knew that to rule Gaul, he would have to win the support of their Christian clergy—neither they nor the Arians would ever bow to a petty pagan king. To win favour with the Christians under his rule, Clovis made Paris the capital of his kingdom, and married a Catholic princess named Clotilde. A strong woman who passionately held her Christian beliefs, Clotilde unsuccessfully attempted to persuade Clovis to convert to Christianity himself. However, in 496, during the Battle of Tolbiac against the tribe of the Alemanni, Clovis promised to abandon paganism if Clotilde's God would grant him victory. The Frankish forces snatched an unlikely victory from the jaws of defeat, and so he relented to his wife's wishes. This worked to his favour, since his newly conquered Alemanni territories were Arians, and so like the Gauls they could not be properly controlled without his conversion to Christianity. Thus on Christmas Day in 496, Saint Remigius baptised Clovis as a Catholic Christian in the cathedral of Reims.

Converting his original Frankish territories from paganism to Christianity proved relatively simple because of their lack of existing ties to any Christian sect. Clovis's conversion to Christianity greatly moved the Gallic-Roman clergy, and they jubilantly accepted his rule. Now secure, Clovis took his newly united army of Franks, Gauls, and Alemanni into the south-west territories of Gaul controlled by the Visigoths, defeating them in a decisive battle in modern-day Poitiers in 507. Grateful to Clovis for his conversion to Christianity and for banishing a tribe from Gaul that had long caused chaos in the region, Anastasius, the emperor of the Eastern Roman Empire, proclaimed Clovis an honorary consul of Rome. He held status far above all the other petty western Germanic kings, and the Gallo-Roman population finally saw his reign as legitimate. Crowning himself the first King of the Franks atop a newly united Christian kingdom, Clovis controlled the vast span of territories that would later become known as France.

INTERPRETATION

Looking out onto the landscape of fifth-century Gaul, one might have concluded that the only way to conquer this vast territory would be to gather an army of immense size and take it all by brute force. Although the once-unstoppable Romans had mostly lost their influence in the region by the time of Childeric's death, the chessboard of western Europe was filled with barbarous kingdoms eager to fill the power vacuum. The Germanic kingdoms that had converted to Roman Christianity squabbled endlessly over their interpretations of Jesus Christ's heritage, while Clovis's tiny kingdom of Salian Franks, far from any Roman influence, had remained pagan.

While tribes like the Alemanni and Burgundians distracted themselves with internal battles and thus did not unite across sectarian lines, Clovis could easily convert his existing Frankish subjects, who had no such emotional ties to any sect of Christianity. By relenting to his wife Clotilde and converting to Catholic Christianity, he would better placate the Roman Gauls under his rulership, who held a significantly better organised society and army than the barbarous Germanic tribes. The influential clergy in Gaul greatly appreciated Clovis's conversion to Roman Catholicism, which granted him a firmer grasp over their armies, and it also won the support and approval of the Eastern Roman Empire. In a single stroke, he brought Syagrius's former Roman lands under his leadership, united the vast Gallic territories into a single Frankish kingdom, and gained a valuable seal of legitimacy from a mighty empire.

Modern-day France would not exist without Clovis's flexible accommodation of the religion that his conquered subjects held so closely to their hearts. If he, like his Germanic counterparts, had rooted himself in his own religion and brazenly imposed it on all of his subjects, he would have gotten nowhere. Not only do people instinctively resist such attempts at domination, they are particularly protective of their religious beliefs. Curiously so, it is across the lines between differing sects of the same core belief that cause the most friction and resistance to conversion—each sect seeing itself as the one "true" interpretation of their professed beliefs. We need not look hard to see this conflict manifest today between the three major religions that all worship differing interpretations of the Abrahamic God: Judaism, Islam, and Christianity. Cruel and tyrannical leaders have long known that stirring up such animosity between factions with religious zeal to be fairly easy and a brutally effective way of keeping a rebelling populace occupied. But softening that resistance and bringing people together in peace, while far more beneficial and mutually rewarding, is decidedly harder.

In the modern world of social media, these beliefs have largely been replaced by distinct ends of the political spectrum and bitter rivalries between popular sports teams. Online media, incentivised to write misleading, overdramatic headlines to maximise their ratings, has only served to further polarise these modern sects, causing visceral hatred and mistrust on both sides. Such needless battles hurt us as a society, driving us apart and making us hate each other, when we ought to unite and progress into a more enlightened scientific age. We may not all possess the power to solve these issues on a mass scale, but we can apply a practice of flexible accommodation to those in our immediate circle. You need not do anything as drastic as converting your religion or political beliefs; you only need to adopt an open spirit, embracing freedom of expression, particularly with those you feel a natural disagreement—watch as your old enemies light up with satisfaction from the validation you freely give them. Clovis consolidated his power and founded the precursor to modern-day France by doing the same with the Roman Catholic Gauls and the Arians.

Be aware, however, that this practice can only originate from inside yourself—if you feel any kind of superiority over others stemming from your differing beliefs, then you must relinquish that perceived superiority now by seeing the damage it wreaks on your mental health. Such feelings indicate a childish need to believe others to be inherently stupid to disagree with us—understand now that it is perfectly possible for someone of equal intelligence and morality to come to conclusions different to yours. By affecting a spirit of empathy with these people instead of hatred, people will naturally gravitate to your aura of mutual respect, and pay you back with an invaluable level of support entirely unlike the fleeting and resentment-filled kind gained by brute force and overt argument.

KEYS TO SOCIAL INTELLIGENCE

In the fifth century BC, the Greek city-state of Athens carried out a practice where once a year, citizens would vote to banish any among their number for ten years. The procedure of *ostrakismos*, the root of the modern word for "ostracism," allowed the Athenians to exercise popular anger against ostracised citizens, a right they enthusiastically partook of for at least seventy years, according to the Greek biographer Plutarch. Before this practice, Athens had suffered at the hands of tyrants and petty despots like Peisistratos, who had ruled the city with an iron fist for thirty-six years. Learning the lesson from electing bullying rulers and taking the fallout from partisan clashes stirred on by the aristocracy, the Athenians introduced ostracism as a countermeasure against dangerous citizens who put themselves ahead of the public good. It worked like this: During the winter, an assembly of Athenians would be asked if they desired an ostracism—if this assembly voted "yes," then an ostracism vote would be scheduled for the spring. The two-month delay would avoid banishments from sudden anger and allow citizens rumoured to be ostracised an opportunity to improve their behaviour. Each citizen would scratch the name of their desired victim on a piece of broken clay tile— the *ostrakon*, chosen for use because of its abundance relative to the expensive Egyptian papyrus—and all citizens named on at least 6,000 ballots would face the banishment. None of their property would be taken, and they could return unscathed after their period of exile, but the remaining Athenian citizens could breathe a sigh of relief that the irritating people were finally gone.

Two victims of the ostracism were Aristides and Themistocles. Although Aristides had served the city-state well, saving it many times from the might of the Persian Empire, in 482 BC the Athenians banished Aristides for his judgemental and haughty manners, and his utter dominance of Athenian politics after his military victories. His nickname of "The Just" had gone to his head, and they ostracised him before he had the chance to seize dictatorial powers and plunge them into the horrors of the years before their democracy. After Aristides, another great Athenian, general Themistocles, fell victim to the citizens' *ostraka*. In a similar pattern to Aristides, Themistocles's victories and benefaction to the city had given him a hunger for applause and further riches, and had treated his fellow citizens with arrogance, hoarding his wealth to prevent others from rivalling his status and power. In one such instance, Plutarch even claimed that "[Themistocles] desired Diphilides, who was a breeder of horses, to give him a colt, and when he refused it, threatened that in a short time he would turn his house into a wooden horse, intimating that he would stir up dispute and litigation between him and some of his relations." What a pleasure to banish such disrespectful and arrogant people! This practice that served the Athenians well and saved them from the creeping dangers of dictators and self-serving individuals unfortunately ended with the banishment of Hyperbolus, a citizen so callow and worthless that the Athenians felt his ostracism had irreversibly spoiled the practice. It was only a few decades later that the Athenians, now ruled by an aristocracy of wealthy and manipulative political types, brought themselves to ruin in their war against the Spartans. Their golden age came to an abrupt, bloody, and humiliating end.

This ancient practice of banishing former military heroes who had once protected and served the city might seem petty or ungrateful, but it's more wise than you might think. When people have served a group well and for a long time, it's easy for them to feel entitled to rewards and credit, and this haughty self-righteousness can reveal itself at opportune moments, like Themistocles hurling threats at a horse breeder. Such anxiety-inducing individuals who forget their duties to the group cannot fail to produce disputes and friction, distracting the group from its work and goals. Empowering citizens to get rid of such people—any people, regardless of status or past service—allowed the city to remain strong and stable for decades of uninterrupted growth because it allowed ordinary Athenians to go about their lives free of distractions from self-absorbed types, by giving them a productive avenue for their resentment. Even better, the public nature of the ostracism completely nullified any kind of counter-attack from the banished individual, whereas an Athenian court prosecution might open up the opportunity to single out the arbiter of judgement in their case—with the ostracism, there's no single individual to take revenge upon, because the entire group voted you out.

You might be right in thinking ostracism to be a bygone relic of the past, but its success alongside a century of Athenian prosperity reflects a deep and important part of human nature. When a member of a group acts selfishly, believing their needs to be above those of the group, the others burn with resentment, even if they don't outwardly show it. In the modern workplace, we despise those who always turn up late in the morning with a smirk on their face, fail to fill up the coffee machine, or promise their help on a project only to let you do all the work while taking the credit for themselves. Due to modern labour laws, it's usually not possible to simply get rid of such types as the Athenians did, unless their contempt manifests in the work they do for their job. Group leaders often fail to punish these selfish individuals perhaps due to cowardice or a desire to show leniency, particularly if the individual happens to do good work. But those leaders who allow this kind of behaviour to continue don't realise that they betray the quiet, conscientious, and hard-working members of the group every time they are lenient to the braggart, the boaster, or the slacker. This betrayal *never* goes unnoticed among the group, and it can ruin any kind of respect and support that the leader might have previously enjoyed. They might ask "Why should we work hard if she can slack off all day?" or "Why does he get to change all of our processes? He's only been here for a month!" The group collectively burns with resentment, and grumblers who were once silent now come forward to stoke the fire—the net effect being the distraction of the group from their work.

The same dynamic happens when individuals join a group for the first time. Eager to impress, they take on all the work, they compliment the boss, and try to make their mark on every aspect of the team's business. While this behaviour might come from a positive place, it is counter-productive at best and destructive to the team at worst. It is easy to discount the insecurity that this arouses as childish and petty, but it is useless to battle against human nature— you may as well shout at your pocket calculator the next time it gives you an unexpected answer. Perhaps it would be better for the existing team members to see the greater benefit brought by the new member's enthusiasm, but only the wisest and least defensive people will see it that way. It is far more productive to adopt a strategy of flexible accommo-dation when joining a new group, whether it's a new job or a casual sports team. There are existing hierarchies and codes of behaviour in every group, and each one takes a different form—we will call this unique identity the Group Mythology. It is something that must be treated with respected and reverence, particularly when joining the group for the first time. Individuals established in the group for a long time will jealously guard their status in the hierarchy and fight bitterly for their entrenched procedures, no matter how inefficient they might seem from your more objective stand-point as an outsider. Attempt to battle with these types and you will face resistance that might cost you your member-ship of that group—you do not understand the influence that the established members have with the leader, after all

—and definitely cost you any trust from them in the long run.

To show this dynamic, let's look at Benjamin Franklin (1706-1790), the great American Founding Father. At the age of seventeen, Franklin left his job in Philadelphia, Pennsylvania for London, ostensibly to buy the supplies to start his own newspaper with the promised financial backing of Pennsylvania governor Sir William Keith. When he arrived in London, he learned that Sir William was a notorious "talker" who would promise everything to everyone but rarely deliver on those promises. There were no funds or parts waiting for him there in London. Stranded in a foreign country and without the money to return home, he started work in a printer's shop as a typesetter. The job seemed fine for a start, since he had gained the relevant experience working at his brother's newspaper back in America.

Soon he noticed that his English colleagues had a strange custom: Five times a day, they would take a break from their work to drink a pint of beer, and to his shock they asked him to join them and contribute some of his wages to their drinks fund. Coming from the puritanical American colonies, this behaviour shocked Franklin, who refused to partake in something he saw as both lazy and unhealthy. Although his colleagues agreed to leave Franklin alone, in the weeks that followed he began noticing unexpected typographical errors in his work. This seemed impossible to him, because he always paid rigorous attention to detail, and such errors, if consistent, usually cost typesetters their jobs. He became anxious, as he couldn't identify the source of these errors, and worried that he'd get fired for the phantom errors he was apparently producing with increasing frequency. He confronted his colleagues about these errors, who laughed and claimed it was a ghost that inhabited the printing shop. Feeling like he was going insane, Franklin relented and agreed to drink with his fellow print shop workers. Loosening up with the alcohol, he felt surprised at how warmly they now treated him. Even better, the errors miraculously stopped, and he began enjoying his job again.

Franklin's experience in an eighteenth-century printing shop shows us that although our work environments may have evolved along with technology, we as human beings have scarcely changed at all. It is likely that you recognised the situation as it unfolded before Franklin, realising that the errors were being made deliberately by his colleagues. This dynamic is easy to spot as an independent observer, but when experiencing it first-hand this is much harder—we feel stressed and anxious as we sense the group rejecting us. Though they may appear polite, there's a coldness in these interactions. It feels viscerally awful to be alone. We might see ourselves as objective and rational beings, but really we are animals that have evolved to live and work in groups, and we can instinctively sense when we are being shunned.

It is likely in this situation that, like Franklin in the print shop, you have become self-absorbed in your own preferred routines. Consider seeing the situation from the group's perspective: "Here is a new member of the group who thinks he is too good for our daily protocols, and maybe he'll want to change them. Ah, see him sucking up to the boss now. Who does he think he is?" Eliciting such responses is fine if you only intend to make a temporary stay, but to survive and thrive in your new group for the long term, you must subsume your ego a little and accept the group's core rituals, no matter how irrational they may seem. Validate their core beliefs, respect their established routines, and they'll gladly reward you with their support for as long as you keep up this practice.

If you feel like an existing routine or procedure within your group is irrational, unproductive, or even toxic, then avoid the temptation to take the direct approach. People will respond by getting defensive, and only entrench themselves further in their patterns, even if they didn't care too much about it before you came along. It's much better to make a show of adopting some of the group's less obnoxious rituals to gain their trust and, only after you have built up a wide enough base of support within the team, question these routines in a respectful manner. Don't outwardly state your dislike for it, but frame your task as a problem to be solved, where getting rid of that irrational procedure stands out as an obvious solution. Frame the interaction as you asking them for advice, being polite in your speech and avoiding coarse language. Your colleagues may still disagree, and that's fine. Don't be so arrogant as to think you can push your beliefs on others, or you will face the same fate as Aristides and Themistocles. If you become known for hammering on the same issues every time you get the chance, your colleagues will avoid you, and reputations like that can take a long time to undo. Arguers and firebrands like that only cause unproductive anxiety and their colleagues are right to shun them. At every step, then, make a show of respecting your colleagues' opinions, accommodating the Group Mythology, and your workplace will become less stressful for everyone involved.

> Think with the few and speak with the many. To want to go against the current is as impossible for the wise as it is easy for the reckless. Only a Socrates could undertake this. Dissent is taken as an insult since it condemns another's judgement. Those offended multiply, either because of the point criticised or the person who'd endorsed it. Truth is for the few; deception is as common as it is vulgar.
>
> — BALTASAR GRACIÁN

REVERSAL

There are toxic work environments that you should do your best to avoid, where adopting their Group Mythology will only bring you to psychological ruin. The best practice in these cases is to watch how people behave, and remain aware of any kind of bullying that seems built into the group and quit before you get hurt. There are also perfectly non-toxic groups that you may have no interest in accommodating, and that's fine. But we rarely have much choice in who we work with, and our workplace is a group whose spirit we can't ignore.

Although you should not take the advice in this chapter at face value and completely subsume your principles, or overtly lie to others to gain their trust, there is little to be gained from ignoring a group's binding beliefs. You can tell yourself all you like that you're staying true to your principles or that your abrasive ideas are serving the group as a whole, but if you irritate others, change their schedules and routines, and rubbish their existing Group Mythology, then don't count on your colleagues' support when times get tough. You will have invalidated and angered them to such a degree that the second you get into trouble, they will see the opportunity to strike and take it without a moment's hesitation.

Remember that the best strategy in a group is to gain a wide base of support, so that your new friends will come to your aid when you need it most. To attach yourself to the boss from day one at the utter contempt of your colleagues might take you to the top quickly, but it will later result in a sudden and hard fall. The principle of group accommodation can bear no reversal—do not bother looking for one.

4

DEALING WITH DIFFICULT MASTERS

A lmost *everyone has a story about a tyrannical boss, and they often tell them with strong feelings of resentment, injustice, and anger. We are social group animals, and we naturally look to our group's leader for cues on how to act and behave. A difficult leader, therefore, can have a disproportionately negative effect on both the well-being and productivity of the group. The most important key to dealing effectively with a difficult boss is to keep your head on straight and refuse to let them control your emotions. You don't need to be insubordinate, but you do need to show that you can't be pushed around, because a tyrant will always tend to bully those who are most easily bullied.*

SURVIVING IN THE MODERN COURT

Dealing with a boss takes great skill and is always a balancing act. We want to do good work and address them with politeness and respect, without being a sycophant. In response, good leaders appreciate your work, pay it the due recognition it deserves, or else give feedback on how to improve it, and help you grow and develop your skills. This represents a fair and equal transaction of labour, respect, and learning between two parties. However, this model is an ideal that rarely manifests in real life. More often we experience misunderstandings with our managers and supervisors that cause friction and mutual difficulties. In these cases, we need to think deeper and assess whether we're communicating up and down these channels clearly enough, and giving our colleagues at all levels the appropriate amount of respect and validation. We can profitably build mutually supportive relationships with most colleagues, including good leaders, by using the techniques described in this book's earlier chapters.

Unfortunately, no matter how hard we might try to understand others, some bosses are predisposed to cause friction and suffering. If we encounter a difficult colleague on an equal level of the workplace hierarchy, it's easy enough to solve this friction using the techniques described in this book—but a difficult boss requires an especially delicate touch. Too direct, and we might lose our jobs; too indirect, and our message will get lost in translation and we'll slowly lose our sanity. In this chapter we will explore the ways you can deal profitably with a difficult master while keeping your head. Before we get into this, a warning: If you feel like you're not getting the recognition you deserve at work, or your boss makes a decision that seems ill-informed, then it's important to not leap to the conclusion that they are a narcissistic sociopath—you may be succumbing to one of the many communication blunders described in this book. But if you're noticing a pattern of behaviour in your boss that's damaging the group then it's time to act. As with any colleague the direct approach is rarely productive, and if you're too direct with your boss, then you may have a new problem on your hands. Dealing with a difficult master requires strategy and subtlety—in a way it is more about what you do *not* do, what you do *not* say. You must keep your head and not get emotional, because that will cloud your objective judgement and give them a distinct advantage.

Whatever resentment you carry, or fantasies you might have of "defeating" this boss, you must recognise that these feelings are self-destructive. There can be no benefit to letting this resentment eat away at you, occasionally snarling at your boss, and not getting the most out of your job. Remember that your goal at work is to learn as much as you can, while helping your colleagues do the same, and earn a fair amount of compensation for the work you provide to the team. Seeking your reward in the form of genuine love and appreciation from your colleagues is a much better long-term strategy, because its results are entirely within your control. Getting credit for your work is outside your control, and whining about not getting it will actually have the opposite effect. While you learn how to deal with difficult masters in this chapter, never lose sight of your goals to learn and support your colleagues—this attitude will take you much further and bring you greater satisfaction than any victory you might think you've gained against your boss.

The following are five types of difficult masters that appear in work and many other areas of life, each with relevant strategies on how best to deal with them. Your own situation may call for a combination of these strategies, for people are complex and often exhibit multiple negative traits at different times. They are culled from history's greatest people-managers and based upon commonly accepted tenets of interpersonal group psychology.

The insecure master. People who harbour doubts about their self-worth are difficult to deal with in any environment, but as a group leader they can hold back their team's progress and force it to sit in stagnation. The insecure leader cannot bear to see any of their subordinate colleagues succeed, and can't bring themselves to give them their due credit. They may even go so far as to hold people back from deserved promotions, and they will often take the credit for a subordinate's hard work as their own. Consumed with envy, this type fosters great resentment in a team that slowly realises it's not being recognised for its hard work. See that the effect of this leader is self-destructive. Insecure masters will often reveal themselves by micromanaging their team, a manifestation of their need for control, which the team usually interprets as a lack of trust from their leader.

The worst way to deal with these types is direct confrontation, because they will only harden and take your criticism as a personal insult. Instead, say that you've learned something from them; or, request their help on a task. All masters, but especially the insecure, delight at such requests and will feel deeply validated that you've given them a chance to show their worth. Demonstrate that you and your colleagues can be trusted to take decisions, keep them informed of your plans, and they may soften their obsessive need for control. Whatever you do, refuse to indulge the cruel temptation to feed their insecurities. It will probably feel intensely satisfying to twist their neuroticism for a brief moment, but you cannot control whatever violent reaction they might show next. You will become a lightning rod for all of their insecurities, and the results will be ugly—smoothness of tongue and a polite tone are a much safer strategy.

The know-it-all master. This type is similar to the insecure master, showing the same defensive attitude when challenged by subordinates. What distinguishes the know-it-all from the insecure master is a more overt need to bulldoze over employees in meetings, claim that your ideas are really just derivatives of their own, and blame others when things go wrong. They consistently exhibit a need to show how clever they are, and aren't afraid to shut down anyone who might prove otherwise. The know-it-all constantly sees threats around them, and will often respond with over-whelming and disproportionate force, using bullying tactics to silence the "offender." In meetings, they will sniff out intelligent but quiet introverts and openly rubbish their ideas, delighting in their confused, stammering responses. Several weeks later, the know-it-all will smugly espouse those same ideas as if they were their own, making their subordi-nates furious with resentment. Their nature, however, often limits their learning, since that would prove they have gaps in their knowledge. They hurt the group by allowing knowl-edge to hoard with the employees strong enough to stand their presence, while never allowing them to make decisions. When those employees have finally had enough and leave, the rest of the team suffers, and the know-it-all exclaims for all to hear that his paranoia was justified all along.

These types are clever, aggressive, and slippery in conversation, always spoiling for an opportunity to prove their worth yet happy to deny any culpability in their crimes. It is unlikely you'll be able to match them in confrontation, because they love fighting and have been doing it all their lives. They see quiet and intelligent people who keep to themselves as a threat and thrive on defeating them by aggravating them into a frenzy and making them humiliate themselves. Research by the pioneering psychoanalyst Melanie Klein (1882-1960) showed that some infants display such ultra-aggressive tendencies from an early age, demanding more nursing and attention from their mothers than others. The child's need to dominate others stems from unusually high levels of anxiety—growing up, these infants cannot bear the thought of anyone showing them to be wrong. Other, less aggressive children may respond healthily to such feedback, but their relatively easy-going natures are easily broken apart by the dominant child plagued with anxiety. Seeing your aggressive boss as an oversized, anxious baby might make you feel better, and it reflects the key to dealing with such types.

The power of know-it-all bosses is that they grate on your nerves, fostering a resentment that grows with each condescending comment. They delight in distorting your mind by clouding it with rage, making it easier for them to dance around you in meetings and other interactions. Deny them this power and you blunt their only tactic. The next time they try to dominate you or openly disparage a colleague, look them in the eye and calmly explain your points, or act as if you didn't hear them and make them repeat their remark for all to hear. You must do this with an innocent expression, otherwise the know-it-all will catch on to your game. It may be particularly difficult to keep your cool if the boss has gathered a group of "yes-men" to support them in such instances—bullies often do this to make their "bravery" easier to display.

Instead of letting a bullying boss twist your emotions, try using their tyrannical energies to your advantage. First gain their favour, and then direct their aggression at the toxic colleagues who try to steal credit for your work or badmouth you behind your back. Aggressive bosses are often very protective of those they have an affinity for. For example, if you suspect that a colleague is planning to complain about you to your boss, or has shown a pattern of cynical comments, then pre-empt this colleague by paying the boss a compliment about some help they might have given you, or giving them a thoughtful gift. When the toxic colleague then tries to ply his trade, your boss will not be impressed, because as far as they're concerned you're a conscientious and gracious employee. Making use of a boss like this is far more productive than getting torn up about their arrogance and dismissive attitude.

Remember that it is alright to contradict a boss so long as you do it respectfully, making a show of putting the group's needs first. Unused to your calm demeanour in the face of their trusty bullying tactics, and unable to refute your arguments, they will grow to respect you and leave you alone.

The over-friendly master. It's good for a leader to keep their team's bellies full, treating them with respect, and occasionally asking to learn more about them when appropriate. But you should be wary of the boss who makes a show of being your friend, mostly because their outer demeanour is so seductive to young or naïve employees. Their friendly manner comes with obvious benefits, such as a decrease in stress across the team, a cheerful and relaxed atmosphere, and an understanding ear when things are getting tough. But it can also come with potential negatives, such as a lack of pressure to make progress in our projects, rewarding undeserving employees to be "nice" and to make them feel included, and a passive-aggressive attitude when office-wide frustrations fluctuate, as they tend to do.

To understand why this master is difficult, it's essential to understand the difference between being *good* and being *nice*. The former entails a leadership style that puts the well-being and achievements of the team first, unafraid to be honest when subordinates aren't performing well, and delivers a fair distribution of rewards based on merit. The latter, typical of the over-friendly type, is dishonest, prioritises pleasing individual people over the team's overall well-being, and doesn't properly communicate feedback in a way that can be effectively used by subordinates. These types will be your buddy one day and then turn nasty the next, without honestly explaining why their tone has changed. This is doubly bad because they offend you without conveying the clear feed-

back that usually accompanies it—and you leave these interactions feeling betrayed by your "friend" without
understanding how to avoid that situation in the future.

The only effective way to deal with the over-friendly
master is to keep them at arm's length. Don't get tied into a
web of what seems like friendship, because it's only ever a
trap. Be polite and friendly with your boss, but make sure
that the relationship is one of professional exchange. These
types are touchy about morality—criticise something they do,
and they'll instantly list their good intentions behind the
choice they made. In these situations, assure them that you
agree with the purity of their motives, but gently ask for
frankness instead of niceties. It's difficult to have a clear,
objective discussion with these leaders because they're so
worried about being offensive. A boss's honesty may sting,
but if they deliver it clearly and constructively, then it helps
us to grow. Encourage the over-friendly boss to be honest
and objective during meetings, giving them plenty of assur-
ance that you won't be offended. The key in dealing with this
master is to keep work strictly professional, and if you must
make friends at work, only do so with your colleagues—it is a
harsh reality of life, but it will keep you out of the firing line
when times get tough.

The political master. This type is focused on one thing,
and one thing only: their rise to the top. They will court,
backstab, take credit, whatever is necessary to climb to the
top of the greasy pole. Nothing is off-limits to the political
type, and do not think they will not exploit you if doing so
will provide the advancement they crave. What the political
master will not do, however, is the honest work necessary to
gain the true acclaim they deeply hunger for. This is the
tragic irony of the political type. To spot them in your group,
try to notice patterns of behaviour that involve sycophantic
praise for their own boss, combined with rudeness to subor-

dinates, or those they don't feel the need to impress. The political master is especially dangerous because they always put themselves above the needs of the group, and will happily run teams into the ground so long as they can deflect the blame onto others. Much like the over-friendly boss they may try to be your buddy, but with a much more sinister motive: to learn more about that coveted project you're working on, or to exploit your existing relationship with someone higher up the chain. They are slippery and possess an indomitable will, always able to slither around "obstacles" in their path.

The best way to deal with political types is to use reverse intimidation. Create the impression that interfering with you will cost more than it's worth. Political types, even when in positions of leadership, are usually cowards and jealously protective of their reputations, so you must be able to threaten that which they hold most dear. Spend time building up a good reputation with colleagues and bosses in other departments. This will give you a wide base of support, and make it impossible for the political master to spread bad words about you. Make some bold and unexpected manoeuvre, creating uncertainty around what you might do next. Even showing a hint of a wild streak will have the desired effect, because no one wants to fight the person who has nothing to lose. Deliberately create a risk that they cannot control, and that can cost them dearly if they attempt to cross you. As always with bosses, be respectful and do your job, but do not be afraid to contradict them if you recognise an imminent attack. Reverse intimidation is the best strategy to combat those who have the most to lose from an ugly, public fight.

The indecisive master. This type of master is constantly bullied, harassed, and misled into making decisions that only serve the stronger subordinates around them rather than the group. Perhaps promoted above their capacity, the indecisive master is constantly anxious, consumed with neurotic thoughts, and too afraid to take action. The result is a team that feels bored and confused, only looking out for themselves. The experienced and skilled people in the group are forced to step in and make decisions, often feeling resentful that someone so weak could earn a promotion ahead of them.

These leaders agonise over decisions, holding meeting after meeting, giving those around them an ulcer. They will argue that they're weighing up all the options, but really they're afraid of failure, and are waiting for someone else to decide for them. They expect the rays of sunlight to shine down upon the office in unison, giving some heavenly omen that the time is right. Good leaders realise that time is limited and that the information available will always be incomplete, nevertheless using it to make the best decision at the time. Where possible, seek such leaders for your team and keep the indecisive ones far away from the positions of responsibility, for the taking of that responsibility is key to a successful team that fearlessly progresses forward.

Most indecisive masters are surrounded by vipers trying to manipulate them in the directions that best please themselves, so don't worsen this burden at the expense of your team. Instead, tell them you have full confidence that they can make a decent decision, and remind them of the dangers of not taking action, showing your points with examples. Don't exacerbate the pressure of looming deadlines, because that will only make them defensive. Encourage them to be less agreeable, so that strong subordinates can't push them around so easily. Give them an image of a proud leader to aspire to and watch them approach meetings with their heads up and shoulders back. Stand up for them in those meetings and show your agreement with their ideas. If these leaders develop in a positive direction, then you will have built up a valuable and appreciative ally with little cost.

* * *

HOW TO DEFEAT A TYRANT

In the summer of 1833, Frederick Douglass (1818-1895) had good reason to feel upset. A slave owned by the Maryland farmer Thomas Auld, Douglass had spent the previous seven years hired out to Auld's brother, Hugh, in Baltimore. To the chagrin of Hugh, his wife Sophia had taught Douglass the alphabet and tutored him in basic reading skills. Douglass had also stolen Hugh's newspapers and some spelling books, using these to learn how to read from white children in the neighbourhood on the sly. While hired out to a plantation owner named William Freeland, Douglass had been caught teaching dozens of slaves on the plantation—Freeland himself was open-minded about their activities, but Thomas Auld and other slaveowners felt incensed about their slaves being educated, and violently burst in on one of Douglass's Sunday gatherings armed with clubs. So in 1833, more than anything to punish his brother Hugh for allowing his slave to read in the first place, Thomas denied Douglass the chance to go back to serve Hugh in Baltimore, and instead sent him to the plantation of Edward Covey.

Covey enjoyed a far-reaching reputation as a "slave-breaker," often employed for his services on young slaves who had showed a pattern of "impudence" to their masters. For six months, Covey whipped Douglass daily, worked him to his breaking point, and fed him barely enough to stay alive. Covey would often slink around behind Douglass and surprise him with the lash, unprovoked. His goal was to break Douglass's spirit down, and he succeeded. One day, in the baking summer heat, Douglass collapsed with a migraine in the middle of working the plantation fields. Hearing that the work had stopped, Covey rode over to the group of slaves working, and commanded Douglass to get up. He tried to obey, but could barely speak in response and collapsed on his face. Covey yelled at Douglass, kicking him repeatedly to rouse him, even smashing a brick on his head before storming off. By sheer luck, this last blow opened a gash and released the pressure from his migraine. When he felt strong enough, he rose and staggered off into the nearby woods.

Overnight, Douglass walked the seven miles back to the Auld house, and pleaded with Thomas to let him come back. Initially, he seemed almost sympathetic to the young slave, angered that his "property" had been so damaged, but ultimately refused Douglass's request. He told Douglass that he could stay the night and take some medicine, but that he had to work the remaining six months on Covey's lease.

After returning to the Covey plantation, Douglass was instructed to attend to some animals in the barn. It was a trap—Covey and a farm hand hit Douglass from behind and attempted to rope him up. Having enjoyed a full night's sleep at Thomas's plantation, Douglass found the anger and strength to fight back. He resisted Covey's attempts to tie his feet, and ended up striking Covey in the head, knocking him hard to the ground. For a split second, Douglass had shocked even himself. They usually hanged slaves who hit white people, but this now meant he had nothing to lose. He continued to beat Covey and, much to the plantation owner's anger, none of his other slave hands agreed to help him. Covey staggered away, and Douglass felt a wave of panic blow over him—he would almost certainly face the hangman, made an example of for other slaves. But, to his great surprise, this never materialised. While Covey maintained his usual nasty manners, he never whipped Douglass again for the remaining six months.

This incident gave Douglass new confidence, and he walked taller while working the Covey plantation, now even firmer in his resolve to gain his freedom. Several years later, having returned to the service of Hugh Auld in Baltimore, Douglass learned a trade, working alongside white carpenters in the shipyards. The physical strength and speed he had gained from years of brutal labour as a plantation field worker allowed him to work faster than any of the other apprentices, and in some weeks he earned as much as nine dollars for Hugh, who was entitled to all of his earnings. Disgusted by having to give all of his hard-earned wages to his master, Douglass pleaded with Hugh to allow him to work for himself. To his great surprise, Hugh agreed—the deal worked out rather well for him, since Douglass's shipyard trade was unstable and he would be entitled to a smaller, yet fixed sum from Douglass once a week, and save all the rest from board, food, and equipment that he would otherwise need to supply a slave from his own pocket.

This arrangement worked fine, until Douglass spent one of his Sundays outside of Baltimore. Hugh felt enraged that Douglass had left the city without his permission and angrily took away his new privileges. Once again exploited and unjustly detained, Douglass gave Hugh a fierce look of violence throughout this exchange, and tensed his large, powerful body as if to strike his master, but calmed himself enough to realise that he would need to earn Hugh's trust again. He obeyed his master throughout the next week, earning him yet another high pay cheque, which Hugh gratefully accepted. But that Sunday, he fled Baltimore by boarding a train to New York City, where he asserted his freedom. He remained a freeman and staunch public abolitionist for the rest of his life.

INTERPRETATION

Let us be clear from the outset: Frederick Douglass was enslaved and legally compelled to serve his master at the threat of horrific violence, and so his circumstances bear many incomparable differences to those we face in the modern workplace. In spite of this, the story of Douglass's early life reveals many facts about tyrants and how to defeat them. Hugh Auld scolded his wife Sophia for teaching young Douglass to read, because education was usually the route slaves took to emancipation. As he watched Hugh explain this reasoning, Douglass realised that his greatest hopes of freedom through book-learning were indeed true, and he later credited Hugh's diatribe as the "first decidedly anti-slavery lecture" he had ever heard.

Masters understand all too well that underlings who educate themselves are the ones most likely to leave for their own ventures. Slave owners in the American South would brutally put down any attempt of their slaves to learn to read, which happened with Douglass's Sunday school and on several other occasions. In his second autobiography, Douglass describes a harrowing scene in which his slave owner encouraged Douglass's slave comrades to drink themselves silly in their free time, ensuring they had no ability or inclination to engage in productive pursuits outside of their back-breaking labour. By learning to read and write, Douglass set himself apart from not only the other slaves but also the free white men he worked alongside in the Baltimore shipyards. Jealous of the eloquence with which the young slave spoke, his apprentice colleagues would beat him to a pulp, attempting to crush his spirit.

Like Douglass, you must understand that the best solution to the tyranny of the master's court is to leave, and that this is best achieved by using your spare time on education and gathering new skills. From his time on Edward Covey's plantation, Douglass learned that by refusing to bow to his cruel lashes, he made himself less liable for such treatment. Douglass was lucky not to have been hanged for his fight with Covey, since in slave-holding America to strike a master usually meant a gruesome public execution to ward off others from trying the same. But Covey had gained a reputation that he valued, bringing him a reliable source of income and prestige. If word got out that he'd failed to break a slave this one time, it would ruin his reputation. It paid him to keep quiet about the incident, choosing to wait out the rest of Douglass's service.

Understand that bullies will only attempt to beat those who are most easily beaten. If you whimper and submit to the bully's blows, then you give him all the pleasure and power he's looking for. Fight back and hurt him, and you show that messing with you is more trouble than it's worth. Above all, what the tyrant most fears is an insurrection from his subjects, for deep down he knows he deserves it. Hold your head up high, be proud of your personal power, and no tyrant will ever be able to touch you. As Frederick Douglass wrote in his book *My Bondage and My Freedom*:

> To make a contented slave, you must make a thoughtless one. It is necessary to darken his moral and mental vision, and, as far as possible, to annihilate his power of reason. He must be able to detect no inconsistencies in slavery. The man that takes his earnings, must be able to convince him that he has a perfect right to do so. It must not depend upon mere force; the slave must know no Higher Law than his master's will. The whole relationship must not only demonstrate, to his mind, its necessity, but its absolute rightfulness. If there be one crevice through which a single drop can fall, it will certainly rust off the slave's chain.

KEEPING YOUR MASTER IN THE LOOP

During the First Battle of Manassas in July 1861, the Confederate brigadier general Joseph E. Johnston (1807-1891) rushed to reinforce P. G. T. Beauregard in the Shenandoah Valley. Arriving at the Confederate line, he found soldiers in complete disarray, all their field-grade officers killed. Even the beloved senior general Thomas J. "Stonewall" Jackson had been wounded in action, discouraging the men left fighting. At great personal risk, Johnston rallied the men into a single unit and reinforced the front line—Beauregard eventually persuaded Johnston not to risk himself there and to return and help with organising further tactical reinforcements. The battle ended in a decisive victory for the Confederates, and Beauregard took most of the public credit, even though Johnston's rallying of the reinforcements on the front lines had played a key role.

For his performance at Manassas, Johnston was promoted to full general by Jefferson Davis, president of the Confederacy. However, Johnston still only stood fourth in the Confederate military seniority, behind three men he had outranked in the US Army before the Civil War: Samuel Cooper, Albert Sidney Johnston, and Robert E. Lee. Johnston had been a brigadier general for longer than these men before resigning his commission in the US Army to join the Confederates, so why should they all be chosen ahead of him? Davis explained that while Johnston had outranked these men in staff rank, his highest official rank in the field was as a lieutenant-colonel of the line before joining the staff. Lee, whom Johnston bitterly envied, had been a full colonel in the field and then promoted to brigadier general just before the Confederate secession, and Davis had decided to place maximum attained field rank over staff rank. Furious for what he saw as clear favouritism for the obsequious Lee, Johnston sent Davis a frankly worded letter accusing him of such. Davis considered getting rid of him for his insubordination and emotionality, but decided against it, since he needed all the experienced leaders he could get, and Johnston was a popular figure among his troops.

In October, Johnston was given command of the Confederate Army of the Potomac and charged with defending northern Virginia from the Union army led by major-general George B. McClellan. Although McClellan's army in fact far outsized Johnston's, the Union general believed that the Confederate fortifications in Manassas would be too strong, and overestimated the number of rebel soldiers under Johnston's command. McClellan turned his army to the sea to prepare for an amphibious assault on Johnston's flank instead. Learning of these preparations, Johnston unilaterally retreated his army southward, leaving northern Virginia undefended and the opportunity to strike at McClellan's own flank to pass by. Throughout the autumn and winter, Davis hadn't received a word from Johnston, and was angry that he had acted so cowardly, revealing to the Union army that the Confederate defenders in Virginia weren't as strong as they seemed. He immediately brought the senior general Robert E. Lee back from the field and appointed him his personal military adviser, using Lee as a proxy to send direct orders right to the forces under Johnston's command. Lee salved Davis's fragile ego by assuring him he was correct to exert such control over the insubordinate general.

In 1863, Davis ordered Johnston to proceed to Vicksburg, Mississippi, as it was then under threat by the Union major-general Ulysses S. Grant. Arriving in the city of Jackson just short of Vicksburg, Johnston learned of two large Union armies on the approach, and ordered a full retreat of his own troops and Jackson's 6,000 defenders.

Grant strolled into Jackson, and soon after took Vicksburg, giving the Union complete control of the pivotal Mississippi River. Instructed by Davis to leave Mississippi for his utter failure to secure the river, Johnston wrote a petulant letter right back to the president claiming that he had misconstrued the meaning of his orders. Facing public outcry for having lost Vicksburg, Davis considered firing Johnston again, but he remained popular both with his men and many key Confederate politicians, so once more he left him alone.

Unable to make a decisive move on Johnston's position in the army, Davis's patience finally ran out in 1864 when the general failed to stop the Union army under William T. Sherman from taking Atlanta, Georgia. Despite having the strength to repulse Sherman, Johnston made an unexpected retreat across the Chattahoochee River, leaving the field open for Sherman to take the key Confederate city. Atlanta was the most important port in the South and taking it meant the Union had achieved its prime objective in subduing the Confederate army's supply lines. Only then did Davis finally fire Johnston from the army, though by then it was only a matter of time until the Confederates lost the war.

INTERPRETATION

Although Joseph E. Johnston's military record clearly demonstrates his failure as a general during the American Civil War, his poor professional relationship with Jefferson Davis was arguably his worst fault. Had he communicated his plans and their intentions to Davis more clearly, his numerous blunders might have been avoided long in advance. Johnston's problem was that he didn't understand his role in the army of a democratic nation, and didn't believe he needed to subordinate himself to civilian superiors like Davis. This was particularly bad in relation to Davis's own personality. The Confederate president was a famously insecure and indecisive leader, unable to rise above personal feuds and in need of total control of both civil and military affairs. Davis could not delegate, and until very late in the war he didn't appoint a general-in-chief, as the Union president Abraham Lincoln had done with George B. McClellan and later Ulysses S. Grant. Had he delegated ultimate command of the army to his senior general Robert E. Lee, self-absorbed troublemakers like Johnston might not have been able to stay so long in the Confederate army.

Lee, in sharp contrast to Johnston, showed the best way to deal with leaders like Davis throughout the Civil War. Having worked closely with Davis for a long time before the war, Lee knew that Davis needed to feel completely in control of his subordinates and took all criticism personally, holding lifelong grudges against his rivals. At every stage of his own campaigns with the Army of Northern Virginia, Lee wrote daily letters to Davis, explaining where he was, where he planned to go next, and what he hoped to accomplish. When Johnston offended Davis, Lee used his seductive personal manner to soothe the situation and assure the president he was doing the right thing. Fighting Davis directly would have accomplished nothing, and with a war going on the Confederate machine needed to keep operating efficiently—constant personal squabbles would sabotage that, and Lee repeatedly had to smooth things over both with the president and his own high command. Learn the lesson from Johnston's story: If you have an insecure, indecisive boss who obsesses over control, then don't fight them and don't keep them in the dark, because that will only worsen their paranoia and threaten your operation.

CONFIRM THE MASTER'S SELF-IMAGE

No woman reached the top of French society as quickly as Jeanne-Antoinette Poisson. At the age of nine, Poisson's mother took her to a fortuneteller who prophesied that she would one day rule over the heart of the king himself. Taking this prophecy literally, Poisson's guardian arranged for her to be educated in drawing, painting, and the theatre, among other subjects, all intended to groom her to become Louis XV's mistress. She married Charles d'Étoiles, her guardian's nephew, and her new marital status allowed her to frequent the multitude of fashionable Paris salons and mingle with figures in French high society and the Enlightenment, such as the writer Voltaire and the philosopher Montesquieu. Poisson became an expert in the bustling social games of these Paris salons, and it was not long until Louis XV had heard her name mentioned at court.

In 1744, she grabbed the king's attention while he led a hunt close to her estate in Étoiles—because of this proximity, Poisson was allowed the rare privilege of trailing behind the hunting party at a distance. For Poisson, this wasn't enough, so she took a gamble and rode directly ahead of Louis in her bright pink carriage. It paid off, and Louis sent her a gift of venison from his hunt. As further evidence of her progress, Louis' current mistress Madame de Châteauroux jealously tried to ward her off with a scathing letter. In December of that year, Châteauroux died—widely suspected to be due to poison—and soon after his mistress's death, Louis invited Poisson to a masked ball at Versailles, at which she dazzled the king and his court, earning her the position of royal mistress she had long coveted. Louis, enamoured by his enigmatic new mistress, made her a marquise, and arranged for a speedy legal separation between Poisson and her husband, which Charles's own father blessed. Charles never forgave his wife and family for their treachery.

Almost immediately on her arrival at Versailles, Poisson sought to gain the good graces of the royal family. She could see that Louis, while royal master of all France, lacked the famed pride of his great-grandfather Louis XIV. Where the Sun King had made his powerful presence known in any room of Versailles, Louis XV was more modest, seeking to blend into the background and rely on the advice of others. He still enjoyed ceremony and being the centre of attention from time to time, but never to the same regularity as his august predecessor. Poisson analysed the situation and noticed that the king would hopelessly give himself over to the mistresses of the court, almost to the point of being undignified—often taking the advice of young guests at the court over his cabinet ministers. The same situation had played out with Poisson herself. The new royal mistress decided on her strategy: She would win the favour of the queen in particular, while lavishing attention on Louis— providing masked balls with him at the centre, and theatre performances where she would star. In daily affairs at the court, she would gain the friendship of those closest to the king to strengthen her enveloping effect on the centre of power.

This all worked beautifully, and by 1750 she had, for all intents and purposes, appointed herself France's prime minister. Jeanne-Antoinette Poisson completely gained the king's ear, for he trusted her above all the other courtiers, who by that time were mostly charlatans and profligates, since the king's weak leadership over his court had attracted swindlers to exploit the royal largesse freely displayed at Versailles. The royal mistress controlled all the goings on, the hiring and firing of cabinet ministers, and even convinced Louis into a war with Prussia. Though she had gained some

enemies who envied her power, gained only from her affection from the king and not through blood, far more in the
court loved her and were afraid of Louis' wrath if they dared
cross her. Poisson had not just conquered the narrow world
of Versailles, she had gained near total control of the entire
French kingdom. As one of Louis' nobles later remarked:

> Louis XIV had been too proud, but Louis XV was not
> proud enough. Other than his excessive modesty, his great
> and sole vice was women; he believed that only his
> mistresses loved him enough to tell him the truth. For that
> reason he allowed them to lead him, which contributed to
> his failure with finance, which was the worse aspect of his
> reign.

INTERPRETATION

Jeanne-Antoinette Poisson, better known later in her life as
Madame de Pompadour, enjoyed a level of power unheard
of for women at the time. She had the complete trust and
confidence of the French king and befriended the country's
highest aristocracy, with none of the heavy burdens of
responsibility that would normally sit on the shoulders of
someone that powerful. The few enemies she had in
Versailles were too afraid of incurring the king's wrath, for
he so depended on her for friendship and counsel.

Poisson set her sights on conquering the king's heart
from a young age, and learned the arts, theatre, and developed her famed biting wit in conversation—gaining Louis'
attention during the hunt was simple and required the
audacity to ride in front of his carriage. But the real key to
her conquest of Louis was in observing his personality and
making herself a force of pleasure and in his life. Louis XV
inherited the throne at the age of five in the shadow of his

great-grandfather, one of the most proud and influential kings in history. From an age when a child should only worry about playing and school, constant court intrigues surrounded him. He needed constant protection from the kinds of exploitative types that often flock to centres of power such as Versailles. It is no wonder that Louis clung to the safe and love-giving people in his life. Poisson embodied this need of Louis' all throughout her time at Versailles.

The reign of Louis XV saw France's treasury drained by foreign wars, and its long-suffering peasantry left to rot in hunger and squalor. Whatever influence Poisson might have had on Louis, it did not help him to realise the decline in the French monarchy and perhaps take steps to reverse it. In fact, she encouraged the kind of royal largesse that both distracted Louis from ruling France and agitated revolutionary sentiment among the peasantry. So let's not pretend that she contributed much to the greater good of France. Poisson's story shows the seductive power you can have over an insecure and isolated master. Rulers like this are made to feel small by a domineering parent, a terrifying childhood, or even a grand predecessor, as was the case with Louis XV. They want to find someone they can trust and who makes them feel safe and wanted. These comforting people are often natural charmers, able to get into the skin of the other person and sense their wants and needs. When such a person comes along, the master clings to them for dear life, trusting them above all others, and valuing their feedback over the types who, while less comforting, can steer them straight and keep them alive. It may not be for the greater good of the whole, but the insecure master is a ripe sucker for positive attention, and if you can move the king, then you can move the kingdom.

REVERSAL

It is so easy, particularly when young, to see our boss as a cruel and dictatorial tyrant. But often this is our ego doing the thinking for us. We enter the work world with a grand vision of what we'll accomplish, how we'll dazzle in meetings and double our salary year after year. The grim reality of daily work quickly ruins this image. We learn to temper our grand visions for the future with the realities of human nature. Our bosses aren't tyrants, they're people with their own motives and desires, acting from a different perspective to you. To them, you might be an upstart threatening their position. Some of us, however, never grow out of this naïve perspective, and continue to rail against our leaders. We let the resentment grow with every passing remark from our boss, every overlooked piece of work we poured long hours into. Recognise that this resentment is actually grandiosity in disguise, and that you cannot bear the reality of someone having authority over you, no matter how temporary it might be. Such grandiosity can only breed negative resentment, for it lives in the ideal and never in reality.

To achieve Social Intelligence, we must put ourselves firmly in reality, watching events happen with a dispassionate eye. We can make career choices to make this easier on ourselves: If we're young and inexperienced, the worst thing we can do is aim for the easy positions with high salaries— such roles are usually interwoven with all kinds of hidden responsibilities that aren't clear from the outside. By orienting ourselves into a mindset of making learning and developing valued skills our absolute priority, we can make ourselves far less resentful of our masters, snapping out of any tyrannical illusions we might have made for them. Once you've achieved this level of clarity, you can then analyse your boss's behaviour with objectivity, studying their patterns over stretches of time.

You might notice flashes of insecurity, or of needing to exert dominance over others, and slowly build up a picture of what you're dealing with. Only then can you know how best to interact with them, playing to your strengths and taking their character into account. Understand that your fantasies of "defeating" your boss are infantile, signs of a toxic grandiosity that will consume you from the inside. It is much healthier to work with your master, understand their motives, and take a less subjective moral view to everything going on in your office. By not taking every little gesture and action personally, you'll perform better and unload the stress you've been carrying all your adult life.

5

F. W. DE KLERK AND NELSON MANDELA

WIN POSITIONS OF LEADERSHIP BY GAINING A WIDE BASE OF SUPPORT

History has proven that power gained through force is never successful in the long term. Great movements are associated with changes in sentiment among the majority, not any narrow minority. Groups may seem to be dominated by an elite class, but there is always a quiet rumbling of contrary dissent among the majority that demands to be listened to. Leaders who make it to the top by attaching themselves to the boss from day one while showing contempt for the common man never last long. To win positions of leadership, you must gain a wide base of support that will sustain you through the bad times as much as they celebrate you through the good. To do this, you must speak to everyone on their level, activating emotions latent across multiple different sections of the group. Uniting groups is, and has proven to be, the most effective strategy for staying at the top once you make it there.

THE GREAT UNIFICATION

In 1988, F. W. de Klerk had good reason to feel pressure from all sides. The newly elected president of South Africa was widely expected to be no different from his predecessor and continue apartheid, the country's policy of racial segregation. Angry that this racist institution would see no end, the African National Congress (ANC) party planned fresh protests at de Klerk's election victory, and the prominent anti-apartheid activist Desmond Tutu said, "I don't think we've got to even begin to pretend that there is any reason for thinking that we are entering a new phase. It's just musical chairs." Even de Klerk's own colleagues in his National Party criticised him for refusing to act against these protests that were technically illegal under the minority government's rule, the more conservative among them demanding a police crackdown. In response to these critics on all sides, the president implored that everyone involved should avoid violence, saying, "The door to a new South Africa is open, it is not necessary to batter it down."

Over the next year, de Klerk held talks with leaders of the ANC, releasing their elderly imprisoned activists. He even visited the activist Nelson Mandela, whose continued house arrest had stirred up controversy around the world, but most importantly among South Africa's black majority. The racist institution of apartheid had continued decades after the American civil rights movement had ended its similar "Jim Crow" laws, and the country clamoured for change. In February 1990, de Klerk announced plans to legalise the ANC and several other banned political parties, to repeal the Separate Amenities Act of 1953 that codified the policy of apartheid in public buildings and services, and to release the activist Nelson Mandela. De Klerk made the proviso, however, that he did not endorse the socialist and Marxist policies that the ANC embodied, instead laying out a vision of a Western-style liberal democracy where all South Africans would enjoy the same rights. Mandela was released a week later and agreed with de Klerk's political sentiments, cautioning his supporters not to give in to the temptation to enact retribution against the white minority that had ruled South Africa since the colonial days:

> I believe the new political order will and must contain the following elements: a democratic constitution, universal suffrage, no domination, equality before an independent judiciary, the protection of minorities and individual rights, freedom of religion, a healthy economy based on proven economic principles and private initiative, and a dynamic programme for better education, health services, housing and social conditions for all... I am not talking of a rosy and tranquil future, but I believe the broad mainstream of South Africans will gradually build up South Africa into a society that will be worth living and working in.

After his release, Mandela led the ANC in talks with the ruling National Party to end apartheid and establish a multiracial government. Conservative critics of President de Klerk accused him of being complicit with the violence perpetrated by the more extreme wings of the ANC, but he also won over older critics on the anti-apartheid side, as Desmond Tutu encouraged others to support the inclusive talks: "It's incredible... Give him credit. Give him credit, I do." Membership of the National Party was opened up to black people, and parliament voted to abolish its racially based land ownership restrictions. Most important of all, though, was the rescinding of the Population Registration Act that classified all South Africans into their respective racial groups. However, racial tensions persisted in practical terms, as white businesses refused to serve black patrons and vice versa.

In March 1992, de Klerk held a referendum, limited to white South Africans, on whether he should continue the negotiations to end apartheid. The referendum resulted in a large "Yes" victory with an unprecedented turnout—the mandate from South Africa's white minority was clear, and an Interim Constitution was later approved to allow universal suffrage in the 1994 general election. In 1993, the Nobel Peace Prize was jointly awarded to de Klerk and Mandela for their negotiations on ending apartheid. De Klerk's inclusion was controversial among the more radical wings of the ANC, though a larger number felt that the joint awarding of the prize embodied the inclusive work done by both parties. Desmond Tutu applauded de Klerk's public apology of the same year for the white government's deprivation of black rights, even during the president's own term, telling ANC supporters that "saying sorry is not an easy thing to do," and imploring them to be magnanimous in the great progress they'd made, rather than give in to feelings of resentment and retributive social justice.

The 1994 general election, the first to feature universal suffrage across the country, granted a sweeping victory to Nelson Mandela and his African National Congress. This general election had increased the potential number of parliamentary seats from 166 to 400, and the ANC won 252 of them. Though this gave Mandela a strong majority, it did not meet the two-thirds majority required to amend the country's Interim Constitution. De Klerk's National Party was the natural choice for a coalition government, with the former president appointed Mandela's deputy. Although this coalition embodied the inclusion that had powered the negotiations to end apartheid, tensions did not end. President Mandela created the Truth and Reconciliation Commission to investigate human rights violations perpetrated by both white and black people, working hard to remake South Africa into a unified country, instead of becoming a mirror image of the racist white regimes that had ruled the land for so long. He proclaimed the inclusive coalition a "Government of National Unity," asking his people to create a "rainbow nation at peace with itself and the world."

Perhaps the biggest step of all was the unity of support for the national rugby union team, the Springboks, at the 1995 Rugby World Cup hosted by South Africa. Many black South Africans saw rugby as a symbol of white Boer privilege, a sport for the privately educated that would not allow black players. Although the Springbok squad included only one black player, the left-winger Chester Williams, Mandela implored all South Africans to unite behind the team. This gesture of solidarity won him the support of white people who felt afraid at a retribution from the burgeoning black population. The Springboks won the competition in dramatic fashion, beating the famed New Zealand team in a final match that has since been celebrated as one of the greatest underdog victories in sporting history.

Mandela and de Klerk's grand unification project came to a culminating point when, in 1997, the new constitution was approved, enshrining the principles of majority rule and equal rights in law. A grand movement across all sections of the South African people had finally banished the institution of apartheid that had oppressed the country's black population since colonial times.

INTERPRETATION

Activism against apartheid had existed long before de Klerk won the presidency, but the ANC and other groups suffered a kind of impotency in their efforts. Consumed with hatred and resentment towards the white supremacy that both dominated South African society and its laws, they would resort to one-sided protests that usually descended into violence. Intending to provoke the government into harsh crackdowns through acts of terror, anti-apartheid extremists only deepened the racial tensions and turned themselves into an unsympathetic group of extremists. Ordinary white South Africans became defensive and lurched to the far right, fearing a repeat of the black insurrections seen in the American South during the abolition movement of the mid-1800s and the civil rights movement of the 1960s. The international community condemned South Africa as continuing the colonial and racially discriminatory practices that the rest of the world had largely dealt with and moved away from. Apartheid was holding back the country. Something had to be done for the country's future, but real progress seemed impossible.

De Klerk's initiation of the apartheid negotiations, and the ANC's willingness to engage, proved that cooperation, compromise, and mutual leniency for each other's crimes are always the most productive methods for solving long-standing conflicts. But these strategies also united the entire country on a single issue, even across the bitter racial lines. Don't forget that both black and white people wanted an end to apartheid after seeing the oppression and horrors it brought to both sides. The referendum result of 1992 showed that even the country's white Afrikaners felt touched by the reconciliation process. There was no lack of tension during the anti-apartheid negotiations—both Mandela and de Klerk had their share of arguments, especially after Mandela's election victory. But these tensions were powerless against the mass, cross-sectional movement encouraged by both sides of the debate. Ending apartheid would not only stop the colonial oppression of black people, it would help the country gain new trade deals and become a strong, democratic nation in a struggling continent. Instead of overthrowing the government with violent revolution, change came through reconciliation and trust—though the country has had its problems since, it has fared far better than those plagued with violent military coups and retributive social justice. See such resentment-driven movements as taking the easy, short-term path—they only worsen divisions and make each side more unwilling to work with the other. It replaces one oppressive regime with its mirror image, and the vicious cycle continues.

When democratic processes decide positions of leadership, cooperation and unification around common issues is not only the right moral path, it is also an excellent strategy. Finding the common ground on issues facing everyone, and representing that cooperation, is far more likely to win support across disparate sections of the group than fomenting bitter hatred. Both sides will appreciate your open-mindedness, feeling that you validate their strongest beliefs. They will also see you as taking the high ground unlike the other contenders for leadership who go for underhanded tactics—this is a strategy we will explore in the next section of this chapter. If the position of leadership is not democratic and instead in the form of a promotion by a superior, then gaining wide support from everyone in the group will have the same positive effects. Instead of resenting your promotion, you will enjoy a near-universal support from your colleagues. Winning over your enemies in the group is even more important since these people will work harder still to prove their support for you. You will have gained a strong base of power that will stand firm for longer than that of the tyrant, because it's supported by a wide majority of the group. There is no better way to win positions of leadership.

KEYS TO SOCIAL INTELLIGENCE

Overt power is not a useful strategy for attaining positions of authority. In the short term, the leader may quickly gain their new position through bullying, force, and betrayal; but in the long term, the behaviour results in resentment, plotting, and an unpleasant end. It produces a singular point of authority supported by nothing other than brute force. It's unstable and relies on soul-sucking tactics to maintain, such as rubbishing any potential rivals, cracking down on dissent, and keeping their subjects in the dark. Deep down these rulers know that they're being plotted against, because they didn't earn their position. The crown does not sit easily upon the authoritarian king's head.

During the Second World War, just as the Allies prepared for the Normandy landings, the Nazi leader Adolf Hitler felt primed for the battle ahead. Even though the Allies had completely fooled Hitler about the actual location of the landings with Operation Fortitude, the Führer knew an attack was coming somewhere across the northern French coast. He welcomed it. Hitler proclaimed his expectation for every German soldier to "stand and die" to protect every square inch of territory. In meetings he would scoff at the "soft liberality" of the Allied democracies, yearning for the chance to show the strength of his authoritarian state.

In reality, Germany was on the defensive by this late stage of the war, and it would be less than a year until they surrendered. A third of the troops defending the Normandy beaches were Ost-Bataillone troops plucked from conquered territories in Poland and the Soviet Union, each forced to shoot at the invading allies with an ethnic German non-commissioned officer (NCO) pointing a pistol at their backs. When American troops invaded Omaha and Utah Beaches, these defenders were often the first to surrender, sometimes having just shot their NCO. Hitler's vain expectation that troops forced into service would show absolute obedience proved false on many occasions in June 1944.

Not only did Hitler's drafted troops fail to fight as expected, but his absolute command structure also failed to allow effective communication on the morning of the surprise assault. By this time, the attempts on Hitler's life and his growing mistrust had driven him to run the war in isolation from his retreat in Berchtesgaden. The immense workload resulting from his refusal to delegate led him into an erratic sleep schedule. On 6 June, as the Allies stormed across Normandy, Hitler slept in until noon. Field marshals Erwin Rommel and Gerd von Rundstedt fumed as they tried to contact Hitler for permission to use the spare SS Panzer divisions in the area. Upon waking, Hitler still didn't believe the invasion was genuine, believing the true attack would come from Calais instead. It was not until after the Allies had gained a firm beachhead that Hitler finally relented and agreed that Normandy was the true invasion point and not a feint.

The utter failure of the German forces to respond effectively to the Allied invasion was largely a result of their power structure. Hitler exerted absolute command across every man in every level of the German military hierarchy, refusing to give true latitude to his best generals. Even Rommel, who had proved himself during the blitzkreig invasion of France and skirmishes with the British in Northern Africa, was kept on a tight leash for his involvements in assassination plots. The authoritarian style of the German Reich made it more rigid and brittle, and less able to respond to circumstances. The Allied generals leading the invasion of Europe saw this as a chance to not only defeat a cruel regime but also to prove the strength of Western liberal democracies. General Eisenhower enjoyed complete delegated authority over the operation, while allowing his subordinates the latitude to carry out his orders in the best way that the circumstances allowed. The Germans may have laughed at the "organised chaos" of the Allied army, but the invaders' loose structure allowed them to respond far more rapidly than they ever could.

Instilling your group with a cause, gaining wide support across all its subsections, will grant you more control than the overtly authoritarian approach. Make your group *want* to follow your lead. Gaining support in this way is actually easier than the blunt approach, because you will spend less time looking over your shoulder and squashing dissent, and more time getting work done with your group. You gain this kind of support in the first place by uniting disparate sections of the group along common lines. The leader who reigns by consent always outlasts the boss who rules by raw power alone.

From one perspective, Hitler may seem a counter-example to this principle. He united many Germans behind his cause by tapping into their latent resentment and anger at being defeated in the First World War. Hitler gained a wide base of support, so why does he fail this test? Because of the rigid command structure of obedience that his authoritarian regime demanded. He was drunk on power and falsely expected that his "subjects" would continue to obey his every command. His high command turned on him several times, seeing him as a danger to his own country. This only made him less trustful, a worsening effect that culminated in the Germans' failure to repel the Normandy landings that led to their ultimate defeat.

Just as F. W. de Klerk and Nelson Mandela did with South African apartheid, you must identify the core issues that your group can unite around, and make a show of paying them due support. Focusing only on a single subsection, pressing the "us vs. them" dynamic, will polarise the group. This is risky because you'll likely alienate the opposing pole. Sure, you have a rabid sect of supporters, but even more would do anything to see you fail. A much wiser strategy is to gain group-wide support. Do not mistake a wide support base for a shallow support base—you must centre your campaign around issues that resonate with people. How will you find out what these issues are? Ask! Talk to people and find out what issues they're dealing with. Take every complaint and resentment seriously. Use the techniques described in earlier chapters of this book to enter people's spirit and empathise with their struggles. They will appreciate your listening ear and confide in you as a friend. This needs to become a regular pattern over long periods of time, so your understanding nature becomes part of your reputation. If you treat it as a one-off then people will see your behaviour as insincere—any whiff of this, and people will stay away from you. Above all, be genuine and start your campaign long before you need the support. Treat each relationship as a long-term investment that appreciates with every conversation and gesture.

Lyndon B. Johnson mastered this strategy. In his first election to US Congress, Johnson was a Democratic candidate in Texas's tenth district. The loyal Texas voters normally returned their politicians until they either resigned or died, so Johnson's opportunity was narrow. Unfortunately for the future president, Texas usually chose Republicans for its congressmen, and Johnson knew he couldn't win by going for the same voters as his opposition. Instead, he went out to the rural parts of the district, often surprising farmers who had scarcely even voted before, never mind been paid a visit by a candidate. Johnson would listen patiently, impressing them by relating a story about someone they knew in the neighbourhood. Polls before election day showed Johnson narrowly behind, but he knew he'd gained votes that no poll would ever show. His strategy of gaining a wide base of support across his district paid off, and he won the election. Travelling so far and talking to so many people took a toll, and on the day of his victory he was hospitalised for exhaustion. Johnson was a master at the one-on-one encounter throughout his political career. Studying his colleagues' tastes, he'd always have just the right anecdote to spice up the conversation. This tactic would win him the support he needed for passing bills in Congress and this popularity ultimately paved his way to the presidency.

Like Johnson, you can build strong support structures by listening to people and getting on their level. In his first election, Johnson paid attention to people who had never even met their politicians, going out to the rural parts of Texas. His victory was an upset in a typically conservative state, and his competition rested on their laurels expecting an easy victory. Your opponents' complacency provides you with a valuable opportunity to connect with traditionally under-served people. This requires observing the people that your opponents are ignoring and knowing what issues they're struggling with. Use empathy with each individual, going with their natural inclinations. These people will appreciate your attention and genuinely believe you'll fight for their cause. Lyndon B. Johnson would tailor his message to every different person who he met. He would talk to a green senator differently to how he would talk to John F. Kennedy. Figure out what makes people individual and respond positively. This strategy will build you a reliable power base.

If you're aiming for a promotion at work, then it's easy to conclude that you only need the boss's favour. This is an all-too-common mistake, particularly with political types, who attach themselves to the boss from day one, treating their colleagues with contempt. They can quickly sniff out who can help them in their rise and who can't, treating the former with flattering praise, and the latter with little more than socially obligated politeness. People are far better at recognising this behaviour than you might think. They know that this type of colleague is only ever out for themselves, groaning at every sycophantic gesture made towards a higher-up. Lacking a wide support base, they operate on tenuous ground, and rather than being able to rest upon the firm, wide base of support among their colleagues, they rely on the daily changing whims of the boss. When the relationship turns sour, the colleagues look on with glee, all too eager to spill their stories about the political type's exploits. This might seem negative or cynical, but it's a dynamic that plays itself out in offices every single day. As a student of Social Intelligence you must realise that the game is social. The overtly power-hungry types fail because they cannot tame their ambition and inner aggression, trying to take the shortest line to the top. You will not get very far in life if you constantly alienate people. The more successful people in history are students of human psychology, able to understand their colleagues' sentiments in everyday circumstances and act accordingly. We're aiming for a gradual rise to the top, not an exponential rise followed by a sharp downfall.

If the above sounds like you, then it's possible to reverse this negative dynamic. As we did in the introduction to this book, it's time to think back to when you might have alienated people. You lost their support, often because you offended their ego or somehow invalidated them. In the heat of a debate or argument it's so easy to push people over the edge with a thoughtless comment. People don't forget these offences, no matter how inconsequential they might seem at the time. We aim to become master empathisers, gaining the ability to influence people and win their support.

The following are five pragmatic techniques for gaining

support among your group and in a public setting. Each technique will make you more persuasive when addressing a group at large and enable you to gain support across its disparate sections. They are all culled from master persuaders in politics, business, and the social realm.

Become a source of pleasure to people. You'll never gain a stable position of authority if you can't elicit feelings of pleasure in others. If you constantly show a crabby attitude, or if you snap at others when under pressure, then people won't enjoy being around you. How do you think you will influence people in a situation like that? You might say *but I'm so moral and support the right causes*, but what is that worth if you invalidate people in one-on-one situations? Try investing your attention in something real for a change, rather than abstractions. You're probably offending people more than you realise—things as subtle as forgetting to hit "like" on a friend's social media post, constantly being late to their meetings, or failing to reply to their text messages can keep you in people's bad graces.

Observe people in conversation and learn what they like and dislike. If they have a hobby, for example, ask them for beginner tips. Report back your progress on this hobby to them and tell others about their expertise. Your new "mentor" will feel validated by your attention and love your company. The power of mutual dislike will also surprise you. If you notice that your colleague hates a particular sports team, then make some off-hand comment about a foul they made at the weekend game. Watch as their face lights up and they become more animated than usual. The pattern here is to enter their individual spirit and resonate with it. As you practise this and get used to your colleagues, this will become natural, and you'll be able to adapt yourself to every different interaction.

Pay attention to people and let them talk. For much of

our lives we're obsessed about what we're not getting out of others, what we rightfully deserve. We're so used to people talking over us, barely listening as we try in vain to get a word in edgeways. This only deepens the self-absorption dynamic, offering the student of Social Intelligence a ripe opportunity to tap into people's intense need for validation. Listen to people to find out what issues they're facing. Every individual person is an intense cauldron of unique feelings, resentments, hopes and dreams. Your task is to find out what these are, and taking this purpose into your interactions will make it much easier to subsume your own ego and really listen to people. Some people are more open than others. For the more closed types, you can get them to open up by letting them know a harmless secret of yours—they will usually relax and offer you a personal fact of their own in return. Building trust with your colleagues in this way will forge strong relationships, and those offer the most support of all.

Offer support to those who deserve it the most. Although the quiet, introverted types like to stick to the sidelines, they are often the most appreciative of positive attention. They find recognition unusually seductive, because they're so unused to getting it. Make a show of understanding and sharing an interest of theirs, and they'll never stop talking. Because these people are less likely to put themselves forward and are so used to being passed over for the louder, more extrovert types, they'll relish the chance to interact with the rare person who gets them. The quiet ones are also usually the most interesting of all, because they've learned to hold back the rich ideas they have in conversation, and often hold deep interests in particular subjects. Stick up for these people in conversations with the louder types and support them if they're being talked over. You will have gained a lifelong friend and supporter.

**Break down people's need to show a façade—banish
political correctness.** No one is more disliked than the
moraliser. Their colleagues brace themselves every time they
bring a political topic up, because they know the moraliser
will let everyone know their opinion. People feel forced to
show a polite façade, deep down resenting the fact they have
to stay quiet and put on a false display of agreement or
neutrality. The moralisers among us are more like bullies
than they realise, and often act shocked when accused of this.
This dynamic plays out during national elections, when a
vocal minority drums up so much noise that the exhausted
majority gladly turns out to defeat them at the ballot box.
The moraliser's daily displays of righteous fury only cause
resentment in their colleagues, and the bravest among their
number will enjoy poking holes in their often faulty arguments (the moraliser rarely seeks or wants feedback) or
winding them up into further anger, much to everyone's
amusement.

Think of the workplace moraliser as a kind of inverse
court jester, making public displays of their cynicism that
only cause laughter and ridicule from their fellow courtiers.
Deep down, the moraliser is acting from a place of deep
weakness. They know they have a dark side, as we all do, and
they can't reconcile it. They feel a need to point out the
moral injustices of others to project their inner disappointment at themselves. If this sounds like you, then it might be
time to switch off the news, log out of social media, and look
at your own life for a change. You may think you're diverting
attention away from your misdeeds towards those of others,
but the more astute among your potential supporters notice
your patterns of behaviour and see that it is really just a
projection. Moralising is one of the most alienating behaviours a person can exhibit, and it is the very antithesis of
Social Intelligence. Accept people as the imperfect creatures

they are, and pay attention to your own circumstances before judging others—you'll be happier and far more popular. People will no longer feel the need to wear a façade and can finally relax in your presence.

Stand up for common issues that your supporters care about. Earlier in the chapter we looked at how de Klerk and Mandela could unite the white and black people in South Africa on the common issue of apartheid. De Klerk stuck his neck out, making him vulnerable to his more conservative colleagues. Remember how the ANC activist Desmond Tutu noted and appreciated the president's magnanimity and willingness to cooperate and compromise. Standing up for issues that cut across the entire population rarely goes unnoticed, and it is an effective way of winning support. In political elections, a candidate's economic policies are never as important to voters as knowing that their leader shares their views, particularly their gripes, resentments, and frustrations. This makes voters feel deeply validated, and it reliably gets them to turn up on election day. Maybe you're not running for president just yet, but standing up to the moralising character in the office that everyone hates will earn you respect, even if it's silently given at first.

The key here is in exposing your vulnerable side and getting people to see that you're willing to face criticism from the opposition for expressing the exhausted majority's long-held beliefs. This is why people like comedians so much, not necessarily for their skills in humour, but because the court jester is usually the only one allowed to be honest about the king. They aren't afraid to expose the hypocrisy that everyone notices, or talk about the policy that's negatively affecting ordinary people. You might wonder at this stage what difference there is between this positive type, and the negative patterns of the moraliser. *Doesn't the moraliser also talk about issues?* They do, but more often from a place of ego, never consulting anyone for their opinion. It's a one-sided lecture. The student of Social Intelligence understands that it's more important to gather allies and sound out their ideas before taking the centre stage. They listen to their colleagues' problems, find commonalities among the feed-back they receive, and then act on it. The allies you gain in the process will be the most supportive of all, and will gladly reward you for sticking your neck out for them.

> It should be pointed out, however, that sheer physical power is an unstable basis on which to found lasting dominance, as the Dutch primatologist Frans de Waal has taken pains to demonstrate. Among the chimp troupes he studied, males who were successful in the longer term had to buttress their physical prowess with more sophisticated attributes. Even the most brutal chimp despot can be taken down, after all, by two opponents, each three-quarters as mean. In consequence, males who stay on top longer are those who form reciprocal coalitions with their lower-status compatriots, and who pay careful attention to the troupe's females and their infants.

> — JORDAN B. PETERSON

REVERSAL

Power is ripe for exploitation. Historical figures, even authoritarian dictators like Adolf Hitler, have repeatedly used the power-gathering strategies described in this chap-ter. To a German who had fought in the horrific trenches through the Great War, bled with his friends, who had come home to a country where there were no jobs and the national pride proved false in defeat, an authoritarian dictator's promises might resonate. If this dictator promises a renewed national pride, a rebirth in industry, and the opportunity to blame some group for the country's failings, then that down-trodden soldier might want to support that dictator.

This is the dangerous side of these methods to gain a wide base of support. In the wrong hands they can be used to create totalitarian regimes, the like of which killed hundreds of millions of people in the twentieth century. Always remember that good intentions never justify bad results. If you tap into too much of people's latent resent-ment, you can start a witch hunt that ends up causing wide-spread pain, rather than make the positive progress you'd hoped for.

This might seem dramatic, but the point is to not let any power you gain go to your head. You must never think you have a "golden touch" and that your wide support base can continue to exist without regular cultivation. To neglect the support structure that helped you towards your position of authority is to commit the same sin as the power-hungry political type. Your colleagues will recognise this betrayal and toss you out at the next opportunity. No matter what stage of the power game you stand at, you must cultivate this support base of yours in the exact manner you used to create it.

II

THE SOCIALLY INTELLIGENT LEADER

So Athens came to flourish—and to make manifest how important it is for everyone in a city to have an equal voice, not just on one level but on all. For although the Athenians, while subjects of a tyrant, had been no more proficient in battle than any of their neighbours, they emerged as supreme by far once liberated from tyranny. This is proof enough that the downtrodden will never willingly pull their weight, since their labours are all in the service of a master— whereas free men, because they have a stake in their own exertions, will set to them with enthusiasm.

— HERODOTUS

Once we reach a position of authority, we realise that the role we thought would be the culmination of our hard work is fraught with entirely new challenges and responsibilities. Leaders not only have to do their own job but also deal with a mirrored reflection from the team, every move accompanied with a reaction that seems arbitrary and hard to predict. As a leader, your group looks to you for direction, how to act, and naturally fits itself to your spirit.

Social Intelligence is vital at every rung of the professional ladder, but the group leader bears a special responsibility. If the leader is too tyrannical, then the group will silently boil with resentment and never truly satisfy the tyrant's demands. If the leader is too weak, then the group becomes plagued with feelings of listlessness, ambiguity, and a different rebellious feeling spreads. Such extremes always come from a tendency for self-absorption. Leaders deal unconsciously with the group's challenges, not understanding why they won't carry out their tasks properly, or always seem to react defensively to their feedback. They rely on old patterns without any introspection on their effects.

The Socially Intelligent Leader reverses this dynamic by practising deep empathy with their group, always conscious of how their words and actions affect their group's temperament. This doesn't mean subordinating to employees or letting them dictate the group's direction—it means that you need to consider how your decisions will affect the group's psychology. Rather than say *I'm the boss, and what I say goes,* consider *If I get rid of this process we've used for years, how will it affect group morale?* When an employee shows signs of being upset, don't ask *Why can't he just shut up and get on with work?* —think *Does he not feel recognised? I'll tell him how well I thought he did on that project.* So-called "bad eggs" who appear to lack motivation for your cause are often created by your dismissive attitude towards their contributions.

Too many leaders ignore their subordinates' individual psychologies or even dismiss them as irrelevant. As a result, the group suffers constant, easily preventable setbacks. These leaders make employees care little about the group's goals; they make valued employees feel like nameless cogs in a machine, and toxic feelings of resentment spread. This isn't just about morality, it's a matter of productivity—your *I'm the boss, and what I say goes* mentality is destroying your best employees' faith in you. Fortunately, it is possible to reverse this dynamic with some simple steps. The following five chapters will show you how to make your team feel like valued and important members of a cause and achieve the respect of the Socially Intelligent Leader.

6

ELIZABETH I AND LOUIS XIV

SERVE YOUR GROUP TO EARN ITS RESPECT

The entitled leader never fulfils their group's potential. Believing themselves inherently deserving of their group's respect and submission, they create resentment and do not inspire creativity. The entitled leader's pride and flippant attitude towards his subordinates and their work only incentivises behaviour that supports and salves his ego. Thus the group rots from the inside as the more productive members leave out of frustration and disgust. The Socially Intelligent Leader, in contrast, can quiet her ego, serve the group's long-term interests, and consider her subordinates' psychologies at every turn. Respect is never a privilege—you have to earn it.

THE PEOPLE'S RULER

Although Elizabeth I ascended to the throne of England and Ireland in 1558, she was no stranger to hardship. At the age of two, her father King Henry VIII removed the infant Elizabeth from the line of succession and had her mother put to death. Henry later agreed to sign a succession act that brought Elizabeth and her half-sister Mary back into the line of succession, though still behind their younger half-brother Edward, Henry's sole male heir. When Edward fell deathly ill after a brief stint on the throne, he tried to pass the throne to Lady Jane Grey, ignoring his father's succession act and the claims of his half-sisters. Through some violent manoeuvres that ended in Lady Jane's beheading, Mary took the throne and became the first queen regnant of England.

Unlike her father and half-sister, Mary was a devout and dedicated Roman Catholic, and married to the similarly devout Catholic King Philip II of Spain. During her brief reign, Mary tried to re-establish Roman Catholicism in England and put hundreds of religious heretics to death. She even had the Archbishop of Canterbury Thomas Cranmer burned at the stake on the same day he had withdrawn his recantation to the Catholic faith—being forced to watch his bishop colleagues burn was too much for him to bear. Mary's advisors warned her that such cruel religious persecution could cause a revolt, but she persevered, and became known during her reign as "Bloody Mary." Even Elizabeth was imprisoned during this time for her supposed sympathies with Protestant rebels, under the constant threat of execution. Mary died during the influenza epidemic of late 1558. Alone, isolated from her people, bitter at her inability to bear children and left depressed by her husband Philip's absence for most of her reign, she had no choice but to name her half-sister Elizabeth as her successor.

The people accepted their new young queen, welcoming her coronation with a deafening din as she presented herself to the public. The evening before her coronation, Elizabeth had spoken to a mixed crowd of impoverished Londoners and wealthy elites. The humility of her tone, the calm dignity and grace with which she addressed the crowd had touched them. The people felt enchanted by Elizabeth, seeing her in a much different light to her predecessor, the arrogant and violent Mary. To their delight and her ministers' relief, Elizabeth's first action as queen was to reverse all of Mary's religious policies, establishing the English Protestant church. Although she resolved to make England a Protestant country, she ensured that her new church would keep Catholic symbols such as the crucifix, and adorn its priests in similar vestments. Although the people and her parliament's House of Commons welcomed these reforms, she faced staunch opposition among England's bishops—fortunately, most bishoprics were vacant, and Elizabeth ensured they stayed vacant throughout her parliament's votes on the proposals. This church settlement formed the basis for the establishment that would later become the modern-day Church of England.

Although Elizabeth could be confident in the loyalty of her chief advisor, Sir William Cecil, she did seem aware of his private intentions. After the horrors of Mary's reign, Cecil determined that ruling was not for women. He believed they were slaves to their emotions, and could not stand up to the strong personalities that usually dominated aristocratic courts. And after the trauma of her imprisonment, threatened by execution at any moment, she could surely not have the resiliency to keep up with the job's demands by herself. Cecil schemed to marry Elizabeth off to a strong European king and insinuate himself as the real ruler behind the throne. To do this, he would need to find a Protestant candidate for marriage, but not one smart enough to resist his intrigues.

However, Cecil's task seemed difficult almost from the start. Unlike her father, Elizabeth preferred to get fully involved in the affairs of state. She would hold daily meetings with Cecil and her ministers, demanding answers and sharply reprimanding any official who could not stay on top of their duties. Elizabeth sought to recover England's finances that her father's costly foreign wars had drained, and so she created a culture of diligence and hard work in her court. Cecil could not help but feel impressed by Elizabeth's work ethic, but she made it very difficult to act out his secret plans. Elizabeth read and spoke all the European languages and was more than capable of understanding Cecil's diplomatic correspondence, surprising him occasionally with her skill in dealing with foreign diplomats. An accidentally curt remark made towards Elizabeth would make her cold and intimidating, refusing to admit him to court for days on end. To Cecil's relief and delight, she would then suddenly entertain talks of marrying some foreign prince, but only on the condition that he help her with some cost-saving measure. He would promptly set up a meeting, only for Elizabeth to withdraw at the last minute, having won yet another piece of saving for England's treasury. Over time, Cecil realised she was playing him like a fiddle, always two steps ahead. It was almost as if Elizabeth could read his desires and dangle tempting concessions in front of him that were clever traps in disguise.

Two great challenges faced Elizabeth's reign: dealing with her cousin Mary, Queen of Scots, and the growing threat of Spain. In 1567, Mary was forced to abdicate the throne of Scotland and fled to England, seeking Elizabeth's protection. The Scottish people hated Mary for her alleged involvement in the murder of her husband, Lord Darnley, and Elizabeth felt surprised at how weak she found Mary's character: Unlike herself, she was self-absorbed, dismissive in her interactions with courtiers, and uncontrolled in her sexual appetites. In spite all of this, and to the horror of Cecil, Elizabeth refused to return Mary to Scotland. This all changed when later, in 1586, proof arose of Mary's involvement in a plot to murder Elizabeth. Though outraged at Mary's stupidity, and at the public outcry her betrayal had caused, Elizabeth reluctantly agreed to sign Mary's death warrant. Cecil was glad that Elizabeth's rule now remained unchallenged, and the people acknowledged that she had taken a personal blow in favour of her country's stability.

The treason crisis now over, Elizabeth and Cecil turned their attention to the growing threat from Spain. King Philip II of Spain, the widowed husband of Elizabeth's predecessor Mary, had been intriguing into England since his wife's death. Despite Elizabeth's Protestant settlement, he was determined to intrigue the Catholic faith back into English society. The beheading of Mary, Queen of Scots, and its popularity among the English people, made it clear that his subversive tactics would no longer work—he would have to resort to military means. Fortunately, Elizabeth and Cecil had already foreseen this as a natural consequence of Philip's aggressive personality, and by this point, Elizabeth's cost-saving policies and refusals to engage in foreign conflicts had brought England's treasury back to parity. Unknown to Philip, Elizabeth had built a vast spy network across Europe, and she was fully aware of his plans to invade England: Philip would take expensive loans with Italian banks and send an unstoppable armada to knock out England's navy. In 1587 she sent Sir Francis Drake to attack Philip's trade ships, and this risk persuaded his creditors to increase the interest on his loans. Drake's antics forced Philip to delay his planned invasion by an entire year. Using this time she slowly prepared an army and navy, bracing for an imminent inva-sion. Philip was becoming desperate, and Elizabeth outma-noeuvred him at every turn.

It was time for the final showdown, and the English braced for the naval conflict ahead. Philip's enormous armada of galleons anchored up at Calais, the point in France nearest to the English coast. Then, one night in July 1588, five unmanned English fireships—light, mobile vessels lit on fire—barrelled towards the Spanish galleons. Fire quickly spread among the Spanish vessels, and just at the peak moment of chaos, light English ships sped into Calais, easily isolating and breaking up the giant lumbering fire-ridden Spanish galleons. The remaining Spanish retreated into the North Sea and, in a desperate attempt to reverse the advantage, attempted to circle around Scotland. The rough waters completely befuddled the Spanish fleet, and once again the English fleet could pick off the sorry vessels. Having risked everything on this ill-advised roll of the dice, Philip's treasury lay bankrupt. Elizabeth's fleet, in contrast, had lost no ships and only a handful of soldiers. With minimal expense and some clever strategy, she had dealt a major blow to Spain and solidified England's long-term security.

INTERPRETATION

The war with Spain would continue throughout the rest of Elizabeth's reign, but her fleet's splendidly bloodless victories at Calais and in the North Sea embodied her style of rule. Elizabeth was patient in working towards her goals, humble with experienced courtiers, and calmly strategic in the face of crises. Her father Henry had become known for his large personality and grand lifestyle; these same prideful attributes drained the country's treasury and caused endless religious rifts that threatened to tear the country apart. Henry had carelessly brought the country to the brink of a religious civil war in his personal mission to marry the right woman and produce a male heir. His people? Some liked his brash disregard for the rich Catholic establishment, but far more suffered. Henry's style was typical for rulers at the time: They would take the throne, having led a life of luxury and privilege, feeling entitled to their subjects' respect and submission. They would continue their lives of leisure, leaving the day-to-day rule to their ministers who would quietly cream off the country's tax income for themselves. All of this would drain the treasury and enlarge the distance between the ruler and his people.

Elizabeth I broke this mould. How could she not be humble after the sadness and uncertainty of her upbringing? Her mother was beheaded when she was two years old, her own half-brother tried to disinherit her, and her half-sister kept her imprisoned for months with the real threat of execution. By the time she took the throne, Elizabeth had gained the proper perspective to empathise with the struggles of her people. She could feel their psychologies and understood how they would respond to her policies. Elizabeth knew there were real threats to her leadership even among her own court, and decided from the start of her reign to become involved in all aspects of her government. In her establishment of the Protestant church in England, Elizabeth kept some parts of the old Catholic institution, validating the beliefs of both sects. She prioritised the country's long-term financial growth over the military conquests that a proud, deluded king might have embarked upon. Elizabeth's choices showed the English people that she intended to serve them with every hour granted to her. In her dealings with Cecil and her cabinet, she cleverly played them by going along with their plans for her marriage only so long as she could extract concessions from them and her suitors. With Philip of Spain, Elizabeth baited an aggressive and melodramatic man into a costly war that sunk its treasury, and England emerged as the pre-eminent power in Europe.

Unlike Philip, Henry, and her other royal contemporaries, Elizabeth firmly grounded herself in reality. She understood that the love of the people was a treasure to be earned, never an entitlement. The arrogance and immoral behaviour of Mary, Queen of Scots so disgusted the Scottish people that they expelled her, and all of England celebrated when she fell to the executioner's axe. This entitlement is a disease that afflicts us all, but particularly those of us who make it to positions of leadership. We believe ourselves to have a "golden touch," when actually some amount of luck or goodwill from others helped us on our rise to the top.

The key to avoiding such feelings is to always stay self-objective, always dwelling in reality. After her tumultuous youth, Elizabeth could have easily succumbed to feelings of resentment and victimhood. But these toxic emotions would have clouded the reality: the threat of intrigues inside her own court, England's dwindling treasury, and the growing danger of invasion by Spain. In each of these situations, she took personal responsibility and immersed herself in dealing with the threats. Like Elizabeth, you must not entertain any fantasies of royal grandeur, or of deserving respect and credit for your amazing qualities—these are illusions. Entertaining them will only result in a resentful team that wishes you would come back down to earth. Assess circumstances as they come, take responsibility, and prioritise results over personal glory. This attitude will result in a workplace where members of the group can only thrive by embracing this positive results-focused spirit, instead of having to resort to politics and supporting your inflated ego.

THE BOY-KING

From an early age, King Louis XIV of France was fascinated by history, particularly tales of past heroes. His first *valet de chambre*, a Monsieur Laporte, read to him every night a chapter of a French history book. The young dauphin delighted in these evening readings, declaring to Laporte that one day he would become a Charlemagne, a King

Richard the Lionheart of his own time. Louis' prime minister, Cardinal Mazarin, found out about his daily history lessons and put a stop to them at once. Mazarin snidely reprimanded Laporte, "I presume the governor of the king must put on his shoes and stockings, as I perceive his *valet de chambre* is teaching him history." The young king was not alone in hating Mazarin. The cardinal always affected a haughty, pompous air, and as prime minister he held more power than even the king and his mother. For all intents and purposes, Mazarin ruled France, and he had no intention of losing his power to the new king. He resolved to keep Louis uneducated and distracted from all government matters. This way, Mazarin could better wrap his tentacles around the royal family and its treasury.

Since Louis and his young brother were forbidden from all intellectual pursuits, they both relied on their natural charm in the royal court. One court chronicler noted Louis' charm when entertaining a royal wedding: "The king, with the gracefulness which shines in all his actions, took the hand of the Queen of Poland, and conducted her to the platform, where his majesty opened the dance, and was followed by nearly all the princes, princesses, great nobles, and ladies of the court. At its termination, the king, with the same grace and majestic deportment, conducted the young queen to her place." When he reached his majority at the age of thirteen, Mazarin decided he should marry a lady of royal blood, and many young ladies from the finest noble families of the realm flooded his court. Louis' mother, Anne of Austria, and Mazarin had succeeded in letting childhood frivolities dominate the young king's mind, and the pair practically ruled the realm themselves. They left Louis practically illiterate, horribly egotistical, overbearing—traits that Anne encouraged, believing her son should stand above all others.

Eventually, the French parliament became tired of the

scheming Mazarin, and an uprising named the Fronde started a brief civil war in Paris. Eventually the Prince of Condé, with 5,000 troops, pushed the cardinal, the king, and their 8,000 troops out of Paris to Pontoise, a few miles from the village of Versailles. Under pressure from parliament, the young Louis yielded to their demands and agreed to banish the cardinal. In return, all those who had taken part in the Fronde were required to swear allegiance to the king. Louis returned home triumphantly leading at the front of his army, having secured control of the French parliament and all those who had previously rebelled against Mazarin.

One evening, Louis' mother gave a private ball in honour of Henrietta, the widowed queen of King Charles II of England. Henrietta was a young and timid girl, feeling embarrassed at the relative splendour of Louis' palace in St Germain. Anne, sitting beside the king, eagerly awaited Henrietta's entrance in the *grand salon*. To Anne's horror, her son refused to even look at the young queen, walking past her as she entered, walking off with one of the other ladies of the court. In front of the nobles assembled, she got up to meet Louis and said in his ear, "You should dance first with the English princess." Louis, unmoved, loudly replied, "I am not fond of little girls." Although Anne rescued the situation, she sharply rebuked Louis after the ceremony. The boy declared right back, "I have long enough been guided by your leading-strings. I shall submit to it no longer." From this moment on, Louis doubled down on his haughty manners and sought to assert his independence in all his royal affairs.

In 1661, Cardinal Mazarin died. On his deathbed, he confessed to a monk through pale and trembling lips that he had extorted 40,000,000 francs from the French people, by levying high taxes on the poor and embezzling all that he could. Embarrassed by the revelations given to him, the confessor declared that the cardinal would peril his eternal salvation if he did not return every penny to the king. The cardinal agreed, and left his vast stores of gold, estates of houses, lands, and farms to his friends in the aristocracy. To the people, he left a miserly 1,200 francs. In spite of this, Louis detested Mazarin, and was glad to see him gone—he could now rule free of the slippery minister's influence. Two days before the death of Mazarin, a minister asked the king "to whom he must hereafter address himself on questions of public business." The emphatic and laconic response was, "To myself." Louis was then twenty-two years of age, left bitter at his poor education, appearing to all to be nothing more than a frivolous, pompous, self-conceited young man of pleasure. After Louis' resolution to rule France himself, his finance minister, Nicolas Fouquet, felt nervous that he might not gain a promotion to Mazarin's coveted position of prime minister. To impress the king, he gave a stunning party for Louis and the entire court at his house. Far from being impressed, the king felt horrified for being so outdone in luxury and grandeur by his own finance minister, and had the man arrested the next day on trumped-up charges. Enraged by the size of Fouquet's mansion, Louis resolved to build his own palace outside Versailles, a grand estate that would dwarf all others of its kind in the realm.

During Louis' reign, Protestantism was spreading throughout Europe. England and the German states had embraced Protestantism as their main religions. These countries had finally come to reject the overt power plays of the Vatican and opt for the simple self-sufficiency that this new movement represented. Louis was a devout Roman Catholic, taking daily Mass and encouraging his family and royal court to show humble devotion to God. But he could neither understand nor countenance the growing number of French Protestants—known as Huguenots, a group that had grown to 2,000,000 French by the sixteenth century. Louis, unable to bear such an affront to his faith, brutally put down the Huguenots. He tried to force them to convert to Roman Catholicism, threatening to send them to the galleys. To his incredulous surprise, many Catholics refused and defiantly subjected themselves to virtual slavery in the French navy. Consumed with rage and frustration, Louis ordered mass bible burnings and executions to teach them a lesson. This "strategy" of Louis' completely backfired. The Huguenots who survived the king's wrath fled to England and Prussia, both kingdoms gladly accepting this influx of devout Protestants. This was all paid for with taxes that forced most of his subjects into miserable poverty. But the sheer luxury of his lifestyle and the many epicurean tastes he encouraged in his own court left the king distracted from the real problems affecting his realm. On his deathbed, Louis bitterly regretted the time and vast sums of money he'd spent on such empty pursuits:

> Loudly, however, he deplored the madness of his ambition which had involved Europe in such desolating wars. Bitterly he expressed his regret that he left France in a state of such exhaustion, impoverished, burdened with taxation, and hopelessly crushed by debt. The condition of the realm was indeed deplorable. A boy of five years of age was to inherit the throne. A man so profligate that he was infamous even in a court which rivalled Sodom in its corruption was to be invested with the regency of the kingdom—a man who was accused, by the general voice of the nation, of having poisoned those who stood between him and the throne. That man's sister, an unblushing wanton, who had poisoned her own husband, presided over the festivities of the palace. The nobles, abandoned to sensual indulgence, were diligent and ingenious only in

their endeavours to wrench money from the poor. The masses of the people were wretched beyond description, and almost beyond imagination in our land of liberty and competence. The execrations of the starving millions were rising in a long wail around the throne.

INTERPRETATION

The example of Louis XIV offers the absolute polar opposite to Elizabeth I's reign. Here was a king eagerly thrust into the shallow world of pageantry, days filled with leisure, endless pomp, bountiful luxury, all at the expense of his poor citizens. His mother and prime minister both schemed to keep him uneducated and distracted from the grim realities of government, encouraging his proud and arrogant manners from an early age. Mazarin's scheme had worked so well, his oppression of Louis so complete, that he practically ruled France as monarch for eighteen years. This oppression totally backfired, since it only encouraged Louis to overcompensate in his fervour to prove his dominance over everyone around him. He created a glorious self-image, the divine ruler of Europe's largest realm. So great was Louis's jealousy of others, particularly those who impressed at court, that he would banish respected ambassadors and start bloody wars over the slightest affronts to his manly pride.

In reality, Louis was a contemptuous, selfish, pleasure-loving man, who had done nothing to merit even the slightest esteem from any of his subjects. His courtiers and various mistresses never dreamed of having any function other than to indulge in luxuries at the expense of others. Tens of millions of French would toil in miserable poverty so that Louis and his court could live in constant plenty and luxury throughout his reign. Instead of being schooled as a normal boy would, Mazarin had consciously raised Louis to be stupid, and his sheer ignorance at anything beyond courtly life only fuelled his pride. Louis knew nothing of the revolting state of French society, not the slightest estimation that a spark of revolution was growing in the grey squalor that most French had to endure. He never even dreamed of consulting the people who paid for his lavish lifestyle. His only goal was to further aggrandise the image of himself and that of the "divine" French monarchy. Stemming from his example, his two successors lived on an even greater level of royal largesse, and drove the country to bloody revolution.

Consider Louis XIV the very antithesis of the Socially Intelligent Leader. Types like him should serve as a constant reminder of the poisonous temptations of the ego, and the dangerous places they can lead. They obsess over their image and only care about work matters if they happen to inflate or threaten their pride. Deep down, jealous leaders know they have no real skill, nothing concrete besides their cunning, and their insecurity drives them beyond rational thought. Without the slightest thought to the goals and needs of their group, or any remote amount of justification, they are happy to live in extravagance. Because the group no longer rewards hard work or any kind of concrete skill, polit- ical types emerge to dominate the group. The members of the group with any real skill either become tempted them- selves or leave in disgust, and the group further declines. When the group inevitably fails, the leader blames all around him for feeding his ego, not seeing himself as the source of all its failings, as Louis howled with regret at the state he left France in on his deathbed. Dwell only in reality, work *for* your team, and listen to the temptations of pride and ego at your peril—they can only lead you and your team to ruin.

KEYS TO SOCIAL INTELLIGENCE

All ineffective leaders, whether tyrannical or cowardly, suffer from the sole nemesis of Social Intelligence: self-absorption. Characters like Louis XIV might seem like dramatic caricatures for this illness, but the impact of their self-obsession is felt so widely because of their authority. Everyone harbours feelings of entitlement, envy, and resentment, but positions of leadership reveal and multiply them. We've all experienced the situation of a colleague becoming a tyrannical monster after being promoted. They jealously guard their power out of insecurity and pride, aggressively shutting down any perceived threats. As Abraham Lincoln said, "Nearly all men can stand adversity, but if you want to test a man's character, give him power." Lincoln's statement becomes even more poignant when reflecting upon the totalitarian regimes of the twentieth century, and to a smaller degree in the experiences we've observed in daily work life—but both respect the same phenomenon, just to differing degrees.

If the leader has any kind of personality fault, some festering wound from childhood, then any challenge to their pride gets lumped along with whatever originally caused that wound. Although these leaders' outward behaviour suggests malice, what you are observing is the manifestation of a sensitive ego. In a position of power and influence, with fewer checks on their demeanour, less need to put up a polite façade, you really get to see their ego projections in full force. This is also why you shouldn't take the demon boss's tirades personally—if you imagine them as the anxious, wounded child that they really are, then what used to become a daily ordeal mutates into something less emotional and thus easier to deal with. When you're in a leadership position, you must realise the negative effects you produce whenever you're rude or unfair towards your team. It isn't just the hurt feelings in that one moment; it's the thick layer of bubbling resentment that lies underneath the surface.

At the time that Joseph Stalin was working his way up the Communist Party ranks, his colleagues would note his charming and seductive nature. He gathered allies, support, and ultimately a lot of power. But when he became the Soviet Union's leader, his true nature revealed itself: the horrific bloodlettings within the party, millions of Ukrainian farmers starved to death, and sending anyone who dared oppose him to the Gulags—hard labour camps far away in cold Siberia. Kulak, a term used to describe a high-earning peasant farmer, one of the original targets for resentment during the communist revolution, became broadened to anyone of even the remotest suspicion. Stalin's paranoia permeated down deep into the system he controlled, and people's latent envy and resentment of others allowed this to spread—people were actually *incentivised* to identify anyone who loosely fitted the kulak description. Stalin even turned on Red Army soldiers returning from the Second World War, fearing that they had been exposed to Western goods and cultural values. This is one reason why he sent the author Aleksander Solzhenitsyn to the Gulags after fighting for his country against Germany, and Solzhenitsyn later exposed the tyranny of Stalin's totalitarian empire in his master work *The Gulag Archipelago*. The good intentions of the revolutionaries who started the Soviet project created a government with such singular totalitarian power in the central bureaucracy, that a vicious tyrant like Stalin was sure to take hold of it at some point. A hundred million dead, all because of one man's paranoia and wounded ego. Taken to its fullest extent, the leader's personality always has ripple effects throughout the group. This effect is the ultimate danger of the entitled, self-absorbed leader on the group.

A 2011 study by the Development Dimensions International group of nearly 2,000 employees and over twelve thousand leaders across seventy-four countries showed three key benefits from good leadership: first, that the difference in impact between a top performing leader and an average leader is 50 per cent; second, that companies with the highest performing leaders were thirteen times more likely to outperform their competitors; and third, organisations with these high quality leaders had up to three times the employee retention rate of their industry competitors. Positive leadership is not merely the "good vibes" option; it directly affects the bottom line. Stop deluding yourself with thoughts that your tough, blunt style of dealing with employees is more "realistic" or "old-school"—it is a sign of thoughtlessness, historical blindness, and an abject lack of real communication with your team. Before you ask whether we can really isolate leadership in an "all else being equal" analysis, consider whether you'd expect a difference in the employees working for a benevolent vs. a tyrannical leader. Do you think that the most skilled workers, highly sought after in the industry, would stay for long under a tyrant with a deep need for absolute control? Leaders are never isolated from their influence—their presence is always felt in every aspect of the group, from its constitution of employees to the dread or the excitement that they feel coming into work every day.

Good leadership can never be broken down into a simple series of techniques or tips because egotism, the root cause of bad leadership, manifests in so many different forms. But it is nevertheless a toxic element we need to identify and deal with. If we can't handle the slightest challenge to our ego, what does that say about the strength of our character? Are we really putting the needs of our group first when we spend all day browsing the Internet, and snap at the employee brave enough to call us out for it? That worker is doing the team a service, and it should be recognised, not punished. Although snapping at them might feel like a momentary thing, you've just revealed your backwards priorities in a very real way, and they won't soon forget it.

At all times, Elizabeth I put the needs of her country ahead of her own, and conversely, Louis XIV put his own needs ahead of his country's. The results speak for themselves: Elizabeth's forty-four-year reign enjoyed incomparable stability and economic growth, turning England from a debt-ridden kingdom on the verge of collapse into a strong and feared power. Louis' seventy-two-year reign saw the French people grow to hate and resent the mere idea of monarchy, and his successors brought about the bloody upheaval of the French Revolution—all because the king sensed that warfare and royal largesse were the ideal ways to enhance his personal glory. One leader subsumed her ego to the good of her team; the other felt so challenged by even the slightest glance, the mere thought that his subjects might worship the same God as him in the "wrong" way, that he would take his country to war. Are you working for your team's good, or for your personal glory? We need to work on our own egos and our own internal issues to solve the pervasive effects of our leadership.

To solve the entitled ego, we first need to identify it—to grapple with the dark forces at play. The entitled ego expects fame and recognition without the good deeds that usually earn them. Ask yourself: Would *you* respect someone who walked into your office and acted offended that everyone didn't immediately bow down at his feet? Or would you respect the leader who, for the last month, has worked past closing time, after the rest of her team have gone home? The entitled ego tells us that, yes, everyone *should* recognise us for our inherent brilliance, whereas the Socially Intelligent Leader understands that her skills, her prior achievements, don't preclude her from the need to continue to prove herself. If you know that there's always more to learn, and put that into practice, then you're already on the right path.

This positive line of thinking is akin to a system that constantly pulls in new ideas, new experiences, and churns out results that benefit not only itself but also those in the periphery. The entitled egoist's system constantly demands respect for little output, while oppressing even the slightest observation that maybe it hasn't done enough to garner that respect. Which of those systems do you think is better for the long term? One seeks learning opportunities in the young upstart employee; the other sees a threat. One cultivates that new team member, guiding them in the proper manner and feeling *delighted* at that young person's success; the other cannot help but put them down in meetings, rubbish their ideas, and make light of their achievements at every opportunity.

The Socially Intelligent Leader is, in all cases, also a teacher, never the presumptuous student who thinks she already knows it all. Becoming a good mentor to a young protégé almost requires a kind of bravery—knowing full well that this young person might grow beyond us and realising that this means we've been *successful* in our job as a leader. If we've built up our ego on the idea that we shouldn't ever open ourselves up to further wounds, then it's no wonder that we get defensive—or even aggressive—when our colleagues accurately criticise us. We've built our ego on the fragile ground of countless falsehoods—just like the prover-bial house built on a foundation of loose sand. Pride doesn't merely stop us from learning new things, it also makes us deaf to warnings—especially if we actively block out any information that conflicts with these falsehoods. We're too busy patting ourselves on the back for past successes when we should be in awe of the rich potential in the unknown that sits all around us. The tyranny of the entitled ego is really a response to the fog of war inherent to reality—are you going to react like the anxious child, or take the leap of faith required to grow?

Carl Jung argued that people need to deal with their internal negativity before trying to enter the world around them. In his book *Answer to Job*, Jung wrote about the paradoxical God-image inside all of us. Jung's idea was that the Lord's own maturity gradually developed over the course of the Old Testament—the cruel, often vengeful God we see ordering Jehu, King of Israel, to slaughter every last one of the Baal worshippers seems a far cry from the God who guides His son to spread the messages of love and bounty. By being incarnated as Jesus, God fully experiences what He made Job and the Israelites suffer in the Old Testament. Jesus takes the sins of humanity entirely upon Himself, and it is this quintessential sacrifice of the ego that birthed the religion of Christ.

Just as the Christian God sent His son into the world, fully embodying Him, we too as leaders expose our egos to the unknown, sometimes cruelly indifferent world. Suffering *is* reality, and the only way we can overcome suffering is to live inside it, to use it to better ourselves. Those among us who want to oppress challenge and pain, instead clinging to entitlement and pride, are really withdrawing from life itself. It's a denial of our shadow side, the part of us we'd rather not show to the world—for the arrogant leader, this is most often constituted by feelings of vulnerability, the weak child that can't fend for itself and must rely on others.

Such a withdrawal from life is essentially a repression of ourselves—and such repression can only produce a swing in the opposite direction: employees lashing out at us, feelings of emptiness, and the need to crush others. We must become aware of the darkness in our shadow sides and finally allow ourselves to become vulnerable. It is impossible to lead others without this integration of the self we want to hide from the world, because we can't help but project these hidden features onto others, lashing out whenever a subordinate threatens to reveal them.

The Socially Intelligent Leader is always at ease, open in her acceptance of others, and never defensive. Why should she ever be defensive? She has nothing to hide, nothing to oppress, because she has no issue with being honest, open to new ideas that might challenge hers. Like Elizabeth I, she is then ready to immerse himself in her work, objective in her view of the surrounding workplace. She's able to be empathetic when employees have problems; her mind is freed up to focus on long-term strategy because her mind isn't clouded with rage, constantly defending her pride from what seem like attacks.

To integrate your shadow as Jung advised, watch yourself for the next few weeks. Stay as objective as possible and take a mental note when you feel pangs of offence. In the moment, you are best able to identify where these feelings of defensiveness are emerging from. If an employee criticises a decision of yours, repress the urge to snap back at any "tone" you might observe, and instead try to see things from their perspective. They have given you a gift: a sign of a sore point in your ego. Go deeper on that sore point, really find out why it's causing you such pain. Even the mere awareness of this sore point will make it *so* much easier to deal with future events like this exchange with your colleague. You will have let go of a heavy load and be better able to view your subordinates with compassion and empathy. The Socially Intelligent Leader is not only the most effective, he is also the happiest and most at peace with his inner mind.

> Win affection. Even the first and highest cause, in its most important affairs, foresees this need and works towards it. Win someone's affection and their respect will follow. Some so trust merit that they underestimate diligence. But caution knows full well that without people's favour, merit alone is the longest route to take. Goodwill facilitates everything and makes good all deficiencies.
>
> — BALTASAR GRACIÁN

REVERSAL

You are a leader, and you should lead the way. Do not make the mistake of allowing your team to run roughshod over you. Nor should you step back with a completely hands-off approach, since employees will come to resent your unwillingness to get involved. Go too far in your empathy, and both paths will lead to *less* respect for you in the long run. Elizabeth I, while empathetic, was not afraid to reprimand a minister if he were rude or acted disrespectfully. In these situations, Elizabeth was not acting out of insecurity. She knew that to command respect in a court full of scheming and aggressive men, she would have to show her teeth every so often. The key is in controlling your reprimands and only using them when necessary. In these moments, you must never show anger or lose your cool—the goal is to communicate that their behaviour is unwelcome, not to show how easily they can rile you.

7

ABRAHAM LINCOLN AND THE TRUNG SISTERS

TAME YOUR TYRANNICAL ENERGY TO PREVENT NEEDLESS DIFFICULTIES

The greatest threat facing the leader does not arise from their competitors, but from their own team. A pattern of dismissive behaviour towards a subordinate will damage your cause more than any rival ever could. Instead of focusing diligently on their work, the resentful employee will plot, connive, and sabotage you until the end of their days. Such threats are needless and easily avoided. Make all your employees feel validated, make all their good deeds known, and actively work for their interests. No matter your mood at the present moment, you must tame your tyrannical energy, or accept the chaos of the inevitable cycles of resentment and insurrection you will create. Seek peace, not victory.

GRACIOUS VICTORY

Ulysses S. Grant and his entourage rushed to Appomattox Court House. The nearby battle with the Confederates had just ended, and Grant had received word that general Robert E. Lee wanted to meet him. The Battle of Appomattox Court House was a culminating point for the American Civil War, a final confrontation between each side's top generals. The battle had ended when Lee surrendered after a last-ditch attack on the Union line had failed, and now it was time for the official terms of surrender. General Grant didn't want to keep the great Confederate leader waiting, and his boots were still covered in mud from the battle.

Lee showed up for the meeting immaculately dressed. He expected to be taken prisoner and wanted to look like an upright soldier. Grant, embarrassed at his shabby appearance, made small talk with him about the Mexican War. Lee turned to Ely Parker, Grant's Seneca aide. When he noticed the man's dark complexion, Lee offered his hand to Parker, saying, "I am glad to see one real American here." Parker shook it and replied, "We are all Americans."

Lee felt touched by the lenient terms that Parker had written on Grant's behalf. No Confederate soldier would face arrest, and once Grant had learned that they had to supply their own horses, he appended a term assuring that they would not be confiscated either. Lee said, "This will do much toward conciliating our people," and offered his sword to Grant, but Grant refused it. The two men shook hands, and Lee's Army of Northern Virginia thus fell into Northern control.

This exchange on 9 April 1865 ended four years of fighting between the North and South. Although people on both sides were glad that the fighting was over, the Southern people realised their futures were now uncertain. William T. Sherman's army had wrecked much of the Southern economy, his March to the Sea campaign having broken train lines, freed slaves, and taken key ports in Georgia and the Carolinas. And less than a week after Lee's surrender, John Wilkes Booth assassinated Abraham Lincoln in Ford's Theatre. The Union president had long advocated for leniency on the Southern rebels, leading many in the

Confederacy to feel upset at Lincoln's death. Much was at stake. What penalties would the victorious North impose upon the South without Lincoln's balanced leadership?

The key battle, in fact, had taken place back in late 1863 and throughout 1864 inside the United States Congress. Abraham Lincoln's Republican Party held bitterly opposing views on how to treat the South following the war. Fervent abolitionists wanted retribution for the South's continuance of slavery, while moderates cautioned against causing yet more rifts and potentially another war. On the opposite side of Congress, the Democratic Party was eager to extend slavery, and they remained bitter at Lincoln's Emancipation Proclamation, which the president had timed to perfection at the height of Union wartime sentiment. George B. McClellan, Lincoln's former chief general, resolved to stand against Lincoln as the Democratic candidate in the 1864 presidential election.

Abraham Lincoln had privately formed a plan to ease the Southern states back into the Union in case of a victory. He had based his plan around his power to issue presidential pardons, to clear offenders of whatever transgressions the Southern people had engaged in. Rather than planning to enact retribution on them, he had long argued that the Southern people were innocents who had temporarily fallen under the sway of evil men. The Union, said Lincoln, was indissoluble, and the Southern states had not legally left the Union at all—they had merely been led into revolt by the Confederate leaders.

In December 1863, Lincoln issued a Proclamation of Amnesty and Reconstruction, offering full pardons and restoration of all property—except slaves—to any Confederate who agreed to do two things: swear allegiance to the United States, and swear to agree and uphold all proclamations and laws of the United States related to emancipation

and slavery. This proclamation did not extend to high political and military officers of the Confederacy. Any Southern
states that agreed to uphold this proclamation would be
recognised and welcomed back into the Union without
penalty—this condition included a "ten per cent rule" which
only required 10 per cent of any state's 1860 census voting
population to agree with the proclamation's conditions to
qualify. Lincoln even accepted "temporary arrangements"
from former Confederate state governments where black
people would remain a landless, labouring, and subservient
class. Offering a moderate peace plan would shorten the war,
while extending his policy of emancipation by insisting any
new governments abolish slavery.

This offer of a smooth reprieve for the rebels infuriated
the radical abolitionists in Lincoln's Republican Party. How
could he be so soft against the people who had blatantly
committed mass treason? How could he be so lenient to the
wealthy planter class, who would get all their land back and
could just rehire their former slaves under the guise of freedom? Freed slaves who had settled on confiscated land
would have to move too, since Lincoln's amnesty guaranteed
that all lands be returned to their former owners—this
included large stretches of Tennessee and Arkansas, former
hotbeds of the slave trade. Pennsylvania representative
Thaddeus Stevens even proposed that the Southern states
had not only left the Union, but that they should be treated
as conquered territories, and thus lie under the sole purview
of Congress. Even among the radicals this view went too far,
because it would only create chaos in the ensuing reconstruction and open up further oppression of freed slaves. Nevertheless, in the summer of 1864, the abolitionists passed a bill
to oppose Lincoln's plan, named the Wade-Davis Bill. This
legislation would revoke his 10 per cent rule, requiring
instead that the majority of a state agree to the Union's

terms. In an unprecedented move Lincoln refused to sign it, stating that it would make the postwar restoration too difficult, and it never came into effect.

In November 1864, thanks to Sherman's overwhelming Union victories in the Battle of Atlanta, Lincoln won the election with a strong popular majority. He could thus form a coalition of moderates in Congress, countering the abolitionist view that Lincoln's offer would create the least friction during the sensitive yet crucial time of war reconstruction, and that it came with the absolute proviso of accepting the president's Emancipation Proclamation. Any harsh retribution against the slave-owning class, they argued, would only attack a tiny minority of the Southern people, and give them an excuse for further rebellion down the line. The moderate view eventually won out, and Grant's complete victory at Appomattox in 1865 seemed to ensure a stable dissolution to the war that had so ruined America for the previous four years. All the Southern states agreed to join the Union on Lincoln's terms of amnesty. And in 1866, Congress passed the Fourteenth Amendment, granting equal citizenship to all people in the United States, regardless of colour or ancestry. Lincoln was not able to see it manifest, but his vision of emancipation had finally won the day.

INTERPRETATION

Because Lincoln was assassinated so soon into his new presidency, we will never know the true extent of his reconstruction plans for the South. Lincoln's successor Andrew Johnson was a Southern Democrat who had run with him on his National Union ticket and wanted to implement his own version of Lincoln's plans. He opposed the Fourteenth Amendment and even tried to destroy the Republicans on a national tour to promote the policies he tried to force through with his executive powers. Many people in the South felt uncertain after Lincoln's assassination, because with his amnesty proclamation he had proven himself willing to extend an olive branch that guaranteed their future safety. Without his calm, objective influence over proceedings, the future now looked hazy.

Johnson's actions may not seem much of a departure from the leniency intended in Lincoln's reconstruction proclamation. After all, didn't Lincoln also fail to guarantee extended rights to former slaves? There is, however, a stark difference in the two men's approaches: Lincoln understood that most people were tired of fighting by this point and wanted to return to the status quo. If those in the South would have to give up slavery for that, then so be it—only a tiny sliver of the wealthiest Southerners actually owned slaves. By the end of the war the Confederacy realised that it could not realistically build a nation centred on slavery, a practice roundly condemned by nearly all the major western powers. Johnson, in stark contrast, showed far less tact in dealing with his political opponents, and much less grace in dealing with African-American rights.

Lincoln knew that any political solution would be messy and contentious, so he instead focused his efforts on delivering military victories. It was Sherman's brilliant campaign that ensured Lincoln's presidential election, and later Grant's victory that ultimately brought the war to an end. Lincoln ensured that both Sherman and Grant demanded unconditional surrenders from their Confederate opponents because, unlike a political solution, it would be impossible to argue with a series of decisive military victories. The Confederate president Jefferson Davis was imprisoned for two years without trial, most likely because Davis would have welcomed the chance to argue his constitutional case for secession in a treason court. Lincoln's goal was not to make grand public gestures, but to bring the war to as swift and decisive an end as possible. In the 1864 presidential election, he and Andrew Johnson ran on the "National Union" ticket. This brilliant move emphasised the national unity he wanted to achieve, and it also isolated McClellan, indirectly positioning him as partisan and in opposition to those goals. Lincoln knew that the long-term stability of the Union was far more important than exacting harsh retribution so soon after the war. In spite of Johnson's bungled attempts to continue his legacy, the United States have stayed firmly bound ever since.

If a subordinate transgresses against the group in some way, consider the long-term interests of the group, rather than allowing anger to cloud your judgement. You will want to exact retribution, and you might justify this with the desire to warn off similar behaviour. Punishing an employee may appear to have the desired effect at first, but in the long term you only create resentment and anger. Does their transgression represent a pattern of behaviour? If not, then ask yourself whether leniency and empathy would work better than yelling or humiliation. Stay grounded and objective in such situations. Your calm demeanour in the face of everyone else's demands for retribution will also do more for your image and reputation as a fair and just leader. Like Lincoln, you are above petty acts of vengeance, weighing the impact of your actions long into the future.

ASSERTING IDENTITY

In the second century BC, forces under the Han dynasty conquered the kingdom of Nam Viet, annexing it into their empire. The Han divided the renamed territory of Giao Chi into nine districts, each ruled by a mandarin. These Han-appointed officials wanted to exploit the fertile farmlands, particularly the Red River Delta, which would also act as a convenient supply point for maritime trade. During this first century of Han rule, Nam Viet was governed leniently, and the locals largely held onto their old customs and way of life.

By the first century AD, however, the Han rulers became greedy, intensifying their efforts to assimilate and "civilise" the former kingdom that they viewed as a society of backward barbarians. The Han governors instituted marriage and land inheritance reforms aimed at turning Nam Viet into a patriarchal society more amenable to political authority, and also forced the people of Nam Viet into paying high taxes to fund the local military and their lavish lifestyles.

Eventually, the Nam Viet had enough. In 39 AD, the powerful Yue lord Thi Sach defied the Han, refusing to let them bully his community into paying such heavy tribute. Fearing he would inspire a rebellion, and to ward off other resistance, the Han governor Su Ding put Thi Sach to death. This act of cruelty infuriated the Nam Viet, and his widow Trung Trac led a full-scale rebellion against the oppressors. She and her sister Trung Nhi, along with other members of the local aristocracy, marched on Lien Lau with the Yue, forcing the Han commander to flee. Within a year the Trung sisters had successfully liberated sixty-five towns and settlements from Han control, and in 40 AD they proclaimed themselves joint queens of an independent state.

In 42 AD, the Han emperor Guangwu ordered a military counter-attack against the Trung sisters. He appointed the general Ma Yuan to suppress the rebellion, giving him the title Fubo Jiangjun, or General Who Calms the Waves. Ma Yuan led 10,000 soldiers through the Red River Delta and broke down each rebel settlement one by one. Though the Trung sisters' army put up a stout defence against the Han invaders, they were ultimately no match for the sheer number of forces under Ma Yuan's command. The victorious Han general captured the Trung sisters and put them both to death. He gathered all the Yue's bronze drums, symbols of their authority under the old system, melted them down and recast them into a statue of a horse which he presented to Emperor Guangwu on his return. The Han ruled Nam Viet with an iron first for the next 500 years.

INTERPRETATION

Although the Trung sisters did not establish an independent kingdom, the modern-day country of Vietnam would likely not exist if they had not rebelled against the Han. Indeed, the Trung sisters are revered in Vietnamese culture today, celebrated as the first prominent leaders to assert the country's national identity. More than just two sisters who sacrificed their lives for their country, they continue as powerful symbols of Vietnamese resistance and freedom.

After they had annexed the kingdom into their empire, the Han governors were wise in their initial approach to the local people. They allowed the continuation of local customs, and ordinary people could largely go about their lives undisturbed. The subjugated territory stayed stable like this for over a century. The locals revolted only when the Han began greedily raising taxes, taking farmlands, and trying to change their society. By executing Thi Sach they also created a martyr, a symbol the Trung sisters used to rally their Yue soldiers. The Han had to send away a large army and talented general for a year, valuable resources they could have used elsewhere.

The swiftness, fury, and popularity of the Trung sisters' rebellion acts as a warning to all oppressive masters. If you get greedy, trying to extract as much as you can out of your subordinates, then don't complain when they leave or rise against you. The huge Han army overwhelmed the Trung sisters, but it was sheer luck that the self-proclaimed queens had not gained a stronger foothold before Ma Yuan arrived. People can subordinate themselves for long periods of time, but there is a powerful part of our nature that creates a burning desire for rebellion whenever we feel oppressed. We want our leaders to lead and serve us as we continue to serve them. The Han could have easily avoided the Trung-led rebellion by continuing with their leniency—as the leader of your group, don't fall into the same trap as them.

KEYS TO SOCIAL INTELLIGENCE

In the 1980s, the primatologist Jane Goodall observed some chilling developments in the chimpanzee community that she and her team were studying. A young chimp they had named Frodo would throw rocks at others in his group, sometimes even throwing them at Goodall and the other human observers. Frodo grew into a large, muscular adult chimp and carried on bullying the other chimps. He became a skilled hunter of red colobus monkeys, and if he ever failed in his hunts, he intimidated the other chimps into sharing their spoils with him. In 1997, the group's alpha male Freud and other members of the community contracted a disease. Freud was Frodo's brother, and had built up his authority in the group by focusing on the other chimp's needs, gaining favour by taking care of the group's children and grooming his friends. Frodo did not interact much with other apes, and used this opportunity to beat Freud into submission, taking control of the group.

Frodo ruled the group through intimidation. If two chimps were playing, and saw Frodo approaching, they would stop. They knew that if he joined in, he'd hurt them. Frodo rarely groomed others and often threatened to beat males who refused to groom him. He sired eight children through the females in the group, usually mating with them by force—he even fathered a child through his own mother, and the sickly child died after a few months. Frodo's reign of terror came to an abrupt end in 2002 when he fell ill. A coalition of smaller males viciously pounced upon him, beating him to a pulp. Frodo retreated from the group and made a full recovery, but he was really never the same chimp again. He travelled with the group, sometimes grooming other males, and died in 2013 from an infected bite wound.

Frodo, unlike his generous and community-minded brother Freud, was a violent and unpopular bully. Goodall noted that he had always shown aggressive and domineering behaviour, even as an infant—he would throw rocks at others and refused to cooperate with members of the group. His influence only became more dangerous to the group as he grew into one of the largest chimps ever observed by Goodall's team. Frodo gained his high status through intimidation and physical beatings, forcing a silent coalition of smaller males to wait in the wings. The minute he fell ill, losing his weight and strength, this coalition of males pounced and nearly beat him to death.

Frans de Waal noted a similar trend in his research into chimpanzee hierarchies. Alpha males could rule through sheer brute strength for a short while, but stood atop an unstable kingdom. This alpha chimp is not good at social grooming, he's not good at forming alliances, and aggravates smaller males. He rapes the females and does nothing to support the resultant offspring, so understandably they're not apt to give him mutual support either. A trio of smaller males, however, can do a lot of damage to one large male if they're brave enough, and this battle becomes even more asymmetric if the alpha falls ill, as Frodo did. Chimps with more of a community-building ethic, like Freud, rule over communities for much longer and with less tendency for bloody dominance feuds. In the chimp world, community support *is* stability.

Power is not the best strategy to attain success. We are not the same as chimps, but we have both enjoyed the longer-term benefits of cooperation over raw strength. Those who argue that human communities have oppressed one another through strength alone are not only taking an unbelievably cynical view of human nature, they're also flat wrong. Dominant groups aren't uniquely oppressive or cruel, they're uniquely good at fostering internal cooperation. Even if you're uniquely strong, two people who are two-thirds your strength can easily defeat you if they join together. That doesn't even have to reflect physical strength either—it can reflect popular support in a group, resources, or money. Hyper-competence and a genuine capacity for reciprocity are the measures for individual and group success, not power.

Denial of this usually reflects an internal justification for failure. If you're not doing very well, then it's easy to think that the game is rigged against you. This can only lead to a heart twisted with hatred and resentment, both of which cloud your mind. It is much more challenging—and consequently much more rewarding—to look objectively at your life and ask whether you're truly doing *everything* in your power to succeed. But unfortunately, many tyrants and dictators across history have exploited this capacity for malevolence in the human psyche. Hitler told war-torn Germany that the Jews were to blame for their struggles. Stalin and his predecessors told starving peasant workers that the most successful farmers were hoarding all the wealth that rightly belonged to them. This capacity for envy is a kind of short-circuit in our mind, and it leads to the violence, cowardice, and ultimately the evil that plagued humanity for much of the twentieth century.

Unfortunately for these tyrants, the same malevolence they themselves stirred up was used to beat them out of power, much as Frodo was overthrown in Goodall's chimpanzee community. Hitler stripped his top generals of power, oppressed his conquered territories, and forced soldiers from all corners of his empire to fight for the Nazi cause. These generals plotted to kill him multiple times, the drafted soldiers were the first to surrender, and the free world brought about a swift and heavy justice upon his empire. Stalin, in a similar vein, starved the Ukrainian populace to feed the key Soviet cities. He routinely purged his country of personae non gratae, killing them outright or sending them to the Gulags. He encouraged communities to turn in their own, promising that they'd receive all their property—a populace living in constant fear would most easily submit to rule, he reasoned. Nikita Khrushchev, one of Stalin's successors, later recounted the horrors of his leader's infamous dinner and drinks parties. Ostensibly such an invitation would seem like a cordial invitation, maybe even an honour. In reality, Stalin forced these men to drink all night, delighting in their struggles to keep control of themselves. Stalin would pull out the gramophone and order Khrushchev and the others to slow dance together in pairs, laughing at the power he held over these men. But when Stalin suffered a major stroke in 1953, these same men refused to come to his aid. Too afraid to take revenge when Stalin was in his tyrannical prime, they let their boss suffer a painful and frightening death.

This dynamic also plays out in less extreme examples. Many conquering leaders have made the mistake of enforcing a harsh, retributive peace on the defeating side. They demand total subjugation, humiliating them with a set of punitive terms. The term "Carthaginian peace" originates from the Punic Wars between Rome and Carthage. At the end of the Third Punic War, the Romans burned the capital city of Carthage to the ground, killed most of its inhabitants, and sold any left into slavery. Carthage never recovered, but this kind of brutal treatment against other subjugated territories eventually led to Rome's downfall.

In modern times, the economist John Maynard Keynes criticised the Treaty of Versailles as a Carthaginian peace. The treaty forced the once proud and mighty German state into humiliating servitude after the First World War, taking apart its industry and forcing it to pay unrealistically high reparations. The Germans were neither pacified nor really weakened in any meaningful way. The German people felt so resentful, their economy having completely collapsed, that Adolf Hitler had ample grounds to lead them into yet another world war as a form of retribution for the Treaty of Versailles. When Germany was once again defeated after the Second World War, some described the proposed Morgenthau Plan as a Carthaginian peace, since it advocated complete destruction of Germany's industry. Allied leaders realised this would make the same mistake as the Treaty of Versailles, and the Marshall Plan won over instead. Named after the United States Chief of Staff George Marshall, this plan instead prioritised the rebuilding of infrastructure in West Germany and the rest of Europe. The Allies understood this dynamic in the same way that Abraham Lincoln had, almost a century prior. The bitter victims of Hitler's war machine wanted retribution, but what would that have really achieved? Exacting a Carthaginian peace over a defeated foe can be especially tempting if they have hurt us in the past, but doing so shows gross historical blindness.

In stark contrast, the Socially Intelligent Leader has empathy for his foe; he's not clouded by irrational hatred. His calmness in any battle or crisis is a distinct advantage, because the destructive emotion of anger is not guiding his decisions for him. He thinks not of what personal slights to his pride he might have taken during the fight, because he knows his team's long-term stability is far more important. That toxic need to have the last word, to get that final insult in before the bell, shows pettiness—a base, animal perspective. This total submission to emotions may feel satisfying as a release every now and then, but it costs us greatly in the social realm. You're better than that—you're a Socially Intelligent Leader with control over your emotions.

The following are five ways to tame your tyrannical energy—we all have it within us, to varying degrees—and attain true long-term stability for your group.

Notice your tyrannical energy. There is no such thing as a person who has completely integrated and solved their self-absorption. There are only people who acknowledge the existence of their grandiose energies and consciously work past them to operate better with people. The trick isn't in finding and killing the inner dragon. It's in charting where the dragon is within the psyche, noting the situations that stir its tyrannical energies. Drawing this map allows Socially Intelligent Leaders to better regulate their aggression and remain an objective observer of their dismissive tendencies. You notice the little moments that would normally pass you by without conscious thought. Without this awareness, the rising tides of emotions and set behaviours easily take control of you. It makes you subject to your paranoia, your urges to have complete control, and the negative results that these toxic emotions inevitably bring about. Awareness is transformative in and of itself. So is the acceptance of the fact that it is not a question of *whether* we possess tyrannical energies, but *to what degree*.

Identify the source of your rage. When you become more aware of your tyrannical energies, you might become defensive, seeing it as yet another foe to be defeated. There is a part of you that knows there is something wrong with this situation. You may have already suffered prolonged stress or anxiety, even heart attacks. This is your body fighting against the unnatural need for total control over others. Not too many of us went through childhood thinking we were Superman, but those of us who did saddled the burden of defending Metropolis all by ourselves. In response to your bullying tendencies, it's likely that you have defended yourself by claiming that you're acting for the greater interests of your team or company. This is a grandiose illusion. No one appointed you to take on this burden, and you must come to see that your overwhelm is causing you issues as a leader.

It is also likely that your rage and violent urges come from a childhood fear of shame and ridicule. You sense all the little jabs to your pride and respond with the vigour you wish you'd had when an adult made a real threat to you during childhood. We all have memories of running to an adult with pure joy and wonder, only to be met with an irritable soul who tells us to go away and quiet down. After enough of these prickly responses, the wonder turns into toxic shame. You fear ridicule because of what happened to you whenever you expressed radiance and joy. Whenever you see the same joy in others, you project that same toxic shame onto them, lashing out in just the same way you so feared from adults as a child. Recognise that you are perpetuating the soul-crushing cycle and resolve to stop it. Any time someone comes to you with joy, take it with gratitude, because it's a rare and beautiful thing in this cruel and uncaring world.

Deal with your need for control. The need for control, predictability, and purity is the greatest disease the mind faces. It twists you into painful knots as events transpire that are utterly indifferent to your desires. Due to childhood pain, tyrants overcompensate for the absolute lack of control they felt as little boys and girls by attempting to extract absolute predictability when they enter the adult world. They oppress the sources of all crises because of the sheer terror that grips them when they realise that not everything falls within their grip. Understand that this need for control does not reflect strength; in fact it represents a stark weakness in your character that your animal urges have long exploited for most of your life. The bully, the person who constantly needs to exert his control others, is always the weakest and most frightened person in the room. Would you give *that* person absolute control over reality?

Another thing that controlling people like to do is build systems that allow them the absolute control they crave. They may think they have good intentions, but who's to say that those intentions will have positive results? With a system that obeys their every whim, there isn't *anyone* who can interrupt the effects of that change. And that system will come to rely upon that person at the top, so the burden becomes even greater over time, and the tyrant is deceived by scheming courtiers. It becomes a vicious cycle of tyranny and further grasps for power and control. And who can say that someone with more consciously malevolent intentions won't take control of that same system?

It is much healthier to cultivate what Friedrich Nietzsche called *amor fati*, or "love of fate." Life *is* pain, and you will waste years trying to fight that fact. Suspend your need to judge and control the outcome of everything that crosses your path. Entertain viewpoints opposing your own. Try to go into work without the need to show how smart you are in every single encounter. Do anything to disrupt your normal routine, break any sense that you already know better and should be the person in control. Step back from the day-to-day and allow events to unfold in front of you. Even try seeing the beauty in this. Embrace the fact that things constantly change. See this constant change as offering new opportunities for learning and growth, rather than trying to oppress it or grab hold of it. You will free up untold mental energy for more productive work and be happier for it.

Express your violent urges through harmless rituals. After reading all of this so far, it's easy to think that you should repress these tyrannical energies. But that will only bury a problem that needs to be examined and explored for new knowledge about ourselves. We'll become even tighter, denying that we have a problem and over-correcting our behaviour. Instead, it is healthier to let these urges out in controlled ways with full consciousness. Great outlets for such energies include creative projects, movies, video games, sports, and competitive activities. Learn to channel your aggression in positive directions. Our aggression is the reason we dominate the world, and it would be foolish to subsume the emotion. Use it to advance yourself in your career, become better at key skills for work and in your hobbies, and manifest your will. This is to accept a funda-mental part of our human nature, without losing ourselves to its potentially destructive power. Zen masters don't shut off their emotions; they accept them and embrace the natural ebb and flow of life.

Develop universal compassion. When you die, all of the fear and resentment you're holding onto will be gone. Why even bother with it? It's a question you'll ask yourself in your last days as you realise how you've allowed these tyrannical energies to eat you from the inside. The people you think are threatening your power are really just you, living a different life in a different set of circumstances. They have many of the same fears stemming from the same core mechanics of human nature: responding to scarcity, threats, and social exclusion. If you take a more universal perspective, realising that other people's pleasure *is* your pleasure, then you're setting yourself up for more enriched life. You'll give your subordinates opportunities for growth because you're not so afraid of locking down their services. You'll be happy giving away your time to help others because then they'll likely carry on the good turn for others, and so on. Commit yourself to elevating the happiness of the world, even if it brings some risk of failure or suffering onto yourself. Being able to look at the world this way is not weakness, nor is it foolishness. It is the highest expression of strength and self-security. If you think otherwise, or if that concept seems too soft, then realise how much misery you've been bringing onto others and decide if that's better. Think about how you've brought suffering into the brief lifespans of others, all so that you can feel a little more secure. The conscious choice of love over fear is a sign of enlightenment.

> Dictators ride to and fro upon tigers which they dare not dismount. And the tigers are getting hungry.
>
> — WINSTON CHURCHILL

REVERSAL

The opposite of the tyrant is the weakling: the leader who lacks the calm centre necessary for group responsibility. The weak leader cannot sleep at night, tormented by fears of his staff disliking him, plotting against him. Their paranoia manifests in a defensive attitude, like Caligula pacing around his palace in the dead of night, muttering unintelligibly about the plotters all around him. They bend to the stronger and more vocal subordinates in their team, losing the respect and awe they ought to wield. This is the leader who always seemed so nice, so pure before being promoted. But we all carry the same tyrannical energies within us, to varying degrees—and this is certainly not limited only to men. Once in a position of power, and subjected to the inevitable challenges that brings, their inner stability collapses and they became just as oppressive as the tyrant.

Much like the tyrant, the weakling is unconscious of the same grandiose, violent urges that live inside all of us. The archetype just lies at the opposite end of the spectrum, with many of the same problems. In general, you should channel your tyrannical energies, not repress them—there is no other way. Now that you are aware of them, there is no turning back. No letting them loose on other people, nor locking them away in a dark cage. Both paths will lead only to oppression and destruction, and you are now responsible for channelling them in a positive direction. There can be no reversal to this core principle of Social Intelligence.

8

THE INTEL TRINITY AND GERMAN UNIFICATION

UNITE YOUR TEAM TO MAKE THE MOST OF ITS DIVERSE STRENGTHS

N*o one person, no matter how skilled, can be a master in all things. Every skill, every trait, every bright light has its shadow side. If you try to go it alone all the time, you'll inevitably come face-to-face with the tasks where you lack skill. Invite people into your team who complement your own deficiencies and give them latitude. Value their unique skills and defer to their judgement on matters in which they hold the most knowledge. To do this, you must critically assess your own skills and deficiencies. Identify your habits and patterns. You cannot do this if you have ego-invested in a grandiose self-image, because you will be too insecure to learn new things. You must accordingly see this influence as a treacherous snake and accept that it is good to integrate your imperfections. Build a tightly knit team with diverse strengths, and you'll be able to deal with any challenge.*

COMPLEMENTARY LEADERSHIP

In July 1968, two scientists named Robert Noyce and Gordon Moore left their positions at Fairchild Semiconductor to found a company they called N M Electronics. Noyce and Moore sought to build a company around semi-conductor memory chips, an industry experiencing rapid growth. Both men were skilled scientists and had excelled at Fairchild. In this new enterprise, their first random-access memory chips were twice as fast as the ones produced at Fairchild, and they quickly won new business and investors. Disliking their company's bland name almost from the start, they renamed their company Intel, short for "Integrated Electronics."

Intel's early growth showed great promise, and they quickly took on new employees. From the start, they ensured that Intel stuck to a flat, democratic organisational structure. Executives received no special privileges. Employees at all levels frequently surrounded Moore's desk, discussing some new idea or sharing feedback on each other's work. Such was the widespread culture of informality that one time a top Intel executive got angry with his wife for turning up to their offices in their luxury Mercedes car, and from then on she only showed up in a cheap sedan. Intel's fast growth and culture allowed them to speed up both their research and production of new chips, but it also provided a host of new challenges for the two scientists.

Robert Noyce was the more charismatic of the pair. He was empathetic with his employees, listening to their problems. People left meetings with him feeling excited and inspired, and he became widely loved within Intel. He was also a brilliant scientist, having co-invented the first integrated circuits with the engineer Jack Kilby. They named these integrated circuits "microchips" and would later form the foundation of Intel. At Fairchild, Noyce had experimented with selling a special $1 memory chip. These microchips were much smaller and cheaper than the industry average, but they proved immensely popular and the company prospered. Noyce foresaw a trend in the electronics industry of iteratively smaller and cheaper microchips. Intel could entice customers in with cheaper prices at first and then increase its margins once production costs fell. Noyce's vision would later become known as "learning curve" pricing, and it remains the standard pricing strategy for technology companies in Silicon Valley today.

Despite his clear technical vision, Noyce lacked key management skills. He was so smooth with people, and so good at listening, that he hated any kind of conflict. He was often indecisive in business decisions, and could not bring himself to fire underperforming employees. He preferred to treat workers like family, and was the primary driver behind Intel's informal, flat management structure. But when in 1975 the company was forced to lay off 3,500 employees due to management mistakes, Noyce was so devastated that he resigned his position as CEO in favour of his cofounder Moore, moving to the position of chairman.

Gordon Moore was almost the opposite of his cofounder. He was quiet and introverted, perfectly happy to study and work in solitude. Even after Intel's rapid success made him a billionaire, he remained humble, and rarely discussed business outside of work. He had deep personal interests in geology and fishing, and could talk for hours on these subjects. As technical leader at Intel, he developed Moore's Law, his observation that the number of transistors in an integrated circuit doubles every two years. This now-infamous principle became a guiding force for the modern technology industry, as the companies themselves seemed to scale and grow at a similar exponential rate.

But Moore suffered from many of the same shortcomings as Noyce. He was more bookish and awkward than his partner and found personal interaction difficult. The research divisions he ran at both Fairchild and Intel were

undisciplined and chaotic. As chief executive, Moore strug-
gled with the day-to-day running of the business, delegating
most of this to Andy Grove, Intel's chief operating officer.
Grove would often say that Moore could answer almost any
technical question instantly, but could rarely solve interpersonal conflicts between employees. In meetings, Moore
would struggle to assert himself and his ideas, even allowing
the more outgoing employees to contradict him openly.
Moore was a scientist at heart, caring more about seeking the
truth than his own personal glory. At Intel, he fostered many
young scientists who would achieve their own successes, and
took this as his greatest satisfaction from the role as company
leader. But Grove would often despair with Moore as he
allowed his good ideas to get overrun by more confident
employees, and he would have to assert Moore's authority on
his behalf.

Andy Grove was the executive who could harness both
Noyce and Moore's technical brilliance, while making up for
their shortcomings. While the two cofounders were vision-
aries and correctly foresaw many industry trends, they both
suffered when trying to run the business. Grove, in contrast,
was highly conscientious, orderly, and operated at top speed.
For example, when the Japanese Motorola Corporation rose
as a competitor to Intel, he brainstormed "Operation
Crush," a marketing strategy to counter Motorola's rapid
growth. By the following week, Grove had reviewed and
condensed his ideas into a concrete plan. By the week after
that, he had presented his ideas to 100 Intel salespeople.
Another week after that, Grove had recruited and organised
over 1,000 employees to his strategy. His management style
proved highly effective—he always prioritised creating
measurable objectives that employees could easily adopt and
deliver. With Operation Crush, Grove instilled in his
employees a feeling that the company's very survival

depended on the plan's success. Everyone felt involved in the project, and that they each had their own unique role to play. It was a resounding success that further solidified Intel's dominance of the technology industry—it also forged a spirit of productivity and hard work that Intel would use in their later growth.

Like his colleagues, Grove also had his own shortcomings. He was vehemently against the decision to change Intel's direction away from memory chips and into microprocessors. Unlike Noyce and Moore, Grove was an employee with a salary, and less apt to take risks that might cost him his job and reputation. He often disagreed with the pair on conflicts between their visions for the market and the day-to-day running of the business. Memory chips were the foundation of the company as he saw it, and he did not share his colleagues' enthusiasm to jump into the new microprocessor market. It was too much of an unknown risk. This, however, was one decision that both Noyce and Moore strongly argued for, and they would not back down. Noyce had overseen Ted Hoff's invention of the microprocessor and knew its potential. Even Mike Markkula, then a product manager of memory components at Intel, expressed the sales potential of these new microchips. (Markkula would later found Apple Computer, Inc. with Steve Jobs and Steve Wozniak.)

Noyce was convinced that microprocessors would revolutionise the technology industry, but he knew that Grove would not approve of taking the company in an entirely new direction. To avoid a conflict, he took matters into his own hands, sanctioning further research and development into microprocessors, which took resources away from ongoing projects. Grove found out and was furious with Noyce for going behind his back like this, and Moore had to act as mediator between the two men. With Moore's calming influence, Grove eventually warmed to Noyce's idea, but there still existed a tension between him and the more visionary Noyce. Even though they disliked each other and frequently argued, they and Moore all reached a compromise strategy: Grove would implement Noyce's plan to change Intel's direction into microprocessors, but as CEO of the company. Noyce reluctantly agreed, and Moore gave his position to Grove.

Their predictions proved correct, and Intel's bet on the microprocessor made it the most successful technology company for several decades—much of the success due to Grove's organisational skills. In 2002, as the technology sector boomed, the company was valued at more than $500,000,000, bigger than the entire automotive industry combined.

INTERPRETATION

While the story of Intel's growth is almost mythic within the technology sector, it is full of real lessons for Socially Intelligent Leaders. Two great scientists, Noyce and Moore, founded the company and proved themselves to be visionary technical leaders. They loved to innovate and find new technologies, and gained a profound satisfaction from encouraging younger scientists and engineers. Each man perfectly complemented the other's deficits—Noyce being more of a people person, and Moore being more of an introvert immersed in his work. This mutual partnership helped them when they first started Intel, driving its early growth. But once Intel grew past a certain size, new problems began to mount. Moore's technical divisions, while flat and democratic, grew increasingly chaotic, and he had to deal with arguments between engineers, individual factions growing within teams. Neither Moore nor Noyce were best equipped to deal with these problems, and if they hadn't brought Grove into the fold, then the company might have collapsed under its own weight.

Being an outsider, Grove brought objectivity and clarity to the business. Though not a scientist, he was much better at organising a company, and provided Intel with the discipline it needed to sustain its rapid growth. Grove's management style also meshed in well with the open culture fostered by Noyce and Moore. Intel's flat management structure might seem familiar to us today, but for the time it was revolutionary. The technology industry we're familiar with today is largely a result of the culture shift that Intel helped spur on. Ideas could be exchanged with employees at all levels, Moore encouraging them to approach his desk whenever they wanted his opinion; Grove revelled in the position of organising the team to put these ideas into practice; by declining the usual executive perks in Intel's first years in business, Noyce stood as a role model for future generations of Silicon Valley CEOs.

It takes great maturity to see one's own failings and bring others into the fold, allowing them to flourish. As narrated in the story, the Intel Trinity, as they came to be known, had to overcome deep disagreements over the company's direction. It took Moore's calmness and maturity to keep Noyce and Grove on good working terms, preventing a battle that might have damaged the company. They were highly aware of their complementary skills, and in spite of any tension along the way, each of them eventually realised their respective strengths and weaknesses. Their distinct personalities and strong desire to succeed in their own ways helped Intel to become the biggest success story in Silicon Valley besides Apple.

You must take this story of leadership as a model for your own leadership going forward. Take a step back from the chaotic daily rhythm of your workplace and analyse where you've made mistakes in leading the team. Consider how you can fill in these gaps with your senior colleagues' strengths. The key is to stay objective. If you become childish whenever someone criticises you, and you cannot bear to even acknowledge your failings, then they will become dominant features of your leadership. Leaders who point out the failings of others, while unable to take a single glance at their own deficiencies, deserve the endless crises they inevitably cause.

GROUP UNITY

The modern-day country of Germany has only existed in its current form for a short time. For much of its recent history, it has existed as a loose group of individual kingdoms: Prussia, Bavaria, Saxony, Württemberg, and numerous others at different time periods. For the 900 years that the Holy Roman Empire existed, this also included modern-day Austria and Czechia. It was a vast empire united by language. After Napoleon invaded Prussia in 1806, the twenty-year-old King Ludwig I of Bavaria saw the need to unite all the German people against this threat. Napoleon had disbanded the Holy Roman Empire as part of his retributive peace terms, wounding the national pride that the German people had enjoyed for almost 1,000 years. Infighting plagued the German states when they were in most need of unity.

In 1807 Ludwig built a massive hall which he named Walhalla, after the majestic hall of the same name in Germanic and Norse mythology. Walhalla contained statues and artwork that honoured distinguished German celebrities, including busts of Ludwig van Beethoven, Nicolaus Copernicus, and the sixteenth-century priest Martin Luther. Ludwig's main criterion for selection was "being of the

German tongue," and so Walhalla honoured a diverse list of 160 people over 1800 years of history.

Martin Luther's inclusion was uncomfortable for Ludwig, since he was a devout Catholic. Despite his own personal feelings, Luther's achievements were points of great national pride among both the aristocracy and lower classes. Luther had long railed against the dogma of the Catholic Church and its worldly extravagance. He promoted biblical scholarship among all classes of people, believing they had the right to a direct communication with God. The Catholic Church's use of Latin prevented this, since only the wealthy could afford a classical education. Luther had therefore translated the bible into German, and made it widely available across the German kingdoms, refusing any of the profits from his writings. Johannes Gutenberg's printing press published over 500,000 copies before Luther's death in 1546. Almost three centuries later, Luther was still such a strong figure of German identity that Ludwig had no choice but to promote his image in Walhalla.

Building on the success of Walhalla, Ludwig further affirmed the consumption of beer as a German cultural institution. Beer had been consumed in the German lands since Roman times, as the historian Tacitus had noted the Germanic proclivity for beer as far back as the first century. So in October 1810, when Ludwig got married in the Bavarian capital city Munich, he celebrated his wedding by sharing enormous quantities of beer with the city's people. The Münchners enjoyed the festivities so much that they have celebrated Oktoberfest every year since. German-speakers and many other visitors from across the world make the pilgrimage to the fortnight-long celebration of beer, and it has since become one of the most recognisable German institutions.

Ludwig's project worked exactly as intended, and the

language-based identity allowed the German states to stop their infighting and eventually bring Napoleon's terror over Europe to an end at Waterloo.

INTERPRETATION

German history is filled with splits, reunifications, and alliances between competing states. It took a threat from a general of Napoleon's calibre to bring together the German states under a strong national identity centred around a common language. The German language, standardised by Luther, formed bonds that brought together people from different kingdoms, and gave the diverse peoples a common cause to fight for against the invading French. Ludwig showed great vision for such a young king, since he clearly understood the power that a single unifying cause can have on a group—especially one based upon a mythic symbol like Walhalla. All this happened soon after the disbandment of the Holy Roman Empire, when German sentiment was at its weakest. So it is even more impressive that Ludwig kept his head, seeing the situation with objectivity, always a key part of Social Intelligence.

We may laugh at national pride over beer, but such things are critical for building a strong Group Mythology, as described in Chapter 3. Ludwig understood this well. As he did, you must unite your group by looking to the past, for common elements that everyone can get behind. These elements must be associated strongly with feelings of pride and pleasure—think of the busts in Walhalla and the beer parties in Munich. In this process, your personal feelings should never play a part. Do as Ludwig did with Martin Luther, and subsume your beliefs and prejudices—the group's morale is far more important. We can easily make figures like Luther into mythic heroes, symbols that fit into the archetypes built inside the human psyche. A wise priest, an underdog hero, a benevolent king; any figure from the past can fill this role. Remember, your goal is to unite people across different factions, so the most effective mythic symbols touch on the most common elements of sectional pride. Just as Ludwig did, you will inspire your people into a strong, tight-knit force.

KEYS TO SOCIAL INTELLIGENCE

An effective team is more important than any plan or idea. This team is tied together with strong bonds, operating with a culture of excellence and reciprocity. Team members freely share ideas, they feel valued for their input, and put in their fair share of the work. They don't think transactionally, instead wanting to put as much excellent work in as possible for its own sake—in fact, they feel honoured to do so. Conflicts naturally arise, as they do in all groups, but they're dealt with in a constructive manner. The team collectively notices toxic colleagues who show patterns of negative behaviour and ask these colleagues to either improve or move somewhere else. You as the group leader encourage the free flow of feedback up and down the chain, ensuring that this feedback is fair and based on evidence. This feedback is received objectively, and members are never punished for reporting their own failures, provided they own their mistakes and learn from them. Senior members gain profound satisfaction from opening doors for their junior colleagues. They actively expose those who exploit others for politics or personal gain. Each member of the team realises that together as a group, with their diverse strengths and perspectives combined, they can move mountains.

We will name this model the Ideal Team State, and use it

as the ideal to strive for when developing our own teams. People will leave for reasons outside of your control, and unexpected challenges will arise all the time. This constant state of flux is the way of nature, and you must see any attempts to fight it as a complete waste of time and effort. Trying to achieve the Ideal Team State is to miss the point entirely, because it is impossible to maintain for any length of time. Instead, the Socially Intelligent Leader must always view circumstances objectively with a keen eye. They compare their team's state to the ideal and schedule regular meetings to fix any problem areas. They consult all members of the team for their viewpoints, no matter how new or junior they might be. Everyone has a unique perspective that is valuable in some way. The key in seeking this feedback is to find patterns in praise and criticism, getting a feel for the group's gestalt. You notice one colleague making a sharp comment towards another, and judge whether this is part of a trend of rudeness or merely incidental. Such things might seem small, but they show sentiments that can destroy group unity. That rude behaviour might spark off feelings of resentment that burn any trust those two colleagues had with one another.

Cohesion is the most important factor in any team attempting to resemble the ideal state. If the team members hate each other, they're unlikely to even communicate, never mind work together productively. You must come to see individual egos as a cancer for group unity. That employee who made the sharp comment earlier might see themselves as the victim of a lazy workplace. He treats his colleagues with contempt, seeing them as worker drones to be whipped into shape. These colleagues resent his dismissive comments and actively seek to sabotage him. Or, some senior colleague always shows up late to meetings. She thinks she has earned this privilege because of her length of service to the group and makes passive-aggressive little gestures to make sure everyone knows it. The others fume at her arrogance and the apparently unequal application of group rules. In either of these cases the leader must recognise the negative dynamics at play and see its reversal as an immediate priority.

The leader explains to the condescending employee that his actions are directly hurting group unity, and that he needs to respect his colleagues—aggressive supervisor types like this often believe in a false dichotomy of utter tyranny and weak laziness, when there is actually a happy medium that embraces Social Intelligence. With the chronically late employee, the leader tells her not to expect special privileges just because she's been around the longest. Give her a taste of her own medicine by making *her* wait—though ensure you carry out this revenge in a controlled manner and make its positive intention clear to the victim, because it can easily backfire if not executed with care. This kind of tactic might seem manipulative, but as group leader your greatest task is to maintain group unity, and sometimes a real experience is the best way of imparting an important lesson

When recruiting people to your team you must screen out candidates that don't fit your group's culture, regardless of their qualifications or even their skills. It is much harder to train someone's character than any individual ability, and people with strong characters are fast and eager learners, regardless of whatever grades they might have attained at school. It's obvious to us that a fancy degree or experience at a competitor does not mean they will do well in the job. But you must go deeper than this and judge a candidate's character more than their skills. How do they fit in with the team? Do they have any irritating habits? Try to notice anything that makes you dislike them as a person. You might think this unimportant in a professional setting, but it's of prime importance to the employees who will have to spend every working day with this person. It's difficult to sniff out such characteristics in a one-hour interview when candidates are actively putting on their best appearances, which is why companies employ multiple rounds of interviews and team exercises. The most effective companies understand that people are their most important asset, and therefore take great care in picking the people they bring inside the fold. Because people naturally put on a performance when they know they're being assessed, it is more efficient to pay more attention to team candidates when they let their guard down. Hold a social event after a group interview session and watch intently for any hints of dismissive behaviour, any personal stories that reveal poor character traits. Your goal is to catch anything that might negatively affect your group's unique spirit, so this will vary between different groups.

All that being said, it's important not to build a group that's too homogenous. In our efforts to recruit team members that fit into our group's existing culture, it's easy to end up with a group of people that are too like-minded. Aim for a diversity of strengths and viewpoints. Not only will this make your workplace a more interesting place to be, it'll also ensure that any given problem has the best chance of being solved. Your team has so many skill sets and personal experiences that you bustle with ideas. To measure the skill levels in your team, run pop quizzes on the common topics in your industry or sector. You can keep the results anonymous if you prefer, but recognise this as an opportunity for your best colleagues to prove their skills—inevitably, your team will want to share their results, so it is almost not worth trying to suppress. Aggregate the results by team member and skill set to see where your team is strong and where it is weak. The weaker members of your team might feel ashamed of themselves, so privately tell them that this is a great opportunity to work on their skills, and reassure them that they're valued for the stronger aspects of their skill set.

As you introduce new recruits to your team, recognise how fragile a time this can be for the existing members. Gently encourage them to interact with the group during downtime. Attach them to a senior member of the team so they don't feel isolated and have a designated person to ask for guidance. When choosing a project for them always pick something new and untouched by others in the team. People are naturally territorial and wary of outsiders. Never criticise your colleagues for this instinct, because it's the same dynamic that drives people's pride in their expertise. The worst thing you can do is take a chunk out of a colleague's territory unannounced and give it to the recruit. This is, in fact, one of the most upsetting things you can ever do to a team member. You might have the best intentions, but you are still telling them "I don't value your expertise and contributions in this area," and "I see you as a replaceable worker drone, not a valued team member." Instead, allow and encourage each of your colleagues to become subject matter experts, with the caveat that they share this knowledge with others where practical. Respect their boundaries, and never tread on toes, even when you're the leader. The Socially Intelligent Leader realises that the happiness of his team is more important than any marginal increase in efficiency. Do not make the mistake of seeing this as protecting against knowledge hoarding or "siloing" as it is often called. That only happens when the team lacks the trust you should already be focused on building.

Team members should always exchange their knowledge with others, and people are usually all too eager and proud to do this when they're allowed to own their category. When Ed Catmull was president of the film production company Pixar, he encouraged the development of a "Brain Trust" of experts. When shown any film in production by the studio, this group would give honest feedback, and it was often frank and brutal. The film's director kept final creative authority, but gained valuable guidance on how to improve their picture. You should consider something similar for your group, building your own Brain Trust comprising your longest-serving employees. This will make them feel valued for their expertise, and by giving feedback on projects they will become invested in your group's success. For more details on this approach, see Chapter 10.

These interpersonal strategies might seem to get in the way of true efficiency. *Why can't people just shelve their insecurities while they're at work?* Or even worse, *I'm the boss, so why don't they just do as I say and shut up?* Holding these attitudes shows a gross ignorance of human nature. Do not be so arrogant as to think you have some higher goals in wrestling with your employees' natural inclinations. You may as well argue with the apple falling from the tree, utterly indifferent to whatever fancy title you've given yourself. We humans are not abstractions, we are animals with primal urges towards jealousy, hierarchy, and aggression. This programming has kept us alive for millennia, so never look down upon it with the dangerous moral lens. For you as the aspiring Socially Intelligent Leader, be careful about abstracting your team with elegant charts and graphs. Such practices are useful and have arguably built much of our modern industry, but you must always take human nature into account whenever using such technology to make decisions about your group. Never write off any grumbling as something that will merely pass— whatever you did to cause it will stick in your team members' minds for a long time and cause irreversible rifts in group unity. People can forget an honest face-to-face disagreement, but they have a long memory for contempt and dismissiveness.

The best way to build good relationships within your team is to keep them close together. Given a shared goal and tasks to get on with, people will naturally banter with each other, forming in-jokes that make the group feel like family. As the leader, encourage this burgeoning Group Mythology and never allow yourself to seem too separated. Lead from the front when it comes to trust, vulnerability, and getting work done. Seeing this, your staff will follow your example. Think back to Gordon Moore in the Intel story from earlier in the chapter. Up to a reasonable point, Moore encouraged engineers to approach his desk with ideas and feedback. Several staff surrounding his desk holding a free, energetic discussion was a common occurrence in the old days of Intel. He never felt jealous of those around him, no matter if they were smarter or more brilliant than he, and was never defensive in the face of criticism. He saw the practice of helping his researchers grow as the greatest satisfaction in his career. Build trust between employees in the same way by ensuring that the group has common goals and a culture of competence and encouragement. Encourage discussion sessions and watch as the ideas fly with passion. You must treasure these moments of energy and reciprocity as the highlights of your working life.

> In the long history of humankind (and animal kind, too) those who learned to collaborate and improvise most effectively have prevailed.
>
> — CHARLES DARWIN

REVERSAL

There is never any time when group unity is undesirable. Any group that lacks unity, that cannot stand together, that has no Group Mythology, is ineffective and open to threats. It cannot organise itself well enough to achieve its goals. Better organised competitors race ahead, taking ground away from you. Your workplace is so plagued with internal conflicts that everyone dreads showing up. Group members feel so disaffected that they see no grand cause to work towards—in fact they may actively work against it. Valuable staff are poached by competitors, all too happy to punish you for your years of contempt. And as the leader, it will be entirely your fault. There can be no reversal.

9

DEALING WITH THE FLOURISHING ZEITGEIST

Human groups naturally morph and change. They respond to changing circumstances in a dynamic and unpredictable fashion. New members bring their unique perspectives. The group is a kind of organism, churning up ideas and behaviours that constantly challenge its status quo. As the leader of a group, you should not concern yourself with this feature of group dynamics for two reasons: one, because fighting it is a fruitless distraction; and two, because fighting change with oppressive measures destroys group unity in the long run. Instead, you must foster open discussion among your subordinates that produces ideas and then select the ideas that best serve your group's overall interests. You are still the group's leader, and they must not see you as a pushover, but you must also move with the times.

MOVING WITH THE TIMES

Times change, and we change with the times. Those words have long been misattributed to Roman scholars such as Ovid; they in fact came out of sixteenth century Germany when times were changing fast. The Protestant Reformation was spreading quickly across north-west Europe, and countries whose kings had once kneeled at the feet of the Pope were ridiculing the Catholic Church's shameless opulence. The Württemberg priest Martin Luther goaded Pope Leo into a public fight on the basis that scripture held higher precedence than the Bishop of Rome. But revolutions are rarely instigated by the poorest in society. The Catholic Church had long irked the German aristocracy as much as they had oppressed the poor—demanding expensive "indulgences" from them as a form of earthly penance for their sins. They resented having to pay lip service to a church that waltzed about so arrogantly, so sure of its own piety. When Martin Luther proposed a new church movement free of all of Rome's pomp (and most importantly, free of its expensive indulgences), they supported him. Though Pope Leo left the Catholic Church in a far weaker state than he found it, Martin Luther didn't escape persecution for daring to challenge the church's authority. He stood before his king and uttered the immortal words, "Here I stand, I cannot do otherwise. God help me." Sentenced guilty as charged, his supporters in the aristocracy "kidnapped" Luther and let him wait out the storm in Wartburg Castle, protected by a disguise and pseudonym.

Revolutions rarely reward their instigators with glory and fanfare—in fact they usually kneel at the guillotine—but Luther's influence on the European spirit is still felt today. Luther understood the changing times, and Pope Leo did not. The latter bitterly resisted the challenges to his rule and only made himself look ridiculous. From Luther's writings, it's clear that he genuinely wanted the scripture-based worship that came with the Protestant Reformation, but he could not have expressed his beliefs at a better time. The aristocracy was sick to death of the Catholic Church's arrogance and the constant harassment from its indulgence sales-men. They wanted to bring its influence to an end, and Luther's clamour for a more austere style of worship was just the ticket. Luther was undoubtedly a revolutionary figure, but he didn't bring down the Catholic Church all by himself. He expressed the resentment that many Germans had held in their hearts for decades and did so in a far more reli-giously pure way than they ever could. Luther sparked the flourishing of the zeitgeist. Pope Leo tried to fight it and paid for it with the ending of his church's 1,000-year domi-nance over Europe..

Comparing the rumble of discontent in an office with a continent-wide religious movement might seem dramatic, but both situations reflect the same pattern in human nature. Pope Leo is in fact the quintessence of all leaders who desperately try to preserve their waning power in the face of unstoppable group change. Such leaders either fail to see the changes bubbling up to the surface and react with force after it's too late, or jealously oppress such change wherever it manifests. In both cases they are fighting the ocean's tides—unstoppable, unrelenting, and utterly indifferent to your position of power. Pope Leo and his church were so used to bullying the people of Europe, extracting vast sums for the church's own grand largesse, that he did not realise the obvious discontent this would bring across the continent.

King Henry VIII of England became so irritated by the Catholic Church's interferences that he created his own, allowing him to annul his marriage to Catherine of Aragon and instead take a younger, prettier queen. Behind the scenes, though, Thomas Cromwell pulled the strings. He persuaded the king that breaking with Rome and forming his own English church would allow him to marry Anne Boleyn, all against Pope Clement's wishes. While this satisfied Henry's carnal needs and created the potential to produce a legitimate male heir, Cromwell wanted a complete religious revolution in England. Henry was grateful for this simple solution and rewarded Cromwell with promotions and riches. The English people didn't mind this change at first, since many had also become tired with Rome's endless intrigues. But when Cromwell knocked down churches, stripped them of their wealth, and forcefully imposed Protestantism, ordinary Englishmen and women decided he had gone too far in his reforms. Many English still had ties to the Catholic Church, and watched in horror as a kind of terror fell upon the country virtually overnight—images of the Virgin Mary being smashed to pieces, church frescoes being torn, worshippers being labelled heretics, on and on. On top of this, Cromwell had levied high taxes to pay for these reforms, bringing back the exploitation they had previously suffered under Rome's thumb. Seeing a revolution brewing, Henry was furious. All he had wanted was an annulment, and now he was facing a mutiny. After he had spent a month locked up in the Tower of London, Cromwell's head fell into a basket in front of a large and enthusiastic crowd.

Cromwell likely understood that the people of England—Henry included—clamoured for change, but he went too far in his reforms. He calculated that the English people would bear the temporary pain, but he failed to disguise his own desperate thirst for religious change, and committed the same sin as Pope Leo in reverse. You want to track your team's deepest hidden desires and go along with them in a conscious manner, but don't make the same mistake as Cromwell, allowing the seductive power this brings to go to your head. You must always stay attuned to the emotional movements of the group, all the patterns in how they interact, and how these evolve over long periods of time. Are people grumbling to one another? Do they want change? Is the change something you can reasonably implement? When talking to subordinates about such things, they'll feel pleasantly surprised at your open attitude towards their suggestions. You're still their leader, but you never feel threatened by any changes because you're aware of them as they appear—and besides, it isn't your job to control such large-scale changes in spirit. Treat this power as a dial that you consciously control. Submit yourself to the group's zeitgeist too far, and you're no longer a leader; oppress the group's zeitgeist, and you're a tyrant. Striking the perfect balance requires a deft touch and will probably demand a series of changes in how you interact with your group.

The following are five strategies for using your group's natural movements to your advantage, keeping them happy and productive and preventing any needless outbursts of revolutionary anger.

Open up channels of free expression. It is much easier to prevent problems from afar than to put out fires on a daily basis. You must see your group's desires as a kind of pressure cooker—allow your subordinates to blow off steam every now and then, without the threat of judgement or ostracisation. If you create a toxic work environment where people feel like they have to be silent at all times, then they'll stew in resentment. That's not a good situation for productivity. When people feel heard, they're not distracted by their boiling resentment. Encourage your team to express themselves. Keep your door open and receive team members with a welcoming warmth. You must foster a culture of trust and cooperation to ensure that team members feel safe in expressing their beliefs and frustrations. Fostering a culture of competition may seem to bring results in the short term, but in the long term employees only hoard knowledge and mistrust one another—they may even sabotage the overall group's goals to further their own—which will make them turn inwards and seethe with resentful rage.

Today there are many computer chat applications available for private and public communication between team members, and you should use them. Allowing your team to discuss things with each other will bring them closer together and deepen the overall spirit of camaraderie. Hold regular open meetings with your group, encouraging them to ask questions, and answer honestly—it is likely that anything they ask has been on their minds for a long time. Your team will appreciate the genuine concern you show for their thoughts and ideas. Most importantly you must act on any promises you make to the team, otherwise they'll see through your ingratiating attempts to win their favour. Remember that you're all on the same team; there is no dividing line between the ordinary team members and the leadership. If the matters being discussed are controversial, then hold anonymous straw polls. You'll get more honest responses and a better sense for the overall feeling of the group.

Establish a set of rules and boundaries. Have a set of principles declared in the beginning of your rule, as early as possible. This will make it known to your group where you will and will not compromise. Stick to these principles in a clear, visible manner. Become identified with these principles if you can. This will make it easier for you to resist being pulled in any direction that the group may temporarily lean towards in its clamour for reform. The boss who visibly panics at the sign of unrest, ingratiates himself, and bends to public pressure, is *never* respected and abdicates his rule. Entire books could be written about leaders who fell victim to revolutions, hastening their own downfall by placating the discontented people's whims, often at too late a stage. They fail to realise that this actually makes them seem more ingratiating and insincere than if they had just listened to their people from the start. It's the "whatever will make you go away and leave me alone" response that shows no great principles.

The Socially Intelligent Leader, in contrast, realises the need to establish a firm yet fair set of boundaries for her group and making them as clear as possible. She makes policies that she will hold herself to, even at her own expense. She follows through on punishments, no matter how uncomfortable, because she made the rules clear right from the beginning. She encourages team members to speak so long as they don't resort to personal attacks, and must base any comments on observable evidence—anything not based on evidence and clear cause-and-effect is classed as mere whining and discarded out of hand. This might seem harsh, but it prevents the spread of virulent ideas and convenient explanations, both of which threaten group unity. The discussion is regulated and metered not for its content, but for the way it is presented.

Creating a firm set of boundaries and sticking to them might seem counter to encouraging group expression. Some will openly whine at the presence of rules, but such types are present in every group and rarely contribute as much as their more conscientious peers. What we're really doing is creating a structured environment for free expression and earning respect from our team by not budging on preset boundaries. This is the foundation of modern liberal democracies! It is likely, however, that you're not running a literal democracy, and you don't always need to consult the group for every decision you make. You're not asking for *permission* to establish rules—you're sound-boarding the rules ahead of time to keep the team informed, and testing the waters for any reactions or feedback. You must ensure these rules are clearly communicated to everyone in the team, not just a select few senior members. One of the biggest causes of frustration in workplaces is the lack of communication of new rules. If your team grumbles at rules, it's unlikely because of the rule itself, but because you were too anxious to tell anyone about it. This may have been due to concerns over morale, but it will be perceived as dismissiveness—and developing a pattern like this will be even more destructive in the long run.

Understand the tyranny of vocal minorities. There is nothing more subversively tyrannical than a vocal minority. You must be able to differentiate a genuine uprising in popular sentiment from what is merely the influence of a small but disproportionately vocal minority. Their desires, often extreme, directly oppose that of the group majority. They bark these views at others without the remotest grasp for empathy or mutual discussion. Because most people naturally avoid confrontation, they may smile at the extremist's proselytising, but inwardly they seethe with resentment at their arrogance and condescension.

Unless others stand up to them, the extremist never understands why they're not listened to and becomes more frustrated. They double down on their beliefs and do one of two things: shout louder, which is rarely effective; or use underhanded tactics, which are often frighteningly effective. Both cases are bad for group cohesion and productivity. Extremists using the latter approach will try to worsen their colleagues' latent resentments by painting you as an evil dictator. They will point to the slightest inequality in treatment as inherent proof of injustice, completely glazing over the fact that some people have unique, useful skills and work harder than others. They will shame people into adopting bizarre behaviours to become a "true ally" of their cause, often doing this in small piecemeal steps to make it more palatable. People feel the pressure of social conformity and bend to the extremist's demands. The group becomes polarised and distracted from its true goals.

Understand now that there is nothing particularly moral about entertaining the demands of a vocal minority—in fact, the reverse is true. Vocal minorities that cannot successfully persuade the majority through open discussion are in every case authoritarian. This viewpoint is likely making you feel uncomfortable. If that is the case, then ask yourself why, in free discussion, such extremists fail to persuade others. Explaining away such failures as "oppression" or "injustice" is the height of arrogance.

As a student of Social Intelligence, you understand that long-term prosperity is most reliably associated with competence, conscientiousness, and mutual reciprocity. People exhibiting these positive characteristics should be the ideal candidates for recruitment into your group. They will recognise the inherent goodness of group unity and the tireless striving for collective results. That isn't to say they don't have their own views to express; such types merely see them as subordinate to the group's greater needs. They listen to all ideas and select the most beneficial among them, always asking *What will benefit the group, not just myself?* Good ideas, when expressed openly and fairly, always stick. When something doesn't stick, no amount of virtuous packaging can justify authoritarian practices. Learn the lesson: Refuse to allow any vocal minority to oppress the reasonable, stolid, hard-working majority—it will make your leadership peaceful, prosperous, and fair.

Keep your ear to the ground. Never fall into the habit of only discussing matters with your immediate colleagues. This may help you to delegate certain responsibilities, but there's a risk that you'll only get a limited top-down view of your group. You need to gain a sense of group sentiment at all levels, because everyone in the organisational structure has some impact on your group's performance. Even a single disaffected employee at the lowest rung of power can have a disastrous impact if he doesn't feel valued or listened to. Such dynamics might be playing out in your group right now, and the first step to avoiding and remedying this is awareness. But you can't only rely on those around you to always present an accurate picture, particularly if their own performance is judged by the stability of their subgroups. You need to do this yourself, or enlist the help of someone who has no personal investment in their findings. Talk to as many people in your team as possible, treat their concerns as valid, and take their ideas into consideration. After you've discussed matters with enough of your colleagues, you'll naturally gain a sense of the group spirit. Try your best to identify common gripes with policies and common obstacles to their productivity. Solving these common gripes and obstacles should be your highest priority going forward, because it'll make your employees' lives profoundly more streamlined, focused, and productive. The benefits of keeping your ear to the ground in this way are twofold: one, you'll gain a thorough cross-section of your group's morale and sentiment; and two, your employees will feel valued and listened to. And if your frontline troops feel like they have contributed towards their group, they will try extra hard to contribute.

Embrace the ebbs and flows in group sentiment. Don't be afraid of human group behaviour. Embrace the changing group zeitgeist as a kind of generator of new ideas, some of which are positive and can improve group performance. Never see such shifts in sentiment as threats to your leadership; in any case, what can you really do to stop it? People can't and won't be overtly controlled. Leaders who adopt a defensive posture against such changes only arouse reciprocal defensiveness and anger in their group. Your job is to protect and serve the group, not forcefully oppress it to serve your interests and lengthen your rule. You don't have to bend to every idea; you only have to *not* brutally oppress or dismiss ideas out of hand. See changes in group sentiment as a manifestation of nature, finding profound beauty in the ebbs and flows that this brings. Life is too short to ward off ostensible threats and attacks—change your perspective and instead see these occurrences as part of an interesting journey with unexpected twists and turns.

Holding onto the past for its own sake makes no sense because it prevents the adoption of new ideas that might be beneficial. Test out new theories in practice and observe the results without personal feelings or judgement. The key is to not personally identify with any idea. All ideas have flaws, and you'll naturally become defensive and react oppressively when these flaws manifest. Instead, identify yourself with positive results, freely interchanging the ideas as they demonstrably help or hinder you. This approach will make you less anxious and stressed because you'll be focusing on variables that lie inside your control. You'll free up your attention to focus on issues that you can actually deal with, while making your work environment more pleasant for yourself and others. Don't fight group change, because it's not even close to a fair fight. Make friends with change, allow the flourishing of the group zeitgeist, and enjoy the natural beauty that it represents.

* * *

THE DANGERS OF REPRESSION

The Battle of Waterloo in 1815 finally marked the end of the Napoleonic Wars that had ravaged Europe for much of the previous decade. Klemens von Metternich (1773-1859), the Austrian foreign minister, had good reason to feel pleased with himself. He had gracefully fooled Napoleon into a marriage with Austrian royalty, and orchestrated a successful counter-attack with Russia on the French capital city, Paris. Now that they had exiled Napoleon for the second time, this time far away on the island of St Helena in the South Atlantic Ocean, Europe could enjoy some stability. Metternich had witnessed the horrors of the French Revolution and the upheaval it caused across the world. Napoleon's rule had represented all that he saw as bad in the rising tide of popular liberalism—long periods of chaos, destruction, and terror. Metternich felt determined to not allow the same thing to happen in Austria, and his resolve was about to face many tests.

In 1817, 500 German Protestant students and professors marched on Wartburg Castle, where Martin Luther had famously been granted refuge after refusing the Catholic Church's demands to recant his beliefs. The students marked the 300th anniversary of Luther's nailing of his ninety-five theses in 1517 with the first Wartburg Festival, a series of protests against reactionary conservative policies adopted by the German and Austrian governments. Two years later, a radical student named Karl Sand assassinated the playwright August von Kotzebue, who had long written derisively about liberalism. This murder gave Metternich the pretext to issue the Carlsbad Decrees of 1819, a set of laws placing German and Austrian universities under strict control: they could no longer organise mass demonstrations, student societies were investigated for liberal sympathies, and guilty students and teachers were blacklisted throughout Germany and Austria. Metternich also imposed heavy-handed censorship on the press and began building a wide spy network across Austria and the rest of Europe.

Metternich continued to interfere in matters across Europe. Through some deft diplomatic manoeuvres, he prevented the Russian tsar from invading the Balkans, and heavily criticised Great Britain's Reform Bill which among other changes made their electoral process more fair and democratic. Between 1821 and 1831, Metternich ordered Austrian soldiers to put down five Italian student uprisings, and his Austrian regime became the enemy of the Carbonari and Young Italy, two radical groups enormously popular among liberal Italians. As further uprisings grew in Austria, he implored the German Federal Diet to renew the Carlsbad Decrees in 1822 and again, indefinitely, in 1833. When the Austrian emperor died in 1835 and his successor replaced him, Metternich declared that "no innovation in policy or principle will take place during the new reign."

Although the thirty years since Napoleon's downfall had been a period of unparalleled peace, in 1848 the Austrian people had had enough of Metternich's repression and attempted a revolution in Vienna to produce a liberal government. They failed in their revolution, but the crisis forced the Austrian chancellor's resignation, sending him into exile in England.

INTERPRETATION

Metternich's name is often associated with repression, but it isn't fair to judge him with the clarity of hindsight. When judged against the backdrop of the French Revolution's Reign of Terror—which claimed the lives of nearly 20,000 French aristocrats, and anyone with the slightest ties to or sympathies with the upper classes—and Napoleon's incessant wars across Europe, it is understandable that Metternich would be terrified of revolution in his own country, and his views were entirely consistent with his contemporaries in the post-Napoleonic years. While we can understand his motives, his methods of oppression have been a subject of controversy ever since. A chancellor more in tune with the spirit of the

times might have made ostensible movements towards liberalism, instead of cracking down on universities and the press.
If he had entertained the liberal protests at the Wartburg
Festival and not used von Kotzebue's assassination as an
excuse to push through his strict censorship laws, the radicals in Austria might have seen him in a better light and not
felt the need to instigate the 1848 revolution.

Critics in the nineteenth century accused Metternich of
preventing the European powers from developing along
liberal lines in a natural and organic manner. Had Metternich not stood so firmly in the way of liberal discussion, the
"pressure cooker" of nationalist sentiment might not have
been powerful enough to trigger the First World War, as it
did with the assassination of the Austrian Archduke Franz
Ferdinand. He was happy to sacrifice freedom of speech to
achieve peace, but this only made things much worse later
down the line. Any time you try to oppress free expression as
Metternich did, you only gain a temporary reprieve. While
people might stay silent to begin with, the radicals in your
group will eventually harden and double down in their
beliefs, now having gained proof of your tyrannical
behaviour. Forcing the dark rumblings of dissent under-
ground will only make them grow more powerful and
subversive.

Understand that all types of repression and reaction to
revolutionary uprisings are gifts to the revolutionaries. As
the political campaigner Saul D. Alinsky wrote in his 1971
book *Rules for Radicals*, "the action is in the reaction,"
meaning that any time you react oppressively you are actually playing right into the revolutionaries' hands. As discussed
earlier in this chapter, you must allow free channels of
expression and never feel threatened by whatever views your
group discusses. Instead of fretting yourself about perceived
threats from all sides, you instead refuse to give the radicals

any ammunition. By focusing your behaviour on the model of the Socially Intelligent Leader at all times, you will have nothing to worry about.

THE FUTILITY OF PLACATION

The 1970s would prove to be a tumultuous decade for Mohammad Pahlavi (1919-1980), the Shah of Iran. In 1971 the shah had hoped that his celebrations for the 2,500th anniversary of the Persian Empire would be a joyful event for Iran, but it only seemed to anger the common people. They criticised the event's extravagance, particularly the consumption of alcohol. Six hundred foreign guests dined for five and a half hours, getting drunk on fine wine while ordinary Iranians starved in the streets; not to mention that alcohol was forbidden for the country's Muslims, naturally excluding them from the festivities. Both the Western press and the prominent Muslim scholar Ruhollah Khomeini laid heavy criticism on what they saw as an event that ignored and insulted Iran's Muslim majority.

In 1976, the shah further incensed Muslims by changing the first year of Iran's calendar from the Islamic *hijri*, when Muhammad migrated from Mecca to Medina, to the year of Cyrus the Great's ascension to the throne. Overnight Iran jumped from the Islamic year 1355 to the Persian imperial year 2535. The people saw this as yet another as anti-Islamic move, and it deeply embittered the opposition from the country's religious scholars. The shah, for his part, saw himself as heir to the kings of ancient Iran and wanted to renew the country into a new golden age of imperialism.

Oil revenues boomed during this decade, and the shah grew to depend on this source of income for his extensive development programmes. He wanted Iran to become the power centre of the Middle East, but in reality most of the oil revenues went to himself and the royal family—by 1976 they had accumulated at least $5,000,000,000 from the oil boom. Little of this money went towards building programmes, and instead of providing Iranians with work, the lucrative oil jobs went to skilled foreign workers. By 1977 the country was wracked with inflation, and a harsh series of austerity measures only made things worse for ordinary Iranians, while the royal family continued with their own lavish lifestyles.

In response to increasing protests, the shah demanded that all Iranians join and pay dues to a new political party; the People's Party of Iran was the only political party allowed by law, and it pushed populist policies such as fining merchants that charged high prices—though measures like these deeply hurt the Iranian middle class, making them *join* the workers in their resentment of the shah's regime. Throughout the 1970s the shah had placated the United States in its efforts to secure Iran's oil exports, which were now under regular threat of protests by the country's angry leftist and Islamist population. Ordinary people saw the shah as nothing more than a mere puppet of the West, ignoring public opinion while profiting from the country's rich resources. The United States president Jimmy Carter privately warned the Shah that he needed to calm down his country's growing instability, but the shah only made piece-meal concessions, freeing some political prisoners and allowing the Red Cross to visit the remaining activists he had jailed.

By 1978 the Shah finally realised that he needed to act and tried to push through a series of liberal forms. But these only seemed like an attempt to ingratiate the millions of angry ordinary Iranians, and the reforms themselves would make the country even more Westernised. After some botched attempts by the American CIA and the shah's intelligence service to quell protestors and assassinate dissidents, Ruhollah Khomeini finally called for a revolution. The shah reacted by dismissing thousands of civil servants and security forces in Tehran, and his new inexperienced police force fired at protesters, which only inflamed the crisis and made the government look desperate. In September 1978 the shah declared martial law, and his security forces massacred 4,000 protesters defying the curfew in a bloody battle that became known as "Black Friday."

In 1979 the shah fled to Egypt with his family, and Ruhollah Khomeini agreed to form a new draft constitution that would be both Islamist and democratic. Khomeini returned from exile in France triumphant, and a popular referendum of Iran's citizens confirmed, with a 99 per cent majority, their desire for a new Islamist constitution. Two and a half thousand years of Iranian monarchy ended in disgrace for the shah, as Khomeini became the Supreme Leader of the new Islamic Republic of Iran.

INTERPRETATION

In hindsight, the shah's actions throughout the 1970s make the Iranian Revolution seem like a foregone conclusion. The shah, his family, and a circle of elites enjoyed lavish lifestyles filled with royal largesse, while treating most Iranians with utter contempt. He severely restricted political and civil liberties through a one-party system and reacted to the growing protests with insincere concessions that only made the Iranian people more angry. His sheer panic at the height of protests in 1978 showed his weakness and ill-preparedness for any kind of strife, almost as if he expected no kind of negative reaction to his rule. In fact, the protests took him by surprise and his actions only highlighted his indecisiveness in times of crisis.

People like the shah react in similar ways when unpopular in positions of leadership. They genuinely can't understand why their teams would want to rebel, because they don't have the slightest awareness of what the people in their team want. They assume that, as leaders, they deserve respect and reverence from their subordinates, and the only way they can react to complaints is to double down and resort to repressive measures. The rest of the group, who might not have had such strong feelings, watch the leader's harsh measures with disgust. It is all a downward spiral with disastrous results.

Desperately holding onto power and wealth, denying the majority any kind of say, is always a reliable way to precipitate a revolution. The shah could have taken several simple steps to avoid the revolution that ended his rule. Had he shown more sensitivity towards the country's Muslims, not embezzled so much of the oil wealth for himself, made real sacrifices in his lavish lifestyle, not allowed the United States to so blatantly interfere in his country's oil industry, and worked harder to make life better for the majority, he would have blunted much of the criticism that drove the anti-government protests. Understand that revolutions are as much the fault of the ruler as the charismatic types pushing for reform. Wise rulers don't fight protests; they *prevent* them by listening to the majority and working for the group. Ignore the demands of the majority at your peril.

MAKE YOUR PROPOSAL THE OBVIOUS CHOICE

Although Abraham Lincoln had won the 1860 presidential election, his path ahead was far from clear. Lincoln was a Republican and a prominent abolitionist, and his election victory sparked the South's secession from the United States. Southern states feared that their way of life could not survive for long with an abolitionist as president, and one by one they split off to form the Confederacy. Lincoln knew that abolishing slavery would not come easily—it was then literally breaking apart the United States. The Union Congress still had many representatives from the Democratic Party who supported slavery, or at least didn't want to see it go just yet. Led by George B. McClellan of New Jersey, these Democratic congressmen wanted return to the status quo that had existed before the outbreak of fighting with the South. Indeed, historians now agree that most Americans in the North went to war to save the Union, not necessarily to abolish slavery. Knowing that he would need support from all sides, Lincoln appointed McClellan a military general with complete control over the Army of the Potomac.

As the Civil War raged, it became clear that the most effective way to break the South was to ruin its overstretched economy. The Confederacy did not have the financial power to maintain a war for any great length of time and had to resort to desperate measures to keep up the war effort. They had needed a nationwide draft to build up their army, and so the men that normally ran the South's plantation-based economy were away fighting. The South's economy completely relied upon its millions of slaves, while the North had advanced in machine-based techniques for farming and manufacturing. Confederate soldiers had to subsist on a quarter-pound of meat and cornmeal every day, hardly enough food to survive, let alone fight a war. The Union's powerful new fleet of ironclads enjoyed free rein around the Southern coast, taking key ports in Georgia, Florida, and Louisiana, all of which choked the Confederate economy.

In spite of this asymmetry between the two sides, the Civil War was still uncertain by 1862, while Lincoln planned the best time to give his Emancipation Proclamation. As the war became more and more unpopular, the calls grew louder for

Lincoln to seek peace instead of pressing on for victory. Although Secretary of War Edwin Stanton supported this move, Lincoln's Secretary of State William Seward advised him to issue the proclamation after a major Union victory, or else it would appear as if the Union was giving "its last shriek of retreat." Lincoln's wish was granted when, in September 1862, the Union won the Battle of Antietam. Though the Union had suffered heavier losses than the Confederates, and George B. McClellan had allowed the key general Robert E. Lee to escape, they had successfully prevented a major invasion of Maryland.

When Lincoln finally gave the Emancipation Proclamation in 1863, he described it only as "a necessary war measure" to break the South's economy and its ability to wage war. Though they could hardly argue with the proclamation itself, Radical Republicans in Congress claimed that Lincoln was, yet again, not going far enough and placating the pro-slavery Democrats. Nevertheless, when put forward in these terms, the Emancipation Proclamation went unopposed. Despite their partisan differences, most saw it as the only way to end the war with the South, bringing forward the peace they desperately wanted.

INTERPRETATION

As a staunch abolitionist, Lincoln would have preferred to end slavery right away, and a less strategic president might have attempted it through an executive order at the outset. But Lincoln knew this wouldn't work in the long term. He knew that while many people in the North felt disgusted by slavery, they weren't much interested in the rights of African Americans. Once the Civil War had broken out, he had to give equal voice to pro-slavery Democrats, since he was president of all the people, not just those who agreed with him on abolition. If he had alienated his political opponents that early on, then the Union would have lacked the cohesion it needed to succeed in winning the war.

Lincoln's genius was in using the Emancipation Proclamation strictly as a war measure, posing it as the only effective way to end the bloodshed. Indeed, the South's absolute reliance on slavery for its society, economy, and war effort gave it a critical vulnerability ripe for exploitation. Once the tide of war began to shift over to the Union's side, it only took Sherman a few months of scorched earth tactics to free thousands of slaves and wreck Southern infrastructure. Sherman did not particularly care much for African-American rights, but he *did* care about ending the war and saving the Union. His campaign was so effective that the economic impact was still being felt as late as the 1920s.

You may think that being a group's leader gives you carte blanche to implement whatever practices you like. But if everyone disagrees with your policies, then they'll find every way to oppose you. If you defy this resistance and try to push your measures through by force, then you'll only be as good as any bullying tyrant. Even worse, whining and complaining will only show your frustration, which is really an expression that you lack power and initiative of thought.

It is a much more effective strategy to win people over to your side gradually and prove that your ideas are the best way to achieve your shared goals, because you'll retain group unity and gain a wide base of support. Align your policies with ideas that already have widespread support. Lincoln told Congress that they *had to* emancipate all the slaves to end the war quickly, a goal that everyone shared at that stage. Never try to fight group sentiment; instead work with it and take your time. You're a Socially Intelligent Leader, not a dictator. Understand that a movement originating from a wide base of support is always much stronger than one forced through without regard for the majority's views. It is for this reason that democracies are always stronger than authoritarian dictatorships.

THE DISEASE OF DELUSIONAL GRANDIOSITY

After the French emperor Napoleon had dominated Europe in the early nineteenth century, he began to show signs of delusional grandiosity. He appointed his relatives to the thrones of conquered kingdoms, anointed himself as a divine emperor, and divorced his wife in favour of an archduchess of Austria. His irrational invasion of Spain and the disastrous forced retreat from Russia destroyed his 500,000-strong Grande Armée, proving that Napoleon had become bloated with power and was now on the decline. His prior victories had gone to his head, and he was no longer objective. Throughout all of this he paid almost no real attention to the French people, assuming they still loved him for his past victories. Conversely, both his foreign minister Talleyrand and minister of police Joseph Fouché knew of Napoleon's impending downfall, and conspired to make his demise more certain. Both men kept faithfully in touch with the French people and knew they had grown to resent Napoleon's grandiosity. The emperor who had once been a model of shrewdness and clear thinking was now resembling the decadent French kings he had replaced.

Talleyrand had lived through the horrors of the French Revolution and knew what the people were capable of if sufficiently roused. Though he had come from the nobility, Talleyrand held democratic beliefs and had seen Napoleon as the man to lead the future of France. But back then Napoleon had been a positive force—creating a new government that centred on the principles of hard work, conscientiousness, and efficiency. Napoleon's mastery of organisational structures and man-management allowed him to blow away the bloated inefficient monarchies. But now the tables were turned, and all of Europe could sense it. Napoleon had made a lot of enemies, and they now had the chance to knock him down. Prussia was eagerly remodelling its armed forces, Austria was building useful agreements, and Britain's naval power was once again on the rise after its loss of the American colonies. Talleyrand recognised that Napoleon needed to be stopped, otherwise these former vanquished enemies would rise up and conquer France, perhaps forcing it into the same retributive peace that Napoleon had pressed upon them. Fouché, always in tune with the spirit of the times, agreed with his former rival Talleyrand. The minister of police had built up a strong spy network that gave him an unparalleled information advantage. This network told him that not only had the people of France turned against Napoleon, they were joined by his Grande Armée, tired of constant wars and demoralised by their recent defeats.

After Napoleon's disastrous retreat from Russia, his enemies smelled weakness. The Sixth Coalition of Russia and Prussia successfully invaded Paris, forcing the emperor's abdication and exile to the island of Elba in April 1814. They gave him a small mansion on the island and a kind of court with its own rituals, all designed to mock the former leader.

In early 1815, Talleyrand and Fouché saw the opportunity to lure Napoleon into a trap that would end his influence once and for all. They told Napoleon that the French people would welcome him with open arms, and the former emperor listened—he dramatically escaped Elba and invaded France with a small army. His former marshals fell at his feet, caught up in the moment's drama, and the restored Bourbon king fled in fear. Napoleon assumed the throne once again, but Talleyrand and Fouché knew this was temporary. Despite the momentum he had created, France's trea-sury was empty and its army depleted. The Allies formed the Seventh Coalition and defeated Napoleon once and for all at the Battle of Waterloo in June 1815, a mere 100 days after his dramatic return to power.

INTERPRETATION

Napoleon is emblematic of all leaders who let their victories go to their head. They become drunk on success and lose all objectivity, forgetting whatever qualities gave them those successes. They make mistake after mistake, leading their team into rash and ill-advised campaigns. The team thus grows to resent the leader's arrogance, counting the days until they're gone. Napoleon's demise fitted this template to perfection, his grandiosity making him lose all sense of proportion. He assumed that the French people still loved him for his past victories, but this was all a delusion. They were tired of constant wars and yearned for some stability. Napoleon failed to realise that the tide had already turned against him long before his rash invasion of Russia. Losing a sense of the times can also mean becoming consumed by the feeling of momentum—the false idea that some abstract force is pushing you forward, not the real factors like your wise strategies and bold actions. Illusions of grandeur will trick you into thinking you have some "golden touch" when in fact you might have just been lucky—groups have a kind of sixth sense for this tendency in their leaders and will punish you for it, as did Talleyrand and Fouché. You must always stay objective and vigilant, starting from square one with each new project. It is the only way to prevent the same mistakes that caused Napoleon's decline.

He was in fact set up for disaster by Talleyrand and Fouché, both men seeing the danger that his uncontrollable

grandiosity posed to France. Avoiding the complete destruction of their country, they conspired with the Austrian
minister Metternich to have Napoleon exiled far away from
Europe. When Napoleon's influence still loomed over the
European leaders, Talleyrand conspired again to lure him
into a trap that would spell his final defeat. Napoleon
became so drunk on success that he did not see what was
really going on around him. He long suspected that
Talleyrand and Fouché were up to something, but reacted
with embarrassing petulance and anger instead of having
them quietly removed. Had Napoleon not been so consumed
with grandiosity, he would have had the objectivity to realise
that these two eminently strategic men had good reason to
work against him. Learn the lesson: Grandiose leaders
always come to an ugly end. Don't join their company.

REVERSAL

Social Intelligence always requires compromise, particularly
when in charge of a large group. You can't ignore the wishes
of the majority for long. But that doesn't mean you can't
stand up straight and direct your team when necessary.
You're their leader and they look to you, particularly in times
of difficulty. Take the initiative and don't look to your group
for permission, as such. Become too obsessed with the trends
of the day, for example, and you'll lose all long-term strategic
perspective. There are times when it is better to act boldly
than to hem and haw, worrying about how popular this or
that action might be. Combine a sense for the zeitgeist with a
sense of timing then, knowing the best time to strike. By
observing people's long-term actions you will sense the spirit
of the times and use this whenever proposing new action or
considering the health of your team. The prevailing group
zeitgeist is an indicator of broad popular support, and

leaders who can tune into it at will are indescribably powerful, though grand changes always take a long time to manifest in a real sense. Learning to use the group zeitgeist to
your advantage is the ultimate reversal to this principle,
then, since dictatorships with a singular rule never last in the
long run.

ED CATMULL AND THE BIRTH OF PIXAR

INSPIRE YOUR GROUP WITH POSITIVE EMPOWERMENT

The secret to unlocking higher levels of productivity and passion within any team is to treat your workers like adults. Let them take ownership of their projects and see how well they rise to the challenge of this new responsibility. They might not always succeed, but you will have gained a team filled with passion and enthusiasm, eager to learn from mistakes and rise to new challenges. Create environments of trust where employees can freely exchange feedback without feelings of resentment or defensiveness. An overt need for control and patronising rules is, in every case, a direct message that you don't trust your team, and they will respond in the exact manner that this attitude deserves.

THE EMPOWERMENT CULTURE

In 1969 Professor Ivan Sutherland, a pioneer in the new field of computer graphics, convinced a young student named Ed Catmull to join his fledgling group of researchers at the University of Utah. Sutherland and the university's computer science department encouraged Catmull and all student researchers to use their high-tech computer lab, regardless of their experience or area of study. The department's inclusive attitude encouraged students from a wide variety of fields to join the workspace, and the result was a collaborative environment that created many ground-breaking new ideas.

Most funding for the university's computer science department came from the Advanced Research Projects Agency, or ARPA, formed by the United States Department of Defense. The US government wanted to support research into new computer technologies in response to Soviet advances during the 1960s, but it saw the micromanagement of such research as counterproductive. They encouraged researchers like Catmull to work on the problems that they were most interested in, and a handful of graduate students all working together throughout the night on a shared project was a common sight in Sutherland's computer lab. Although some complained that the hands-off approach would give the researchers license to slack off, Catmull and his fellow researchers greatly appreciated the trust given to them and worked harder than many other departments. Early on Catmull saw that each researcher, given the freedom to choose their favourite areas of research, would feel ownership of their projects and put far more effort into them than if they had been directed into some area they weren't passionate about.

In 1972 Catmull created a short animated film with a digital representation of his hand. He had made a physical model of his hand and drew hundreds of interlocking polygon shapes on its surface, which he mapped into his 3D computer animation program. When Catmull showed *Hand* at a computer science conference in 1973, his colleagues were stunned by the hand's realistic movements. By the time of the conference he had added smoothing effects to the digital hand's surface, making it almost lifelike. No one in Sutherland's department had replicated Catmull's feat, and everyone saw the potential in what his young student had created. Sutherland believed that this technology could eventually revolutionise Hollywood, and set out to create an exchange programme where students could learn about the movie business, and animators could learn more about how to tell great stories. For Sutherland the mutual benefits seemed obvious, and he sent Catmull to Disney Animation to sell them on the idea.

Unfortunately, the executives Catmull met at Disney did not seem interested in Sutherland's ideas. They had tried to integrate computers into their animation process for *Bedknobs and Broomsticks* in 1971, and it had caused endless headaches in production. Catmull tried to explain that the technology was improving and that Disney could play a major part in developing it to meet their requirements, but it was no use. The executives instead offered Catmull a job in their Disney Parks ride design division, which he turned down on the spot. Sutherland was furious when he heard that Disney had not only failed to see the potential in his exchange programme, but that they had also tried to poach Catmull away for an irrelevant job. Though discouraged by this setback, Catmull graduated from Sutherland's department with a PhD and a much clearer sense of his goals— most of all, he wanted to rejoin a collaborative, supportive environment just like the one he had enjoyed under Sutherland's care.

In 1974, the New York Institute of Technology's founder Alexander Schure called Catmull, asking him to create and lead a new computer graphics research group. For Catmull, this was a dream come true. Schure wanted to hire computer scientists to help him create the world's first computer-animated film, and money was no object. Catmull hired the most brilliant computer scientists he knew, including Alvy Ray Smith and David DiFrancesco. He felt determined to create the same kind of environment he'd enjoyed in his graduate programme, with a flat non-hierarchical structure that encouraged the free flow of ideas and technical support. Catmull's new group were not alone in trying to create a fully computer-animated movie—many competitors were attempting the same thing. But he noticed that these competitors were obsessively secretive, holding onto their discoveries. Catmull and his team had all come from an academic background and believed that industry-wide collaboration would solve their key problems much more efficiently. They took a completely different approach from the rest of the industry: sharing their work, publishing their findings, and actively taking part in the computer science community. This approach caught on with other studios and proved Catmull right—it helped to quicken the advancement of computer graphics research. Over the next five years, by taking the lead in their attitude of transparency, the NYIT team became a pre-eminent force in the growing new field they were helping to create.

While the team made significant strides over this period, something seemed amiss. Catmull and Smith both felt that they needed real experience inside a movie studio, which no one in their team possessed. While they appreciated Schure's support at NYIT, the group had reached the brink of financial collapse more than once, and it became clear that they needed a more stable environment. Fortunately, the industry was learning the value of their work. The directors Francis Ford Coppola and George Lucas invited Smith to discuss their visions for the potential of digital filmmaking. Both Smith and Catmull felt delighted that two such prominent directors seemed so fully sold on their work, and in 1979 Lucas persuaded both of them and four other NYIT scientists to join his production company Lucasfilm and lead its development of computer-generated film animations. Over the next four years, Catmull's new team grew into a significant division of Lucasfilm. Working alongside Lucas's Industrial Light & Magic division, they successfully developed groundbreaking new filmmaking technologies that would help in the production of pictures such as *Star Trek II: The Wrath of Khan* in 1982 and *Star Wars: Return of the Jedi* in 1983. This was exactly the sort of work that Catmull and Smith wanted.

From the beginning they realised that the technology available to them at the time would not suffice. Overlaying special effects onto real camera footage required the use of awkward, clunky optical devices that took years to learn how to use. Both Catmull and Smith knew that a sophisticated digital solution was needed to seamlessly combine their computer graphics effects with camera footage, and so they spent years developing a powerful device with the processing power to achieve this for feature-length films. They named this device the Pixar Image Computer, and it would become the core of their business for the remaining decade.

On top of this groundbreaking piece of technology, Lucas wanted Catmull's team to develop video editing software that would work on the computer. At the time, editors would literally cut and paste pieces of film together to make full sequences, a slow and laborious process. Lucas envisioned editors being able to cut pieces of footage, drag and drop them to make scenes, and implant digital effects, all in the same software program. Catmull's team successfully built software with these features, but to his surprise the Lucasfilm editors bitterly opposed the imposition of new technology onto their work. They didn't want to learn how to use computers and saw this software as a threat to their jobs, which they had spent years mastering. Catmull could not understand why the editors refused to learn what was clearly a superior process—it enabled the use of computer animations within real camera footage, and it also made cutting and reordering film scenes much easier. He had been so consumed with developing this new technology that he hadn't taken into account how stubborn the editors would be, and it disrupted his work. Catmull despaired at these new, unfamiliar challenges. Although he had the enthusiastic support of Lucas, none of them had bothered to consult the editing team, or tried to win their buy-in to this new system, and the ongoing battles with film editors made him feel overwhelmed and exhausted with stress—he wasn't used to these kinds of interpersonal battles as a manager.

Lucasfilm's future suddenly became uncertain in 1983 when George Lucas and his wife divorced. Catmull's technology division was valuable but also ran up high costs for the business, and so Lucas decided he would sell off the group. But there was one problem: To stand on its own as an independent company, the computer division needed an additional $15,000,000 of investment for the ongoing development and production of its Pixar Image Computer. Lucas was not pleased with this, since he himself was short on cash following the divorce. Potential buyers baulked at the need to put so much money down to invest in Catmull's proposed new business, and it wasn't until 1986 that they found their buyer. Catmull's editing technology captivated Steve Jobs, who had recently been forced out of Apple. He believed that the Pixar Image Computer was far ahead of what was available and wanted access to the technology behind it. Although Catmull and Smith found Jobs' personality abrasive and intimidating, they knew that after a dozen failed attempts to sell, this was their last chance to save their division and keep their employees' jobs safe. With Jobs' funding, the three men spun the Lucasfilm computer division off into an independent company, which they named Pixar.

Their new company, now focused on building and selling hardware, did not have a promising start. They priced the Pixar Image Computer at $122,000 per unit, and the company would only ever sell 300 units. But Catmull resolved not to let his company go the way of so many failed Silicon Valley startups, and he studied manufacturing techniques to make the production more efficient. He learned that after the Second World War, an American statistician named W. Edwards Deming had travelled to Japan, where he helped several companies implement new quality assurance practices. Japanese products were seen as notoriously poor in quality at this time, and Deming believed this was because of an over-reliance on hierarchy and cost-saving. If workers in a factory saw issues on the production line, and management had created enough of an incentive for them to keep the line going at any cost, then problems would go unreported. Deming proposed that factories install a cord that any worker could pull to halt the production line. This simple change to the manufacturing process had a profound impact: By empowering employees at all levels of seniority, from factory floor workers to senior managers, they made quality control the equal responsibility of everyone in the organisation. After companies such as Sony and Toyota implemented Deming's suggestions, Japanese manufacturers enjoyed unprecedented levels of quality, and their sales revenues skyrocketed. These stories struck a major chord for Catmull, as he realised he could cultivate a working culture that was not only supportive and collaborative, but also where no single employee had to ask permission to take responsibility for the quality of its products.

Despite these valuable lessons, Pixar was still in deep financial trouble, and Steve Jobs was growing impatient.

Because the Pixar Image Computer had failed to sell due to its unaffordable price tag, the company was burning cash with little return to show for it—Steve Jobs had sunk over $50,000,000 of his personal wealth into the company by the late 1980s. Catmull had supervised the production of short animated film projects that had garnered critical acclaim— the short film *Tin Toy* won Pixar their first Oscar in 1988— and had long thought that this direction would be much less risky for the company. Jobs had tried and failed multiple times to sell Pixar and justify his investment, but Catmull eventually persuaded him to abandon the selling of hardware and invest fully into the production of animated films. Though this was not at all Jobs' original intention for buying the company, he respected Catmull's fervent belief in the potential of this new direction and relented. In 1991, Pixar agreed a deal with Disney to produce three fully animated films in exchange for majority financing and distribution.

In early 1993, Disney executives green-lit a story concept proposed by John Lasseter, one of Pixar's lead filmmakers: A boy named Andy loves his toys—most of all a cowboy named Woody—who are all secretly self-aware and walk around when humans aren't looking. But Woody's world is turned upside down when Andy brings home Buzz Lightyear, a brand new toy that consumes all his attention and makes him forget his other toys. Though this story had promise, Lasseter's first storyboard meetings with Disney were discouraging. They said that Woody was too easygoing and should have a meaner character. Lasseter dutifully obeyed, and Pixar later unveiled a new story centred around Woody, but they had severely over-corrected—though they had followed Disney's recommendations, Woody was now bullying the other characters, showing a character full of malevolence and envy. The change had completely ruined the core story. To Lasseter and Catmull's horror, Disney shut down the production of this film until they could fix Woody and get the story right.

Though they felt demoralised, Lasseter and Catmull knew that this was only one setback in their journey. Back in 1991, their CAPS system—an advanced version of the software Catmull had designed for Lucasfilm—was instrumental in the blockbuster films *Beauty and the Beast* and *Terminator 2*, as well as 1993's *Jurassic Park*, which completely relied upon Pixar's technology. Jobs reassured Catmull that this film was part of a much bigger movement, a complete change in the field of animation. Lasseter and the rest of the Pixar team worked for months to fix the story, and in 1995 *Toy Story* broke box office records as the first fully computer-animated feature film. Riding the wave of dizzying success from this film, the company went public and renegotiated a much more favourable deal with Disney. Catmull had finally achieved his goal of creating a fully computer-animated film, and Pixar now possessed the firm foundations to create more.

Although there was a long-lasting feeling of euphoria within Pixar, this quickly turned to shock and panic. As they prepared to assemble a team for their next film, *A Bug's Life*, they found that their production managers were reluctant to sign contracts to continue working at Pixar. They complained that during the production of *Toy Story* the creative crew had treated them with contempt, as if they were impediments to the process. Catmull learned that this poor treatment was apparently a common dynamic in the film industry, and it was why so many production managers worked as contractors rather than full-time employees in a studio. Being treated as second-class members of the production was considered normal, and complaining about it to management usually meant losing their jobs. Catmull and Lasseter were shocked to hear this—they had made a conscious effort to give everyone a voice within the *Toy Story* production, so how had they failed to make these production managers feel valued? Deeper conversations with the production crew made them realise that the key cause was a restricted flow of information. Feeling under immense pressure to deliver *Toy Story*, production managers had scrambled to keep control of the project's budgets and schedules, demanding that artists and technical crew only report information and requests directly through them. This greatly restricted the flow of information—someone who needed to talk to someone in a different department would often choose not to, because it wasn't worth the hassle of dealing with an over-stressed and paranoid manager. This resulted in strained relationships and a production that suffered in its quality.

To Catmull, the rift now made perfect sense. Though it was well-intentioned, the production managers' micromanagement of the creative staff had in fact made *them* feel underappreciated and resentful, and they had treated the production managers snobbishly in turn. The solution to this problem was clear: Catmull decided that communication would no longer go strictly up and down chains of command. Animators could now immediately talk to modellers without having to go through their direct manager, and thus the flow of information became much faster and more efficient. Instead of making the production managers a resented group, this new policy made them equal colleagues in the production process, all while the creative employees felt trusted to work on their projects without interruption or babying supervision.

Along with this major change, Pixar's next films would see the rise to prominence of its "Braintrust," a group of senior colleagues all experienced in the company's key areas: animation, computer graphics, and storytelling. This group formed organically during the production of *Toy Story*'s sequel, and its key role became to hear story ideas from directors and then give honest feedback—these were not intended as orders for the directors to follow, but helpful advice for improving their stories.

When work on *Toy Story 2* began, it became clear soon after that the project was heading in a poor direction. Disney only expected this film to be a direct-to-video sequel—at this time, their CEO Michael Eisner's home video campaign was in full force—and so the film's animators weren't under as much pressure as before. Because they weren't creating a "real" Hollywood movie like the crew working on *A Bug's Life*, they felt like they had been relegated, as if management had judged them as less skilled and valuable than their counterparts. Creating a product of lower quality didn't feel right to Catmull and the other Pixar directors, and when Lasseter and Andrew Stanton showed the film to Disney executives, they felt so embarrassed that they remade the entire film. They reluctantly dropped the film's two directors and took charge of the film themselves. The story's premise was solid —Woody's arm being ripped, and then him having to make the choice between an immortal life behind glass in a museum and being left on Andy's shelf as a broken toy—but it needed more emotional stakes to make it into a great film. Through endless story meetings over the next few months, the Braintrust helped Lasseter to strip the film down into its most resonant emotional beats, dissecting why some scenes fell flat and others worked.

For instance, the Braintrust suggested adding a character named Wheezy the penguin, who warns Woody that since breaking his squeaker, Andy has left him on the shelf and never played with him since. This piece of foreshadowing would establish that any toy can get thrown away for any reason, using a very real threat to heighten the story's tension. They also added the character Jessie, an abandoned cowgirl doll, whose role was to warn Woody that Andy, once grown up, would inevitably forget about him and toss him away.

With the story fixed, animators worked day and night to make their changes and, in just six months, Pixar successfully delivered *Toy Story 2* in time for its cinematic release. It smashed records and proved that Pixar's groundbreaking filmmaking formula worked. The crucible of *Toy Story 2*'s troubled production forged Pixar's identity for the decades to come: a creative machine that consistently produced animated films of the highest quality.

INTERPRETATION

The story of Pixar's genesis and growth is a fascinating insight into the birth of computer-generated animation technology; but it also offers a variety of crucial lessons for students of Social Intelligence, particularly those in positions of leadership. Ed Catmull's self-awareness and honesty were key factors in his successes at Lucasfilm and Pixar, helping him to identify problems in his teams without feelings of defensiveness or arrogance.

This is perhaps the most important takeaway from the story. Self-reflection and objectivity are natural prerequisites for Socially Intelligent Leaders—without these qualities, Catmull would likely not have spent as much time digging into the hidden reasons for discord in his company. He correctly saw this analysis as absolutely critical to Pixar's long-term success, and you should too.

Catmull's time in Professor Sutherland's computer lab gave him an early lesson about the benefits of a collaborative and supportive environment. The academic world, free of commercial influences, is often better at building such environments than the private sector, because it is easier to collaborate when the principal goal is scientific truth. Sutherland's eagerness to bring together research students from a diverse range of fields was key to the laboratory's spirit of openness, because it introduced an array of unique perspectives and skill sets.

Socially Intelligent Leaders like Sutherland understand that bringing in smart people with diverse skills and opinions should never be seen as something threatening, but actually of profound benefit to the group. Catmull later used this lesson when hiring Alvy Ray Smith, who at first intimidated him with his raw intelligence, but was later instrumental in Catmull's group at Lucasfilm. He didn't let his feelings of fear and insecurity take hold, instead choosing to trust colleagues like Smith to do their jobs. The perceived risks from such a choice are rarely realistic, and the payoff is usually profound.

With the *Toy Story* production managers, Catmull did not dismiss the rift as temporary unrest, nor did he let the problem fester underneath the surface. Deeper analysis of the problem revealed that it was actually the creative crew who felt micromanaged. Implementing a new policy of free communication between departments and across hierarchies empowered the creative staff to do their jobs. This action made the creative staff happier, made the production more effective as a whole, and also prevented the production managers from becoming the targets of resentment and isolation within their teams, all in a single stroke.

In your group, you may think you have good reasons for restricting the flow of information between people and teams. But these reasons boil down to a lack of trust. Your employees are not cogs in a machine or points on a diagram; they are human beings. They are more astute and better at reading your actions than you might think, down to your body language and the way you address them—all behaviours that reveal your true attitude. Whether or not you mean it this way, enforcing tight restrictions on your employees' behaviour is a direct message that you don't think they're competent enough to behave in the right manner. Even though it is implicit and nonverbal, they hear the message loud and clear, and its effects on their morale are deep and long-lasting.

Catmull learned this lesson best when he saw the positive effects of the Braintrust. Group meetings with Pixar's Braintrust are an exciting exchange of ideas between its film directors and elder statesmen. Employees freely give honest feedback on story plans where it's needed, and the directors never feel defensive or offended by this feedback for two reasons: one, because the suggestions are incredibly valuable; and two, because there is no obligation or hierarchy implied in the meetings. The suggestions aren't orders for the directors to follow—think back to the disastrous results when Lasseter obeyed the letter of the Disney executives' suggestions for story changes—the environment is filled with a spirit of collaboration, respect, and trust. Directors are granted full ownership of their projects, entrusted with the creative freedom necessary to create the classic films that Pixar has consistently made. Far from being a scary council of judgemental and callous corporate bosses, the Pixar Braintrust is an invaluable advice panel of passionate individuals enthusiastic to offer their advice, and their attention is in demand within the company.

When you give employees ownership of their projects and trust them with the responsibility to produce a quality result, they will work extra hard and become fiercely proud of their work. A group structure that is too rigidly hierarchical may look nice on a diagram and give the illusion of control to its managers, but really this restricts the team's creative output. Your people come into work dreading what humiliation they'll face that day, and never lift a finger for the group that so deeply invalidates them, all because the responsibility and trust is out of their hands.

Like Catmull and his colleagues, you must continually look for hidden dynamics that threaten your group's creativity. Create safe environments where feedback is given on a level playing field, not as orders to follow. The only way to allow free expression is to lead the way: be vulnerable, admit your faults first. Your workers will respond by helping each other rather than seeing their colleagues as competition. Learn the lesson: Empowered workers trusted to complete their tasks will move mountains for you.

KEYS TO SOCIAL INTELLIGENCE

We humans are the dominant animal species on our planet, and our ancestors achieved this dominance because of several factors: Chief among these is what scientists call "theory of mind," or the ability to attribute unique motives and perspectives to other people. This gave our ancestors the ability to predict the behaviour of animals who are trapped inside easily predictable patterns, and we became brutally efficient hunters. Our ancestors enjoyed a rapport with their fellow early humans unparalleled even by other ape species, making it easier to form organised groups with divided roles and social hierarchies. This allowed individuals who were part of groups to prosper far more than the unfortunate souls who were forced to fend for themselves. If you think Social Intelligence is critical to us in the modern world, try stepping back in time a few hundred thousand years and see how well you fare by making enemies and refusing to work for your group.

This deceptively simple yet immense power must have

given our ancestors a profound feeling of control—and in some ways, a profound grandiosity too. Humans across all cultures passed down creation myths with clear similarities— all of them human-centric. In terms of our mythology, we are not modest. But should we be? Compared to other animal species we have *immense* control over the very planet we live on. Carl Jung explained this grandiose tendency to place ourselves at the centre as a kind of interplay between the self and the ego, two archetypes built deep into our psyches. In other words, we are born egotists.

It's easy to sneer at this supposition, but consider how much it helped us as a species. Any creature who *believes* himself the centre of the universe is a lot more likely to try to manifest it than the humble chump who placates others. But there is, undoubtably, a dark side to this egotistical tendency of ours: We frequently lose all proportion of the amount of control at our fingertips, presuming ourselves able to run every facet of an entire organisation. We discount the more likely roles of luck and being in the right place at the right time, choosing instead to believe in our "golden touch." We fall into believing we can control the world at will, and that anyone who defies us should be suppressed violently.

During the late stages of the Second World War, after the Allies had successfully gained a foothold in northern France, the tide of the war was turning against Germany. But Adolf Hitler, so consumed by his personal grandiosity and posi- tively megalomaniacal attitudes towards those around him, only became more tyrannical. After surviving multiple assas- sination attempts, and believing his top staff to be incompe- tent, Hitler exerted his personal control over every aspect of the war.

Hitler's delusional need for singular control is emblem- atic of all leaders who pay the price for centralising their command structure. The need for everyone to get explicit permission before doing anything inevitably ties down the organisation into a slow lurch. Not only does the organisation move slower as it relies upon a single power centre, but the junior leaders and their teams slow down even further. Rather than humiliate themselves by going through tedious channels to gain permission from a condescending leader, they decide it is less stressful to not act at all. They stagnate and their skills dull, because they're not allowed to express those skills in their positions. Responding to the inevitable downturn in productivity, the paranoid leader lashes out at a group he sees as lazy and unwilling to take the initiative, responding with complex rules and procedures in an effort to "fix" the issues he has created. This only makes his workers feel patronised, resentful, and thus *even less* likely to fulfil their roles. The leader's desperate need for centralised control causes a vicious cycle towards massive failure.

After a group reaches a certain size, no one person, no matter how brilliant, can run it effectively all by themselves. Micromanagers experience a great deal of unnecessary stress from the amount of power and control they desperately cling onto. No one can deal with the work of ten people for long without some kind of blowback to their health and their sanity. Unfortunately, we humans have a tendency to attempt such autocratic, centralised control even after it is shown to be a doomed exercise. In the late 1950s, the communist government of China led by Mao Zedong attempted to create a fully planned economy centralised in Beijing. In a process known as "collectivisation," land-owning farmers were forcibly stripped of their property and forced to join collective farms, where families would work for the greater group and everyone received an equal income, all the produce going to central planning committees. As an effort to restructure the country's economy and achieve full socialism sooner rather than later, Mao's government named this policy the Great Leap Forward. Although Mao and the communist party expected this to lead to an egalitarian utopia, it was a horrifying disaster. Because all output went towards the collective group, there was no longer any incentive for individuals to work hard—everyone was guaranteed an equal share of food regardless of how much they produced. This was a manifestation of the "free-rider problem," as less successful farmers joined the collectives and enjoyed the shared output without having to put in a proportionate amount of work. The amount of food and income people received was a function of their needs, not a function of their competence. Even worse, community leaders in charge of collectivised farms felt pressured into lying to their party superiors, giving wildly inflated figures. Mass shortages of food were the inevitable result of the collectivisation policy, and at least 45,000,000 Chinese people died from the resulting famine between 1959 and 1961, according to the Dutch historian Frank Dikötter.

As a leader, Mao reacted to this failure in the worst possible way. Instead of reflecting on the clear evidence of his policy's downsides, he affirmed that the problems were due to laziness, and "class enemies" sabotaging farm production by hoarding it all for themselves. Forbidden to leave their farms or produce their own food, tens of millions of Chinese were forced to eat clay soil and the bark off trees, all because of a megalomaniacal leader who could only deny the failings of a strictly planned centralised economy. He cruelly suppressed all talk of modernisation from party moderates such as Liu Shaoqi and Deng Xiaoping, resorting to one egotistical tantrum after another. After suffering years of intense criticism throughout the party, in 1966 Mao initiated a Great Proletarian Cultural Revolution as an attempt to reconsolidate his power, which only caused further damage to the country's economy and society.

It was only several decades after Mao's death that China would learn the benefits of a more decentralised structure. In the 1980s a new Chinese leader, Deng Xiaoping, seeing his country's decline and sensing a growing anger against the horrors of the 1960s, encouraged a new experimental system of entrepreneurship throughout China. Suddenly, young Chinese with an appetite for work were given an incentive to earn more than others were willing to. As the government relaxed its strict ideological restrictions on production, factories became more efficient, able to produce goods that people actually *wanted* to buy. Although they did not come without tensions or mistrust from communist party traditionalists, Deng's economic reforms resulted in a blossoming business culture in China that has not stopped growing since.

For China, a centralised command structure resulted in inefficient production on a mass scale that ultimately led to the deaths of millions (although an egotistical, idealistic leader at the top didn't help). But don't just see this as a mere historical note—it is eminently relevant for students of Social Intelligence. *All* centralised command structures suffer from the same problems, though perhaps not to the same extent as seen in China's Great Leap Forward. Stripped of all individual power and recognition, the individual feels little incentive to go above and beyond the minimum work necessary. Because all meaningful control is concentrated at the organisation's centre, and there is little distinction between workers and their pay, the same free-rider problem occurs. Junior leaders aren't entrusted with enough power to make a difference with their sub-teams, but are still expected to hold a great deal of responsibility on their shoulders. During China's Great Leap Forward, this led collective farm leaders to lie or exaggerate about their output, because with no power to control pay or fire lazy workers, they had little real influence over their group's performance. A centralised command structure always creates a perverse system of incentives, which in turn grounds the organisation to a halt.

The military theorist Carl von Clausewitz (1780-1831) observed similar problems in the Prussian army's heavily centralised command structure 200 years ago. In his book *On War*, Clausewitz wrote about his contemporaries' blind observance of military traditions at the expense of clear working strategies and objectivity on the battlefield. Prussian soldiers were drilled to perfection, but this only made them predictable to the enemy and unable to respond to circumstances. When Napoleon fought the Prussians early in his career, his loose structure of smaller forces led by marshals literally ran rings around the slow, immobile mass of Prussian troops. Clausewitz's experience in these battles, and later as a prisoner of war, likely taught him a harsh lesson. An ideal army, Clausewitz later wrote, should consist not only of drafted citizens inspired by a charismatic leader like Napoleon but also of professional soldiers. A body of men who had dedicated their careers to military service would fight out of sheer professional pride, and that sense of pride would drive them to much higher levels of cohesiveness and effectiveness than any micromanaging leader could ever induce:

> An army that maintains its cohesion under the most murderous fire; that cannot be shaken by imaginary fears and resists well-found ones with all its might; that, proud of its victories, will not lose the strength to obey orders and its respect and trust for officers even in defeat; whose physical power, like the muscles of an athlete, has been steeled by training in privation and effort… that is mindful of all these duties and qualities by virtue of the single powerful idea of the honour of its arms—such an army is imbued with the true military spirit.

Not all of us command troops of infantry, but Clausewitz's description of the ideal army ethos is a great model for all Socially Intelligent Leaders to strive for. At its heart, Clausewitz's ideal has the professional regiment, fiercely proud of its distinct identity, yet also equally proud to serve the greater whole. The typical modern workplace, in contrast, is full of petty politics, depressing rules, and hierarchical structures that look nice on a chart but actually *suppress* creativity and free expression. Workers trudge into the office each morning filled with dread, when they could be filled with excitement. Deep down they know they're not fulfilling their potential. All of their time, trust, and privileges taken away by a centralised command structure, they feel like they have no control over the direction of their daily lives. This depressing scenario plays itself out day after day, and it is a far cry from Clausewitz's ideal of the professional regiment. Instead of empowering our junior leaders and letting them take pride in their work, we take that pride away from them by trying to place absolute control on their work.

But the need for empowerment is not black and white. In his book *The Dichotomy of Leadership*, former US Navy SEAL commander Jocko Willink explains that optimal leadership lies in the middle of a continuum. At one end of the continuum is the micromanagement approach, and at the other is the laissez-faire approach. Both extremes are bad. We've discussed at length the failings of the micromanagement approach, but it also turns out that *too much* empowerment has just as much of a negative influence on group performance. Recounting a story from a military operation in Iraq, Willink shows that when he gave a subordinate too much freedom, without exerting his influence at all, it led to a series of embarrassing failures. Willink's laissez-faire approach in this instance led to a lack of direction for his junior officers, and they resorted to chaotic behaviour that

did not align with the goals of the group. Without the necessary clarity from the top, the task force's individual platoons
failed to coordinate and resorted to acting in self-interested
patterns. It was chaos, and Willink concludes the story with a
lesson that perfectly captures the need for a balanced middle
ground: "Own it all, but empower others."

No one struck this balance in Willink's leadership
dichotomy better than Napoleon. As described earlier in this
chapter, Napoleon structured his army for optimal mobility
by segmenting forces at every rung of the hierarchical
ladder. While his opponents sought to maintain absolute
authority by concentrating their forces in massive, oversized
centres, Napoleon had the bravery to take a risk by
entrusting his junior leaders with latitude over their own
independent sections of the French army. Undertaking an
enormous reorganisation between 1800 and 1805, he split
the Grand Armée into several corps, each with its own
infantry and cavalry divisions—so each corps was effectively a
kind of independent army. Each of these was led by a
marshal, a young officer who had proved his ability on the
battlefield, full of energy and new ideas, yet also strongly
aware of a battle or campaign's overall objective. Napoleon
could thus build a large army unprecedented for its quick
thinking and movement, since he could relay an order to a
marshal and it would be done in that officer's own way,
freeing up Le Petit Corporal to focus on grand strategy
rather than on petty details of corps command—completely
bucking the traditional trend of huge yet immobile armies.

This empowering approach not only freed up the
leader's mind for other tasks, it also allowed his junior
leaders to learn and develop as leaders in their own right—
far from feeling threatened by this, Napoleon encouraged it,
and it is why we now know a lot about Marshal Ney, who had
risen from being the son of the cask-maker to a great

general, and less about other officers of similar rank in other European armies. Napoleon's genius lay not in any superior weaponry or technology, but in his superior understanding of command structures. Seeing such a fast-moving army split and merge at will from the opposing side is frightening, even for the most battle-hardened soldier, and it is the prime reason for Napoleon's successful early campaigns. This approach seems entirely logical to us now as students of Social Intelligence, but at the time it was positively revolutionary—indeed it forced a complete rethink of military strategy across the West.

This lesson became clearer to Ed Catmull later in his career. In 2006, Steve Jobs sold Pixar to Disney, with Catmull and John Lasseter placed as leaders of both Pixar and Disney Animation. When the two men started working at Disney, they assessed the situation. They noticed that unlike Pixar, the Disney Animation crew worked in a culture that was rigid and afraid of failure. Management had far too much say in creative decisions, with the former Disney CEO Michael Eisner often getting involved in petty matters, bullying directors and animators alike. Staff working on films would receive notes ordering them to change key aspects of a film's story at the last minute, forcing them to work long hours with little credit or reward. Animators at Disney Animation had become terrified of upsetting management and stopped taking creative risks, a major cause of Disney's slump in the early 2000s. Catmull knew that this toxic culture had to change immediately. Meanwhile, he turned his focus to a new film in production called *Bolt* that the team had decided to scrap. Asked why the production was so far behind schedule, the animators answered that the story and technical changes required to fix the movie would take six months.

Catmull had heard enough. Assembling all the Disney production staff in one room, he gave his "Toyota Speech," assuring them that in future every one of them, regardless of rank, could and should speak up if they see such production problems appear, as early as possible. The speech, while uncomfortable, had its desired effect. That weekend, three animators took it upon themselves to complete all the changes, and Disney could release *Bolt* on schedule, to both critical acclaim and box office success.

What changed? Nothing, except for one key change in Disney's working culture. In the time before Pixar's acquisition and Catmull's appointment at Disney Animation, a toxic culture caused by micromanagement and rigid protocol meant that the animators felt terrified of any failure. When the animators on *Bolt* originally claimed the changes would take six months, they weren't wrong—they simply meant that it would take six months to produce a flawless, bug-free animation. Once Catmull had eradicated this oppressive, controlling culture from Disney Animation and replaced it with a more open and democratic one, the studio flourished creatively and produced one box office hit after another. Empowering animators to take responsibility for the quality of their work produced tangible, long-term benefits for the business. Learn the lesson: Bring intelligent, conscientious, and creative people into your team, give them clear direction, and never impede them.

We have come to a stage where we understand the benefits of empowering our junior leaders to take ownership of their tasks, but with a caveat that you, as the leader, must provide a clear overall direction for the team and promote a culture of pride in the quality of their work. Rather than create an organisational structure that concentrates power at a single central point, you create an efficient, decentralised command structure that operates with equal strength and cohesion at each of its hierarchical levels. You keep an eye on key performance indicators, but you also place great trust in your junior leaders and communicate your goals. They beam with pride as you explain that they're the ideal person for the job, with all the right experience and skills to see the project to its conclusion. You express your disappointment in the team when they don't meet their goals, and this is usually enough to bring their performance back up to expectations. You instil these positive values into each of your junior leaders until they themselves create similar decentralised command structures of their own, and the entire organisation runs like an efficiently designed machine. Building this kind of structure is not just the optimal way to build a group; it is the height of Social Intelligence. Leaders who give their juniors the right amount of empowerment understand that this not only eases stress on themselves, it also makes their team happy to come into work and proud of what they accomplish.

> If you treat an individual as he is, he will remain how he is. But if you treat him as if he were what he ought to be and could be, he will become what he ought to be and could be.
>
> — JOHANN WOLFGANG VON GOETHE

REVERSAL

It is possible to give too much latitude to your junior leaders, but this only happens when you do not give your team a clear direction to work towards. Your biggest problem when using a laissez-faire, directionless leadership style is junior leaders creating their own personal fiefdoms, building their own power bases for self-interested reasons. This most often happens in political environments, where the measures of performance and competence have become unclear. It is the leader's job to instil a positive culture, and an abdication of this responsibility leads to slow, lurching systems.

During the 1930s, General George C. Marshall (1880-1959) became Chief of Staff of a US army that over previous decades had become bureaucratic and slow to move. With turmoil rising in Europe and war on the horizon, Marshall realised he needed to restructure the army for efficiency and mobility. But there were many older generals who had amassed great influence, mostly to satisfy their own egos. Marshall replaced these men with young, energetic officers— one of them Dwight D. Eisenhower, later commander of Allied forces and US president—and ruthlessly cut down on waste in military spending. By cutting the army down and spreading a culture of efficiency and speed of communication through the army, he ensured the US military machine prepared itself for the series of wars on the horizon.

Had Marshall not recognised the problems in the army's structure at the outset of his tenure, and had he failed to deal with these problems as quickly as he did, then the twentieth century would have looked very different. A lurching bureaucracy dominated by generals out for their own power was not a good shape for an army about to take part in a war. To prevent this from happening, you must stay aware of the middle ground between micromanagement and the laissez-faire approach. Give your team direction and don't be afraid to punish slackers when necessary. A leader with an ambiguous, indecisive style will create a team that resorts to looking out for its own interests.

III

THE SOCIALLY INTELLIGENT
WARRIOR

Kind-hearted people might of course think there was
some ingenious way to disarm or defeat the enemy
without too much bloodshed, and might imagine this
is the true goal of the art of war. Pleasant as it sounds,
it is a fallacy that must be exposed: War is such a
dangerous business that mistakes that come from
kindness are the very worst.

— CARL VON CLAUSEWITZ

As a student of Social Intelligence you have so far learned
how to win friendships through competence and reciprocity,
develop strong alliances with strategic generosity, and build a
cohesive team that will follow you to the ends of the earth.
Making these lessons into regular practices is likely to earn
you a long, peaceful career.

But it would be foolhardy to assume that everyone shares
your inclinations towards social cohesion and mutual gain.
There are plenty of people out there with aggressive tenden-

cies and malevolent intentions who are all too happy to bully others, prey on the weak, and capitalise on others' misfortune. They are not interested in cooperation, but dominance —they want what you have and won't shrink from taking it by force. On the other hand, a perfectly good friendship can quickly turn sour, going in a way that you can't reverse.

In either case, to study only the positive aspects of Social Intelligence is to leave yourself defenceless. Showing yourself to be toothless and impotent in the face of workplace bullies can be career suicide, and all the strategies from earlier sections of this book will have been for nought. You must extend your study outward into aspects of war and strategy, building a defence in case an aggressive colleague goes on the offensive, or a tyrannical boss places you in his sights.

Such conflict is inevitable in life since we humans are, to varying degrees, aggressive. It is folly to assume you can avoid it and stay ignorant of strategy. When the time comes, you must stand up and fight for yourself. You will be glad you armed yourself with strategies to defend yourself in the often tumultuous social and professional realms. The Socially Intelligent Warrior stays prepared for all battles, staying happy and secure while retaining the ability to ward off threats.

This section will arm you with a series of effective strategies to keep you alive when things get ugly. This third aspect of Social Intelligence will tread into the darker realms of human nature. You will learn how to manipulate, control, defend, and attack. This might conjure feelings of unease, but do not get discouraged; understand that there is nothing moral in letting others bully or exploit you. Recognising a bully's strategies, outmanoeuvring them, and ultimately defeating them at their own game, is one of the most satisfying experiences we can have in life.

Each of the following five chapters contains historical

examples from war and other less overtly violent realms. Absorbing the lessons from a broad range of victories and failures will give you the best chance of surviving in any conflict. Throughout it all, do not forget that you are a diligent student of Social Intelligence. You seek peace before war for its own sake, but when a fight is inevitable, you will be more than prepared.

11

ZHOU ENLAI AND THE FRANCS-TIREURS

BECOME UNFIGHTABLE TO AVOID DANGER AND FRUSTRATE THE ENEMY

Always be unfathomable. When weak, hide and blend in with the crowd. When challenged, answer sweetly. When criticised, agree and amplify. Those who show too much of themselves, presenting a clear front, invite the brunt of the enemy's attacking strength and pay the price. Putting layers of heavy armour on yourself is not the best way to defend yourself; instead, you must nullify attacks by refusing to engage. Your enemies cannot fight what they cannot see, and they will exhaust themselves trying to pin you down. Offer no discernible target. Smile at your enemy. Appear as a friend. All of these passive tactics represent the highest form of defensive strategy. And once you have grown sufficiently in strength, and you have seduced your enemy into letting his guard down, you can bury your fangs and attack. He will never see it coming.

THE DIPLOMAT

In 1949, the newly proclaimed People's Republic of China emerged bloodied from a long civil war. Though they had roundly beaten Chiang Kai-shek's nationalist army, Mao

Zedong and the communist party knew that a fresh new challenge lay ahead of them. By that point, China's international influence had all but disappeared: The doomed Qing dynasty, overthrown in 1912, had presided over a century of humiliation, with European powers taking Chinese territory virtually at will. Allied leaders later questioned China's ability to deal with repeated Japanese incursions throughout the Second World War. But now that the communists had finally unified China, Mao had a fresh blank slate to work with, and appointed his long-serving revolutionary compatriot Zhou Enlai both as China's premier and minister of foreign affairs.

Zhou was the perfect man for the job. He was respected as a senior revolutionary and had gained a reputation as a skilled negotiator during the power struggle with Chiang Kai-shek's nationalists. When the Japanese invaded in the 1930s, Chiang's own officers were so frustrated with his obsession with exterminating the communists before dealing with the invaders, that they actually allowed Mao and Zhou to capture Chiang. But this was not the last surprise for Chiang. Zhou, without the knowledge of his colleagues, planned to let Chiang go, on the condition that they fight together against the invading Japanese. Expecting a humiliating execution, Chiang felt surprised as the calm, handsome Zhou instead addressed him with respect, asking for his help as a fellow Chinese soldier. Chiang gratefully agreed, secretly wondering if the communists had turned soft. While some communists were angry at Zhou for letting him go, Mao saw the wisdom in this move. To have killed Chiang would only have emboldened the nationalists' hatred of the communists, a foolish mistake when they needed their support. The communists could develop their rag-tag army into an experienced fighting force, while the nationalists took the brunt of the fighting. Zhou had seduced the nationalists into a position of weakness, allowing the communists space and time to gather strength and popular support. Now the communists had won and expelled the nationalists to the island of Taiwan, they hoped Zhou could help China do the same thing again, allowing the bruised nation to recover and gather strength.

From 1949 onwards, Zhou persuaded prominent figures outside of the communist party to accept jobs in the Chinese government. His biggest coup was in recruiting Zhang Zhizhong, one of Chiang's fiercest supporters, in a meeting with a delegation of nationalist leaders. Zhou promised Zhang that his family could safely return to Beijing from Taiwan, and every officer in the nationalist delegation accepted similar terms. These men who had once bitterly hated the Reds were, like Chiang had been years earlier, surprised by Zhou's conciliatory tone. He won them over with promises of safety, understanding the precarious situation that defecting to the communist party might pose to themselves and their families. Zhou appreciated the risk he was asking them to take, and went out of his way to ensure that his promises did not go unfulfilled. His new government recruits—once his and Mao's most bitter enemies—became some of communist China's strongest supporters.

Although China longed for a period of peace after the revolution, the Korean War and Franco-Vietnamese War had both ratcheted up the tensions between Asia and the West. In Korea, America had overplayed its hand in its attempt to quell a communist revolution in the north, and most of China saw the conflict in Indochina as yet another attempt by arrogant Westerners to cling onto their waning imperial influence. Both conflicts had seen horrifying acts committed by their combatants, with North Korean soldiers engaging Americans in near suicidal frontal attacks, and the Vietnamese making use of booby traps and mutilation on French soldiers and civilians alike. The 1954 Geneva Conference was organised to settle the Franco-Vietnamese War, and tensions were high. Everyone expected the conference to be a stormy series of tirades, especially between the Soviet and American emissaries. Knowing that these two powers wanted to exert their own influence over the discussions, both Zhou and Mao saw Geneva as the People's Republic of China's first opportunity to stand up and make itself known on the international stage.

People did not know what to expect from Zhou on his arrival in Geneva; they had only heard stories and rumours. When Zhou's limousine arrived outside the Palais des Nations, an unusually large crowd had gathered to get a glimpse of one of China's new communist leaders. Just as the soldiers and spectators outside eagerly watched the mysterious figure emerge from the car and stride towards the conference, no one on the inside knew what to expect from him either. He smiled and shook hands with leaders from all countries, who felt pleasantly surprised at this friendly gentleman's manner. During one early meeting, Zhou encountered the US Secretary of State John F. Dulles. Dulles was a staunch anti-communist and would later advocate an aggressive posture through the early Cold War, but Zhou nevertheless gave a warm smile and offered his hand. Several onlookers had, out of mere curiosity, turned around to watch this encounter. Dulles looked the Chinese leader up and down, said, "I cannot," and stormed out of the room. To this rude response, Zhou merely gave an amused shrug, which the many onlookers admired and regarded as a small victory for the Chinese premier. Dulles argued throughout the rest of the conference that the Chinese did not deserve to even attend, to which Zhou calmly responded that it was natural that China involve itself in matters of Asian importance.

As it happened, the talks resulted in a way that best

served China's interests, with French Indochina divided into several new independent states—including a socialist republic in Vietnam—free of Western influence. Dulles, who had meanwhile fallen out with the British delegate, future prime minister Anthony Eden, refused to sign the agreement, merely stating that it "took note" of the agreed ceasefire. Zhou, having wowed the international community with his dignified and friendly posture, celebrated his victory by having lunch with Charlie Chaplin, recently exiled to Switzerland from the United States for his alleged communist sympathies.

Despite these early victories, the late 1950s and 1960s proved much more challenging for Zhou and the long-suffering Chinese people. Through his constant battles with the Russian leaders Joseph Stalin and later Nikita Khrushchev, Mao had become frustrated with the lack of progress in turning China into a socialist state, and in 1958 he initiated the Great Leap Forward. Aggressive land reforms, collectivised agriculture, and mass dishonesty about productivity resulted in a nightmarish disaster. Tens of millions of Chinese farm workers and their families starved to death, while Mao enjoyed rich meals and an ever-changing succession of young women—he was a notorious womaniser. Managing Mao's constant tantrums and finger-pointing about the Great Leap's failure became a Sisyphean task for Zhou, as other communist veterans from the old days such as Liu Shaoqi and Deng Xiaoping became louder in their criticisms of Mao's idealistic policies. After Mao stepped down from the chairmanship of the communist party, Zhou, Liu, and Deng spent the early 1960s putting China's broken economy back together. The three men became popular among the Chinese masses after the horrors of the Great Leap, but something dark was brewing. The Soviet Union, joined by the hard-line ideological types in the

Chinese communist party, increasingly mocked Mao for his failure to bring his ideal of an egalitarian economy into reality. In private the Chinese leader seethed at Zhou for taking apart his policies.

In 1968, following media pressure after the Vietcong's Tet Offensive, US president Lyndon B. Johnson announced a steady withdrawal of American troops from Vietnam. For China, then deep in the anarchy of Mao's Cultural Revolution, this was good news. It signalled that the US would no longer pose a military threat in Asia, and it could not have come at a better time: In August that year, the Soviet Union sent troops into Czechoslovakia to remove Alexander Dubček from office after he had threatened to liberalise the country's failing economy. For Mao this intervention was both astonishing and appalling. The Soviet leader Leonid Brezhnev asserted that the communist world was a single global entity with Moscow as its capital, giving it the right to unilaterally "intervene" in the operations of any one of the world's socialist nations. China was ill-prepared for a Soviet invasion. Mao had no choice but to swallow his pride and soften relations with the American imperialists.

In early December 1969, the US ambassador to Poland, Walter Stoessel, had a chance encounter with his Chinese counterpart at an international fashion show in Warsaw. Stoessel was under standing instructions from the new US president, Richard Nixon, to issue a verbal message to the Chinese ambassador at the first available opportunity. Chinese diplomats throughout the Soviet bloc, however, had their own standing orders to *avoid* all communication with American envoys. Stoessel chased the anxious Chinese ambassador down the frozen steps of Warsaw's Palace of Culture, and after a long pursuit described by onlookers as both surreal and comedic, he caught up with his Chinese counterpart and breathlessly delivered his message: "President Nixon... would like to have... serious concrete talks... with the Chinese."

For his efforts, Stoessel received no direct response. But some time later, the Nixon White House learned that two American citizens arrested for sailing into Chinese waters were now being released. This move was later revealed to be a direct intervention by Zhou. A year later, under instructions from Mao, the Chinese invited the US ping pong team to tour China, resulting in an unexpectedly friendly embrace between the players Glenn Cowan and Zhuang Zedong. While hanging out together, one Chinese ping pong player was photographed wearing a T-shirt with the message "Give Peace a Chance," gifted by a player from the American team. Though seemingly unscripted, these sporting partnerships were all orchestrated by Zhou, laying the perfect ground for Nixon's historic visit to the People's Republic in 1972. With Mao secretly in the late stages of ALS, or Lou Gehrig's disease, Zhou would take centre stage.

The meeting between Nixon, Mao, and Zhou had all of its desired effects. Nixon's visit to the Great Wall of China was a media sensation, and many onlookers in the West watched with rapt curiosity as they gained a rare insight into the normally closed-off China. But more importantly, it caused the Soviets great concern. A year earlier, Nixon's announcement of the visit had by itself shocked the world and put Moscow on the back foot, but now the hundreds of photographs of the president surrounded by smiling Chinese officials at the Great Wall, and toasting drinks with Zhou and the visibly frail Mao, showed a burgeoning new friendship.

After the 1972 state visit, the US and Chinese jointly signed the Shanghai Communiqué. Washington acknowledged China's claims control over the oft-disputed island of Taiwan—as well as the island's assertion that it was the *true*

Chinese republic—and agreed that it did not support any move for Taiwanese independence. Détente between the two former enemies appeared complete, and the Soviets quieted down their veiled threats of intervention in China. Zhou had pulled off one of the key diplomatic and geopolitical masterpieces of the twentieth century.

But Zhou would not receive much reward for his masterful diplomacy. In one of his frequent mood swings, Mao resented all the favourable attention shone on Zhou Enlai, and decided that he had become *too* friendly with the imperialists. It was the suave, handsome Zhou, not the frail, drooling Mao who was credited with being the chief architect of China's opening to the outside world. In 1973, Mao ordered Zhou to attend a series of humiliating criticism sessions organised by the party's hardline leftists. Mao's own wife, Jiang Qing, said to Zhou, "you have fallen to your hands and knees to the Americans." Slamming his fist onto the table, the normally dignified Zhou exclaimed, "I, Zhou Enlai, have made many mistakes in my life, but I cannot be accused of rightist capitulation." Having sent the message of who was boss, Mao signalled for the humiliation to end. He had never wanted to purge the useful Zhou, only humble him.

Still not satisfied, Mao denied Zhou treatment for his bladder cancer, and the premier died in agony in 1976. Mao refused any official acknowledgement of Zhou's death, but once word got out, to his great shock, a massive outpouring of grief came from the Chinese people. In their eyes, their beloved premier had been killed through sly political manoeuvring motivated purely by jealousy. Riding this wave of grief, Zhou's old friend Deng Xiaoping returned to politics, taking Mao's place shortly after his death less than a year later. Laying to rest three decades of famine and chaos, Deng instituted a series of business-friendly economic reforms that laid the groundwork for China's transformation into a truly modern power.

INTERPRETATION

Zhou Enlai was a key stabilising figure in the Chinese communist movement, and perhaps one of the best models of Social Intelligence in modern history. Without Zhou's political skills and practical approach, Mao's grandiosity and obsession with ideology would have likely destroyed China. While Mao's popularity waxed and waned through the cumulative pain of the Great Leap Forward and the Cultural Revolution, Zhou remained a consistently beloved figure in the hearts of ordinary Chinese, even though as premier he arguably played just as much of a role in those disasters. His critics have often characterised him as a timid yes-man to the ruthless Mao, a kind of cowardly henchman who failed to stop the cruel bully when he was at his worst. Why then, upon his needlessly painful death, was there such an outpouring of grief throughout China and the outside world?

Zhou outmanoeuvred all of his enemies with a smile, always keeping his suave, dignified pose. When he met the captured Chiang Kai-shek during the civil war, Zhou knew that torturing or executing the man, as his comrades would likely want to do, would only stiffen the nationalists' resolve. Rather than succumb to petty rivalry, Zhou softened Chiang's resistance by treating him with respect as a fellow Chinese leader. His warm, enthusiastic manner took Chiang off his guard, making him more pliable. It made Chiang second-guess his rivalry with the communists, clouding his mind with confused, conflicting thoughts. Zhou would repeat this seductive manoeuvre with many of his political enemies in the communist party: Instead of offering the hard, resistive front they expected, he assumed a posture of disarming charm, reassuring them that they were fighting for the same thing, while really pushing China's interests.

Where the failed Qing dynasty had been haughty, mono-lithic, and patriarchal, Zhou's new China was spirited, proud of itself, yet also ineffable and hard to pin down. Zhou was more than just an able politician or skilled diplomat: He was a mysterious, even romantic figurehead. At the Geneva Conference, he could not have provided more of a stark contrast to the United States. The combative Dulles bluntly opposed every motion and treated the Asian nations with disrespect. Zhou, in stark contrast, offered a polite, charming front while pushing for a solution that best served China's interests. He enchanted the conference with his attractive manners, and they paid him back with favourable terms. As for the Americans? Their arrogant, combative style only won them enemies on all sides and an unfriendly environment in Asia.

While Mao threw one tantrum after another at the Chinese people for what he perceived at their failure to turn his dreams into reality, Zhou remained calm and pragmatic. He realised early that the pace of the change was impractical, causing millions to starve to death because of dishonest productivity reports and poor harvests. Seeing that the people were angry at the reforms, Zhou did not shrink from criticising the policy of ranking ideological "redness" over the twin virtues of competence and patience. This encour-aged Liu Shaoqi and Deng Xiaoping, two other eminently pragmatic administrators, to emerge and help heal the coun-try's shocked economy. During the Cultural Revolution too, as Red Guards ravaged the country in a path of chaos and destruction, the Chinese people appreciated Zhou's interven-tion in the mayhem. The Chinese were tired of Mao's egotis-tical adventures and petty battles, the obese chairman

enjoying champagne, enormous meals, and a constant rota-
tion of eager young girls. But Zhou, perhaps motivated by
more than mere popularity, had a far better sense for the
Chinese zeitgeist, and could use it to take political risks that
others would usually shrink from. Like a twentieth-century
Zhuge Liang (the celebrated Chinese strategist from the
fabled War of the Three Kingdoms era), Zhou protected
himself by appearing to offer no resistance at all, and then
going on the offensive when Chinese society depended on
him for it the most.

Understand that in any fight, a hard exterior is often the
worst form of defence. Closing ranks and acting defensively
against a bully will only reveal a sore point that he will jab at
again and again. It is also to play into the hands of the many
aggressive types who *want* to provoke such a reaction. In
either case, the Socially Intelligent Warrior practises a much
higher form of strategy: assuming an unfightable pose in his
behaviour and attitude. Rather than taking the attacker's bait
and risking a costly social blunder, you retain a dignified
pose as your enemy exposes himself. You refuse the enemy
the frightening, scrambling reaction he craves, reversing the
dynamic entirely with a wry smile at the knowledge you're
above such petty battles. You nullify the enemy's attacks,
making him frustrated and liable to fall into embarrassing
tantrums, like so many of Zhou's enemies. While they
desperately look for somewhere to attack, they make themselves appear overly aggressive or even downright crazy—
never a good look. Defeating your enemy in this way, leaving
him isolated from the group while advancing your own prestige, is the height of Social Intelligence.

KEYS TO SOCIAL INTELLIGENCE

Since early childhood we have had to deal with attacks that put us on the defensive. Whether it is a bully trying to intimidate us or a rival trying to make us a social pariah, life offers constant pinprick attacks to our ego. Large threats are easiest to counter since they are so rare and often telegraphed; instead, it is the frequent small jibes and setbacks that get under our skin. Subtle attacks in the social realm are unsettling and difficult to counter because of our need to feel accepted in social groups, and we feel powerless to stop them, since to give into our frustration and overtly react makes us look ridiculous. We constantly ruminate on the intentions of people's words and behaviours, and this concern puts us on edge in future encounters. Skilled "attackers" can cut you into pieces before you can form a coherent word in response, and they often relish dominating others by unsettling their minds in this way.

The natural response to such attacks is to form a defensive wall around the ego. We close off and act guarded in interactions with others, rarely giving away details that leave us vulnerable. We assume the worst intentions in the most innocuous statement, sometimes snapping at our perceived assailant. This defensive approach might protect the ego, but in the long term it only drives people away and makes you more prone to isolation. People with defensive attitudes are most unpleasant to be around, constantly picking apart every word and body language signal for perceived attacks, never relaxing or being truly present. You must see such a desperate need to protect the ego as a sign of profound inner weakness. It fills us full of dark emotions, like anger and resentment, yet gives us no concrete target to fight against.

This high emotional state puts us in a dangerous position.

We throw away all semblance of strategy and instead regress into a kind of "react mode," throwing jabs that don't land, making ourselves look foolish. If you find yourself in this position often, then you must deal with it to achieve your potential as a Socially Intelligent Warrior. You should explore the parts of yourself you feel the need to defend so badly—shining light on dark, sore points and accepting them instead of letting them fester. This process is vital for keeping the defensive attitude at bay. Watch yourself when you next feel angry or resentful and try to think objectively about what is triggering it. Through deep, honest reflection you can accept your deficiencies and the next time they're threatened you'll have more control of yourself. This practice will help you immeasurably with the defensive aspect of this chapter.

In war, this propensity to give pinprick attacks without giving a concrete form is best characterised by guerrilla warfare. When a large army invades a space, then a small defending force may find it heroic and valiant to fight to the death—but what does that really achieve? Fighting a head-on battle only plays to the invader's strengths, and martyrdom is a messy and inexact strategy that fails more often than it succeeds. The guerrilla warrior denies his foe the advantages of frontal attacks and instead yields territory, diffusing into the surrounding wilderness and blending in with the local populace. He makes small yet constant pinprick attacks, irritating the enemy to no end while offering them no concrete form to grab hold of.

The worst form of response to a guerrilla attack, and historically the most common, is to crack down on the local populace to drive out the guerrillas. This "strategy" plays right into the guerrillas' hands, because it makes them seem like brave, sympathetic heroes fighting against bullying oppressors. Far from scaring the guerrillas, this actually serves to swell their ranks. The only way to defeat a guerrilla threat is through kindness: instituting popular reforms, removing the harsher aspects of their prior rule, and respecting their most valued customs. This approach robs the guerrilla of the local support he desperately needs, while in the background you can work at removing his valuable supply chains. By refusing to fight on the guerrilla's preferred playing field, you have nullified his only form of attack.

This principle applies equally to the social realm where guerrilla warriors of the mind love attacking others in the subtlest of ways. If you have a toxic colleague who likes to attack and test people, then the best way to inoculate against such types is to use the support-gathering strategies discussed earlier in this book, since a strong reputation for generosity, competence, and fair dealings is by itself a potent shield against toxic types. But regardless of your social standing in a group, if you don't handle yourself well when under attack then you will embarrass yourself through displays of anger and frustration, losing that precious popular support. Learn to become unfightable, and you will gain the ability to suck all the energy out of negative interactions, reversing any attack back onto the aggressor. There is no more essential defensive skill in the social realm.

In the late nineteenth century, France and Prussia fought a short war with huge implications for Europe. Almost immediately after the French parliament declared war, a German coalition quickly formed under Prussia's lead, sending many well-trained, well-armed troops into northeastern France in 1870 (so quickly that some historians concluded that the war was in fact a deliberate ploy orchestrated by Prussia's wily chancellor, Otto von Bismarck), and this superior army easily overwhelmed the weak French in a matter of months.

Although the German coalition blew away France's

conventional forces, they faced a new threat once they began occupying their new territory. While on parade, a high-ranking officer would get fatally shot through the head, in broad daylight and in front of his troops, and no one could tell where the shot had come from. Attacks like this happened many times across a wide area, and these incidents caused a shock wave of fear and tumult through the occupying Prussian troops. The shooters were, in fact, a loose brigade of French marksmen, who were waging a new—and horribly effective—style of war against their strong invaders. These French guerrillas, who became known as *francs-tireurs* or "free shooters," became so feared and notorious that both the Spanish and Portuguese named their terms for a sharp-shooter after this group (*francotirador* in Spanish and *franco-atirador* in Portugese).

Embarrassed that a few young men in rags could tie down entire companies of apparently well-drilled soldiers out of pure fear, the Prussians executed all captured marksmen on the spot, arguing that by fighting in civilian clothes they were violating normal codes of warfare. Unseen shooters continued to pick off invading soldiers, and Prussian leaders reacted with fits of frustration in their sheer inability to deal with this constant and growing threat. The Prussian mistrust of French civilians became so violent and cruel that they pillaged and burned entire towns full of innocent people. Naturally this bred a long-lasting hatred between the French and Germans that manifested in the two world wars of the twentieth century.

During the First World War, French snipers used the same tactics as their ancestors, often operating plainclothes and hiding in plain sight among civilians. This new generation of *francs-tireurs* became so efficient at killing German soldiers that the German General Staff, who had not forgotten the lessons from the Franco-Prussian War, carried out unusually harsh occupation of the French areas they conquered to pre-empt any guerrilla resistance. This, predictably, only added to the sharpshooters' ranks and many of the later sniper attacks on Germans were by French-speaking Belgians, after they too had learned the unexpected power of guerrilla warfare. In the Second World War years later, after German Panzer tanks rolled into France, the Nazi Gestapo came prepared to deal with the inevitable French guerrilla tactics by publicly torturing and beating known *francs-tireurs*, sentencing them to years of back-breaking labour.

It is clear to see the repeated patterns across three different conflicts, each separated by entire generations: a strong invading force blows away a country's conventional forces; the weak locals have no choice but to respond with covert guerrilla tactics; unsettled and frustrated with their inability to deal with this threat, the invaders resort to harsh retribution upon anyone with the slightest link to the guerrilla force, more often being mere indiscriminate violence. Guerrilla warfare creates a cycle of increasing barbarism on the side of the invader, as its soldiers become increasingly terrified by the random attacks that come at any time and from any place. Since the invading soldiers can't easily identify the source of these attacks, they see the surrounding environment in general as a threat, getting nervous chills whenever tasked with leaving camp. A few pockets of resistance here and there can strike more terror into an invading soldier's heart than a conventional army of 100,000 enemy troops.

A similar form of guerrilla warfare flared up in Northern Ireland during the late twentieth century. The Provisional IRA (Irish Republican Army), much like the *francs-tireurs*, used deadly sniper teams who planned their attacks with absolute precision. They went to great lengths to ensure their secrecy through several methods: importing guns from sympathisers in America and Libya, keeping teams compartmentalised into separate cells to minimise the threat of betrayal, and hiding their weapons in secure locations not linked to any home address. Sniper teams would use "dickers," children who acted as lookouts, and post signs in neighbourhoods boasting of the PIRA's watch over the area. Once a sniper took a shot, whether it hit the target or missed, they would move to a new location, because in a firefight an enemy can easily identify the location of a shooter who continues firing from the same spot.

Every part of this strategy contributed to the feeling of an all-pervasive threat that could strike with deadly force, even though the conflict with British forces was starkly asymmetrical. Much like the Prussians a century earlier, the British Army and local police, furious with their ungraspable enemy, responded by arresting anyone based on the slightest link to the terrorist threat—often using advanced forensics techniques to identify gunpowder on a shirt, and then humiliating captured PIRA soldiers as a deterrent to their friends. These harsh, unpopular measures split the community further and forced the PIRA to increase their counter-forensic measures and become more aggressive in their sniper campaigns, which hurt their own credibility by making them seem too extreme. It took decades for the conflict in Northern Ireland to simmer down, and a latent resentment still exists on both sides to this day.

Understand that in any conflict, your true enemy is the opponent's mind. You can make the strength of his forces irrelevant if you successfully cloud his thoughts with feelings of confusion, rage, and fear. If you assume a polite, dignified front and offer no upfront resistance to his barbs, then it becomes socially distasteful to attack or even suspect you of wrongdoing. If your attacks seem to come from all sides with little rhyme or reason, you close him down into a kind of reactive terror that nullifies all of his strengths while pressing down on his greatest weaknesses. By becoming unfightable, even the most ostensibly weak warrior can gain an almost spiritual kind of power over the strongest foe. This should come as an empowering realisation for those who normally feel helpless.

Another tactic you can use is to devise a smokescreen, a campaign of deception. Using feints, realistic indications of movements towards an ostensible goal, can confuse your enemy about your strength and whereabouts. Unsure about what or who you truly are, the enemy feels a kind of paralysis. The lack of any clear information robs him of the certainty he needs to form a concrete plan, and you force him into the frightening situation of sailing into the unknown, nervous and ill-prepared for the fight. On the other hand, your feints can be used to suggest a sign of your strategy that is actually false. But this takes subtlety and an understanding of human nature: Because we are naturally egotistical and *want* circumstances to prove our suspicions correct, you must only make indications that fit with his preconceptions. If he is paranoid, show threats spread widely all around him. If he likes to fight, then show weakness. If he also uses his own form of strategy, then indicate a random, patternless approach. To devise an effective smokescreen deception, you must always take your enemy's mind and inclinations into account.

During the Second World War, Allied forces used a vast number of secret deception operations designed to fool the Nazi leadership. Operation Bertram, led by Bernard Montgomery and devised by Dudley Clarke in 1942, consisted of building dummy tanks, artillery, and other military *matériel* to fool German forces in Egypt of the Allies' strength and location. From the air, it was impossible for reconnaissance to distinguish real tanks from the fake, giving the enemy no clue about where a possible attack might come from, and how powerful it would be. German soldiers stationed in El Alamein could only guess, though there were strong indications that a great number of Allied tanks were positioned for an attack from the south. This seemed logical, since an attack from the north would risk pinning themselves down against the sea, and reports had showed tank movements near the Qattara Depression to the south. To their great surprise, the Allies attacked unexpectedly early with mobile tanks and heavy guns. Where had they come from? They had seen these tanks moving towards the south only a few days earlier. Those tanks in the south had in fact been real, but they were only a strategic feint. Perfectly lifelike dummies had replaced the real tanks soon before the Allied attack, reinforcing the guns moving in the north. This splendidly executed surprise attack gave the Allies an unlikely victory against a strong defending force.

After the battle, a captured German tank general told Montgomery that he had genuinely believed an Allied offensive would come from the south and in greater numbers than they possessed, and two weeks later than it actually did. Using a brilliant smokescreen, the Allies portrayed a convincing picture that contradicted the situation's reality, and caught the defending Germans unprepared for the true offensive. The deception was a splendid execution of deception warfare.

The Socially Intelligent Warrior, understanding that strong enemies lurk around him at all times, hides his true intentions and refuses to expose a weak point, while facing everyone with a friendly yet bland and unreadable front. It is understandable to feel uncomfortable with being closed off or mistrusting, since it is exhausting to live and work in such a closed-off manner all the time. You *should* be polite and generous when people show that they deserve such treatment. But just as often there are environments where you feel unsure of your surroundings and can't risk opening yourself up to attack. Rather than blurting out your intentions for all to hear, it is much safer to operate with a base level of politeness that betrays no strategic details. Remember that you're here to work, not make friends or debate the meaning of life. When an enemy confronts you, react with a disarming charm that makes them feel confused and, later on, guilty for their rash behaviour. This might seem manipulative, but it is a practical tool that you pull out when required and in self-defence, and it is particularly effective at that. It is impossible to fight an enemy who provides no true form, and becoming unfightable is to take back one's personal power over both the relentless bullies and unpredictable circumstances that would otherwise dominate us.

> Mao dominated any gathering; Zhou suffused it. Mao's passion strove to overwhelm opposition; Zhou's intellect would seek to persuade or outmanoeuvre it. Mao was sardonic; Zhou penetrating. Mao thought of himself as a philosopher; Zhou saw his role as an administrator or a negotiator. Mao was eager to accelerate history; Zhou was content to exploit its currents.
>
> — HENRY KISSINGER

REVERSAL

Although Zhou Enlai was indeed a master at the social game, he suffered greatly at the hands of the cruel Mao. His ability to deflect attacks and deal with troublemakers in the most oblique fashion possible won him many political victories, but it could not save him from being dominated and toyed with in a humiliating way.

Becoming unfightable, using the fighting style of the guerrilla warrior, does not work out in every single situation. No strategy can be the single answer to all circumstances, and you must stay fluid and respondent to everything that happens around you. Sometimes you should speak up and fight for yourself, lest you spend your life in humiliating misery with a false smile on your face. If you let bullies trample all over you, then you are not a Socially Intelligent Warrior; you are a coward.

There is little more to say on this except to listen to your gut and to always keep your overall goals in mind. If something feels wrong to you, then the wisdom inside your unconscious is telling you something *real*, and you should listen to it and act accordingly. There is no virtue in becoming a pushover, because no one will ever respect you until you're able to show your teeth. The next chapter gives a full description of this opposite side to defensive warfare.

12

ROBERT E. LEE AND GEORGE B. MCCLELLAN

MAKE THE PROSPECT OF FIGHTING YOU COSTLY AND DANGEROUS

I f people know you to be a pushover who will meekly accord with the dominance of others, then you will become a ripe target for the overly aggressive types. Balance your polite, gentle front with the ability to show your teeth when the time calls for it. It is impossible to respect someone who lacks any measure of danger. When under attack, stand up and defend yourself in a respectful manner for as long as the situation—and the aggressor's behaviour—calls for it. Take the initiative and smite the enemy with a strong counter-attack —you will quickly find out that many aggressors are really just big cowards looking for an easy fight, and will leave you alone after your display of defiance.

AGGRESSIVE DEFENCE

In May 1861, the Confederate States of America moved their seat of government from Montgomery, Alabama to Richmond, Virginia, where state legislators had just voted to secede from the United States. Virginians had previously voted to stay in the Union, but changed their minds after the capture of Fort Sumter near Charleston, South Carolina in April. Realising that an armed conflict was now inevitable, both the North and South began recruiting soldiers and forming military strategies.

Although the North was more industrialised and had a far larger population than the South in 1861, they had a much different task ahead of them. The North had to mount an active offensive against the South to bring them back into the Union by force, whereas the South only had to resist the North's advances and survive for long enough to keep their new independence. If Lincoln stood idle, then the South won by default. But this didn't mean the South had an easy task ahead of them either, since they had an overwhelmingly agrarian economy heavily reliant on slave labour, and any threat to farm production would completely hamstring their war efforts. Although the North was the only side with a professional army, it only had 15,000 active soldiers. Both sides needed to recruit and mobilise an army quickly, accepting that these new soldiers would be green and unused to fighting.

Winfield Scott, the Union's commanding general, came up with a series of ideas to put down the Southern rebellion with an economy of both resources and manpower. His Anaconda Plan called for a widespread constriction of the South's economy, including the blockading of key Confederate ports down the coast; sending forces to control the Mississippi River, a key source of trade; and seizing control of Richmond with a large army of men. This strategy was sound and, incidentally, how the North eventually won the war, but it had just one caveat: The North had no navy capable of the mobile, heavy manoeuvres Scott demanded to carry out coastal blockades. Transforming their meagre, deep-water navy would take time, and the Northern public clamoured for Lincoln's military to lead the charge into Richmond right away. Unable to ignore the democratic tide, in July 1861 Winfield Scott sent his subordinate Brigadier General Irvin McDowell south from Washington, D.C. with 35,000 men, confident that a quick, heavy blow would knock the South out of the war quickly.

The Confederates, well aware of the Northern public's clamour for a quick advance, concentrated their forces near the Manassas Junction under the generalship of P. G. T. Beauregard, a Louisianan. Both sides had armies full of green recruits, and Irvin McDowell's plan for a surprise attack on Beauregard's flank turned out to be highly ambitious, and the first fighting was a nervous and messy affair. Because McDowell's ineffective charge had taken so much longer to manifest than expected, Confederate Brigadier General Joseph E. Johnston and his army of 12,000 men had time to arrive with fresh legs, and the course of battle quickly changed. A forceful counter-attack by the Confederates proved decisive, and a Union retreat quickly turned into a scattered rout. A group of civilian onlookers who had come to watch the battle even tried to block the retreating Northerners. One previously unknown Virginian general named Thomas J. Jackson earned great praise during the battle for standing his ground against a fresh Union charge—another Southern general calling, "There stands Jackson like a stone wall—rally round the Virginians!" The name "Stonewall" Jackson stuck, and the South quickly associated his conduct with the stout defence of their home soil.

Although both sides suffered moderate losses compared to later encounters, the First Battle of Bull Run (or First Battle of Manassas as the South called it) had huge effects to their respective expectations of success. Northern leadership's hopes of a quick victory were severely blunted, while the South took heart and expected to win independence. One thing was certain: This war would be a long-drawn and bloody affair. Winfield Scott, blamed for the Union's failure to take northern Virginia, was forced out of the army by George B. McClellan, a political general appointed by Lincoln to represent the Democratic Party in the North's military leadership. McClellan cut a dashing figure and was immensely popular with his men in his Army of the Potomac, a stark contrast to the obese and enfeebled Winfield Scott, who had been seventy-five years old at the time of Bull Run.

McClellan was, however, a know-it-all who believed himself far more capable than both Scott and Lincoln. With one eye on the upcoming presidential election in 1864, he thought that a large victory in his name at this early stage would give him the popularity to defeat Lincoln in the next election. In March 1862, McClellan moved south with 50,000 soldiers, now well-trained and a little more battle-seasoned, towards the tip of the Virginia Peninsula, which would hope-fully allow him to approach the heart of the Confederate capital state from behind and force the South onto two fronts.

McClellan's Army of the Potomac landed successfully at the eastern tip of the Virginia Peninsula, but quickly faced surprise opposition. Confederate Brigadier General John B. Magruder had received word of McClellan's amphibious movement early and pinned McClellan down with a counter-attack to discourage any further advance. Frightened and dismayed at this obstruction, McClellan turned a long path northwards towards Richmond. Exhausted and emotionally drained by some unexpected heavy fighting at the Battle of Williamsburg on the path to Richmond, the Army of the Potomac doggedly pursued the retreating Confederate forces who were moving quickly to defend the capital, a far more strategically important location to both sides. As McClellan finally approached Richmond, his army faced even more stout Confederate defence on the city's outskirts, at Hanover Court House followed by a strong counter-attack by Joseph E. Johnston at Fair Oaks Station that appeared to come out of nowhere.

Unprepared for such a heavy assault, the battered and bruised Army of the Potomac lost 5,000 of its remaining 34,000 soldiers. Despite the roughly equivalent losses on both sides, the fight was yet another blow to McClellan's naïve and egotistical expectations of a quick and heroic campaign. He made a hasty a retreat down the Virginia Peninsula to regroup.

The Battle of Fair Oaks had another effect that would prove both fateful and decisive in the final months of McClellan's Peninsula Campaign: Joseph E. Johnston had been wounded by artillery during the battle and was replaced the next day by a general named Robert E. Lee. Unlike the cautious and sometimes timid Johnston, Lee understood the situation before him in clear terms. The Army of the Potomac was severely demoralised and spread thinly across the rain-swollen Chickahominy River. But with a charismatic leader like McClellan at its command, this army could easily rally and send for more forces. Thus, Lee could not afford to engage in a long and drawn-out battle of attrition, because that would give the North the time they needed to recruit from their large population and fully activate their immense industrial war production effort, a system that the South lacked entirely. Lee's strategy was to send Stonewall Jackson to overwhelm both of the Potomac's flanks with a force amounting to 90,000 men. It was an audacious plan, but such a risk was necessary to scare off any prospect of future incursions into Virginia by the North.

On the 25 June 1862, McClellan made a pre-emptive strike on the newly organised Army of Northern Virginia, with a force totalling over 110,000 men thanks to some last-minute reinforcements from the sea. At first the fight seemed to go strongly for McClellan, until Lee began executing his plan to smite his army at both of its flanks. Over the next seven days, both armies fought virtually non-stop at eight different battle sites. Though McClellan had been forced into yet another retreat down the Virginia Peninsula, Stonewall Jackson, in his sixties and exhausted after a severe lack of sleep over the previous week, failed to cut off the North's escape towards a strong defensive position on Malvern Hill, close to the southern side of the peninsula. On the last day, Lee launched a series of frontal attacks right at McClellan, suffering heavy losses at the hands of the Northern general's infantry and artillery guns. Over 20,000 Confederates died in the week of fighting, but they had driven the Army of the Potomac from Virginia. The capital state was safe for now.

After the Seven Days Battles, as they later came to be known, both Lee and McClellan returned home feeling disappointed: Lee bitterly regretted the final charge's heavy losses, and McClellan wrote a series of petulant letters to Washington claiming he was facing at least 200,000 Confederates (a wild overestimation) and demanded a new army of at least that strength to carry out a fresh offensive. He had heard that a rival general named Ulysses S. Grant had grown in popularity after gaining some success in the western theatre and relished draining his forces to place his waning fame on firmer ground. McClellan saw Grant as a depressed drunkard who had merely gotten lucky in a less critical side of the war, and felt confident that the failed businessman's popularity would wane if he isolated him.

To McClellan's dismay, Washington flatly denied his request for a number of reasons: Lee's aggressiveness, the sheer impossibility of raising such a large force so quickly, and the unfavourable mosquito season due in the late summer. McClellan raged to anyone he came across about how unfair he thought this was, but he knew deep down that he had failed in his last attempt to gain glory and stayed unrepentant until the rest of the war. Robert E. Lee, in contrast, received great widespread praise across the South for his heroic resistance with a small, rag-tag force. The fight was still far from symmetrical, and the losses had been heavy on both sides, but the reports of Lee's fights at the Seven Days Battles breathed fresh energy and optimism into the Confederate war effort.

INTERPRETATION

The South's repulsion of early Northern advances were costly and often involved clumsy execution of audacious battle plans—from Beauregard's fumbled flank attack at Bull Run to Lee's suicidal frontal assault on McClellan at Malvern Hill. But the North's failed invasion campaigns had a much deeper and pervasive effect than either side could have predicted: They showed that any incursion into Southern territory would come at a high cost in casualties, time, and morale. This gave the South the confidence they needed to continue fighting, and those at home the spirit to keep working to supply the war effort. Even abroad, the Seven Days Battles showed an unexpected reversal of fortune in the American Civil War. In October 1862, British prime minister William Gladstone spoke with relief at the Confederacy's efforts to a crowd in Newcastle, since the South's survival was critical to England's burgeoning textile trade (slave labour driving all of the South's cotton exports).

The strategic situation was favourable to the South during the war's early stages. All they had to do was repulse the North for long enough and make the fight as costly as possible—if they could stretch the war out until 1864 without allowing the North a meaningful victory, a pro-slavery

Democrat such as McClellan could end the war on the South's terms.

The North, although stronger on paper, had a leadership full of competing egos vying for political dominance. It took Lincoln several years to find the right balance in his military team, cycling through several generals each proving themselves lacking in some critical way, with McClellan proving himself overly cautious and prone to jealous fights with his colleagues. The North also had no choice but to compel the South to rejoin the Union, giving them a much higher bar to pass than the South. The South's task, however, was only easier by comparison, since they still had to raise a large army from a sparsely populated country of men who had never fought a battle in their lives, and in fact often resented being forced to fight what they perceived to be a rich man's war, since only a small minority of wealthy Southern families owned slaves.

The South knew, however, that they could not rest on their laurels. Soldiers can fight a lot harder to defend their homes than an invading army far away from theirs, but allowing too much of the fighting to occur on Confederate soil would be a disaster in the long run. They would lose valuable farming land and slaves would likely run away to join the invading Northerners—this was, in fact, exactly how the North won the war with William T. Sherman's March to the Sea in 1864. Lee therefore decided that the way to win the war was not to wait for the North to advance into their territory, but to smite them, discouraging any attack through sheer aggression. Upon taking control of the new Army of Northern Virginia, his first action was to regroup and organise a forceful series of flanking attacks on McClellan's flagging army. This positive plan alone had an inspirational effect on both his subordinate commanders and the soldiery alike, and its eventual success at driving out the Northerners from home territory had a euphoric effect throughout the South that cannot be discounted.

Just as Lee made the North think twice about invading the South in future campaigns, you must respond to aggressive types with sudden counter-attacks that surprise and demoralise them. They might see you as weak and quiet to begin with, but that will quickly change once you launch an offensive of your own. Don't merely wait around for the enemy to make the first move; take the initiative and smite him. *Show* him you won't go down without an ugly, bruising fight. Expecting an easy victory, your sudden move will put him on the back foot, clouding his mind with doubt, and make those around him second-guess his later moves. To double the effect, find an unexposed flank covering something he craves and strike there, inducing the fear in his heart that he could lose more than he bargained for in fighting you. Bullies are usually big cowards on the inside and like easy victories. Given enough of a push backwards they will choose to leave you alone, rather than risk everything on an offence that turns into a costly gamble. Deterrence, namely in the form of a spirited offence, is truly the best form of defence. As George Washington wrote a century earlier in similar circumstances to Lee:

> It is unfortunate when men cannot, or will not, see danger at a distance; or seeing it, are restrained in the means which are necessary to avert, or keep it afar off. I question whether the evil arising from the French getting possession of Louisiana and the Floridas would be generally seen, until it is felt; and yet no problem in Euclid is more evident, or susceptible of clearer demonstration. Not less difficult is it to make them believe, that offensive operations, often times, is the surest, if not the only (in some cases) means of defence.

KEYS TO SOCIAL INTELLIGENCE

Being on the defensive can be quite terrifying, particularly if we don't expect the aggressor's attack. We feel threatened, and our animal instincts kick in, which are much stronger than our higher powers of conscious rationality. These instincts aren't without their worth, since they kept our ancestors alive when life was harsher than it is now. It is nevertheless easy for these instincts to overwhelm us when we're attacked, and we react on the sole basis of these fleeting emotions. We end up making the situation worse for ourselves and better for our attacker, since this fit or irrationality is exactly what they wanted to induce in us. There is no use in denying that there are people out there who are not only aware of this effect, but *enjoy* using it on others. They often have very little control of their own lives, and are so twisted with bitterness and resentment that they get a kick out of making others feel the same way (there is also a small minority of people who are legitimate psychopaths, people disconnected from any feelings of empathy or emotion and who see you merely as a tool to use in their games).

Although as students of Social Intelligence we try to uphold the virtues of competence, reciprocity, and empathy where possible, it is suicide to ignore the very real threat of people who want to take our hard-earned support and resources away from us. Human beings are inherently aggressive. This is a fact with which we must deal, not an inconvenient truth we discard because it doesn't fit in with our ideals. As a Socially Intelligent Warrior, you must see the need to dwell in reality as more important than any individual strategy or tactic.

Aggressors in most realms seek easy victories. If they can dominate an opponent sitting on some valuable resource, like a successful company or a strong network of social allies, then the cheaper they can acquire that resource, the better. They will try to achieve this goal by seeking victims who will most easily yield to pressure, using shock tactics to frighten them into a rash surrender. Aggressors *hope* that their victims don't give themselves enough credit for their own strength, and so they will sometimes use nasty manipulation tactics like trying to persuade the victim that submitting will actually bring them benefits they hadn't thought of, or appealing to the victim's attachment to some group they're responsible for ("If you *really* cared about your family's wellbeing, wouldn't you sign the merger?"). If you are on the verge of becoming a victim to such a subversive attack, then anger is actually the correct and healthy response, so don't repress it. No one has the right to enter your life and alter your circumstances without your conscious, rational agreement. Anger is not evil; it's a genuine reflection of the circumstances bubbling up from deep within you—in many remarkable ways, your body is often a better judge of scams than your conscious mind. Anger is, however, a destructive emotion if left unchecked. It can lead you into burning valuable bridges and soiling existing partnerships. Like all emotions, you must channel anger consciously so it doesn't take unconscious control of you.

Aggressors fear victims who, upon being attacked, turn into furious, unpredictable, and therefore *dangerous* enemies. If you can signal to your aggressor that an attack on you will come with a heavy price, then they will most likely cut their losses and leave you alone. Responding with aggressive counter-attacks, hurting things he values, will prove that fighting you is not worth the price. Only those on a holy crusade, or those out to trigger you will continue on such terms (in that latter case, the best response is no response; remember your reaction is their goal, so deny it to them). When someone strikes you in a way that proves their betrayal, lack of trust, or even as an existential threat, you have a responsibility to strike back. Not out of some irrational emotion like honour, because that can quickly spiral out of control; you're doing it consciously because you know it's a time-honoured strategy.

In the American Civil War, Robert E. Lee repulsed the North's advances on Richmond with aggressive, forceful counter-attacks. Lee *punished* the enemy for daring to encroach on his home territory, and the Confederate people loved him for it; in fact his brave defence has become part of the South's mythology, remaining a heroic ideal for many in the former Confederate states to this day.

The spirited defence against a foreign aggressor is a highly resonant archetypal structure, and we respond to this theme strongly in stories like *The Lord of the Rings* where the people of Rohan and Gondor heroically fight off an enormous invading force of evil warriors. It's deeply embedded in us.

Being on the defensive grants certain strategic advantages. Like the Union in the American Civil War, your aggressor has to work to compel you, otherwise he will lose by default. As the defender you have more control over the situation than the aggressor, because you have no pressing objective except to survive, and you can make the aggressor's job as difficult as you want. The very fact that he has to outdo you gives you strategic options, and the side with the most options usually wins. In the Second World War, the United Kingdom, the Soviet Union, and the United States took bruises at first, but rallied together and launched brutal counter-attacks on Nazi Germany from two opposing fronts. Both sides took heavy losses, most of all the Soviet Union, but were willing to do so for the sake of freedom and to repel the very real existential threat that Nazi Germany posed. In the Vietnam War, the United States was actually on the verge of exhausting the North Vietnamese of resources, until General Võ Nguyên Giáp saw that public support for the war in America was on the wane, and used the Tet Offensive to cast an image in the American mass media that the war was far from over. The offensive was actually a huge gamble and took a heavy toll on the North Vietnamese, but it produced enough political pressure to convince the Americans to leave.

When an enemy attacks you, he naturally exposes himself on a weak salient. He shows his hand early, hoping that you will submit quietly and not have enough time to recognise his true intentions. In either of the twentieth-century conflicts mentioned above, the aggressor used shock tactics in their early waves of attack. This strategy, while intended to show strength and power, is actually always a gamble, the risk being that the early attack is not strong enough to frighten the defender into submission. Hitler and Rommel's blitzkreig attack worked on France at the outbreak of war, but it did not work on the armies of the western Allies or the Soviet Union. Keeping a calm head, General Dwight D. Eisenhower saw that a blitz offence always exposes a weak rear, and used it to bait Germany's aggressive Panzer divisions into what he called his "Meat Grinder." On the Soviet side, Joseph Stalin did what all Russian leaders on the defensive do best: forestall the invading force for long enough to mobilise the country's enormous population towards a vicious winter counter-attack. Stalin's Red Army could absorb the attacks for long enough to force the German invaders into an unpleasant war of attrition that Hitler was too arrogant to prepare them for. This is the result that *all* aggressors fear, regardless of culture or geography.

While a firm, decisive counter-attack can be effective in putting aggressors on the defensive, you should also take steps to prevent attacks from happening in the first place. If a potential aggressor looks at you and sees a strong, proud person with lots of allies, then he will think twice before starting an offensive or give up the idea altogether and find a weaker target, of which there are usually plenty. The strategies in this book lay out an array of proven methods for gathering strong allies, building a competent and conscientious team, and gathering a support network, all of which make up a formidable defence to ward off potential attackers. If you have such a strong network around you, then any attack on you risks the very real possibility of a fight with your entire network. This is the strategic value of military alliances: If you're in a three-person game, then it's much more effective for two of you to team up against the now-isolated remaining player than engage in a bloody free-for-all. Friends may abandon you when times get tough, but that's never really inside your control; all you can do is ensure that you're paying enough attention to your allies to maximise the probability that they'll stick by you, and those are your real friends.

From the 1980s up to the late 2000s, Bernie Madoff made use of his unshakeable reputation when faced with inquiries into his Ponzi scheme. Because he had provided investment "returns" on such a reliable, consistent basis for so many decades, and built such a strong network of allies in the Jewish community over that time, his friends and clients angrily denied any suggestion that he was doing something wrong. Madoff emphasised a loyal family culture inside his firm, and chose new employees who would most readily respond to that culture, even though he guarded his investment "strategy" with secrecy. The federal authorities investigated Madoff's operation *six times* and found no evidence of wrongdoing. Each time investigators visited Madoff, he charmed them with his friendly manners and confident command of his field in conversation. If clients asked to withdraw their funds, they received a cheque in the mail soon

after, without question. It both looked and felt like a proper
Wall Street investment firm.

When an accountant named Harry Markopolos looked
into Madoff's trades and reported that they were impossible,
he was correct in his analysis, but he often treated federal
investigators with a condescending tone, and later became
paranoid about his safety for turning in such a reputable
figure. This nervous, jittery, and socially awkward accountant
didn't stand a chance against the ironclad reputation of a
confident Wall Street giant. During the 2008 financial crisis
clients asked for their funds back and, like all Ponzi schemes,
Madoff's accounts ran out of money and the truth finally
came out. If someone running an audaciously large con can
use this principle to his advantage for decades on end, then
so can you.

In the modern social realm, attacks are unlikely to be
violent. Unwilling to risk ostracisation—and obvious legal
penalties—we have learned to criticise others in the most
oblique manner possible. Giving firm counter-blows to such
attacks makes us seem mad, which can help ward off attacks
in some situations, but more often damages our reputation
in the long run. Despite this new, elusive form of attack, we
feel their effects in hurt emotions and spend months rumi-
nating over the smallest, often inconsequential comments. If
you feel someone giving you oblique criticism, don't get
emotional or show your defensiveness. Some aggressive types
give such barbs on purpose to test for sore points, so reacting
emotionally is to give them what they want. Instead, it is
sometimes better to take a mental note of that person's toxic
nature, dismissing their attack as something not worth your
valuable attention. If the aggressor persists with their jibes,
then feel free to give it right back, but only in a humorous,
light-spirited manner. You show that you're neither a
pushover nor easily provoked into defensive anger. This is

also a good approach to take when you're on the receiving end of aggressive, tyrannical energy from a superior at work. If you think their criticisms of you are unfair, then don't just roll over and take them. Without being rude or disrespectful, calmly explain why you think they're wrong, giving examples where possible. In doing so you skilfully defend yourself without risking your job, and your boss will look at you with greater respect.

Earning the respect of both your enemies and allies alike is the real lesson from this chapter. The ability to display your strength in a fashion measured to the circumstances will go a long way to preventing aggressors from taking advantage of you. Often, doing this passively with a strong support network can work just as well and save you the risk of a costly blow to your reputation. But don't be afraid to hurt your enemy when necessary by jabbing them in one of their sore points. If this makes you uncomfortable, then don't think this strategy makes you a bad or aggressive person; just see it as a measure taken temporarily and in a posture of self-defence. Don't be afraid to recognise and integrate your more aggressive side.

> Whenever you and your enemy defend a common border, if they make incursions to plunder and disrupt your settlers in the contiguous region, you can establish ambushes at critical points and erect obstacles to block and intercept them. Then the enemy will not recklessly advance. A tactical principle from *The Art of War* states, "What can cause the enemy not to come forth is the prospect of harm."
>
> — THE TSO CHUAN

REVERSAL

The most important reversal to this chapter is the great risk of becoming addicted to the aggressive, polarising counter-attacks that deterrence strategies often require. If you don't pick your battles wisely, you'll launch a counter-offensive against someone with a mean streak, and you'll wish you hadn't poked the bear so carelessly. Whether you go down as a martyr is your choice, but consider whether temporarily yielding to such a strong foe would keep you alive to fight another day when you've gathered up a sufficiently strong base of support. There is no wisdom in offending the wrong person, so make sure you know your foe. Lee's aggressive attacks on the Union armies in the Virginia Peninsula worked because of McClellan's cautious nature—above all, the Union general was a scheming politician out for his own personal glory, not a brave warrior like Ulysses S. Grant or William T. Sherman, and Lee took advantage of that. You should also note the situation you're in: in wartime, anything goes; but in peacetime, you need to consider your long-term wellbeing. The Socially Intelligent Warrior doesn't rattle her sabre for the mere sake of it, because she knows the good faith of her allies is far more important.

13

PETER THIEL AND GAWKER

BAIT RASH ENEMIES INTO COSTLY ATTACKS

R *ather than needlessly bloody yourself fighting strong enemies, use their aggression to your advantage. Appear weak, like an easy prey. Dangle valuable prizes in front of them. Feed their natural feelings of arrogance and grandiosity. Let them come to the battle ill-prepared. By baiting a rash enemy, you encourage him to charge forward on lines of your own choosing, and you therefore gain a form of indirect power over the conflict. Blinded by their fury and eagerness for an easy victory, they will make themselves look scrappy, impetuous, and antagonistic, saying or doing things that damage their social standing within the group. Confident, aggressive enemies look for fights, opportunities to show their strengths. Learn to manipulate this hostile tendency of theirs, and you will always control them.*

THE DEADLY TRAP

In December 2007, the media blog Gawker published one of its biggest scoops of the year. In a short blog post it claimed that Peter Thiel, the billionaire investor in both PayPal and

Facebook, was gay. The news itself didn't come as a complete shock to everyone who read the blog post—the reclusive investor's sexuality had been an open secret in Silicon Valley for a long time. But Thiel had always kept his sexuality to himself, not seeing it as relevant to his work or his network of friendships. He could not help but feel humiliated. Not only had Gawker failed to notify Thiel of the upcoming post, they had thickly laid their trademark snark in the post's title: "Peter Thiel is totally gay, people." The post's writer ostensibly used it as an opportunity to congratulate Thiel on his immense business success, but Thiel saw it differently: Gawker had no right to out people; that right was a personal privilege exclusive to them alone, when they were ready. He couldn't let them get away with such callous cruelty. He wanted revenge.

Between 2008 and 2011, Thiel brooded over his outing and considered his options. He wanted to do something about Gawker for its propensity to embarrass both public and private figures, and he wasn't alone. Gawker, and its founder Nick Denton, had naturally made a lot of enemies. Thiel's friends talked to him about directly suing Gawker, but he knew this would be a lost cause. Gawker, and other media outlets, enjoyed strong protection under America's First Amendment—the right to free speech was enshrined in the US Constitution, and Gawker had used it to defeat the dozens of lawsuits it faced from the angry people it had so callously humiliated in its blog pieces. Also, getting into a fight with a media outlet would make Thiel look petty, and Gawker would likely double down in finding and posting more embarrassing details about Thiel's private life, as it had done in other lawsuits. Thiel wanted revenge on Gawker, but the odds seemed stacked against him.

After coming to terms with the fact that direct retribution would be unlikely, Thiel decided on a new strategy. He used a team of lawyers and investigative journalists to sift through Gawker's blog posts, searching for any hint of legal wrongdoing. They avoided any potential cases that Gawker could defend under the First Amendment, looking instead to other forms of legal wrongdoing. One such area was the right to privacy, namely where the infringement of that individual's right had caused them damages. Thiel was sure that his team could find a suitable case that could stand up in court, and when they did, they would fight that case tooth and nail, sinking whatever resources it took to hurt Gawker.

In 2012, one such case raised its head, and it was the best yet. Gawker published a sex tape of Terry Bollea, better known as the professional wrestler Hulk Hogan. Without his knowledge or consent, Bollea had been recorded having sex with his best friend's wife, and the footage had somehow found its way into Gawker's hands. Mortified by the publication of the tape, Bollea issued a cease-and-desist order that Gawker arrogantly brushed off, claiming that because Bollea was a public figure, his concerns weren't warranted.

Watching all of this unfold, Thiel and his team knew it was the perfect opportunity. Cases brought to court based on privacy were much less challenging than those based on free speech, and according to Thiel's legal experts, being a celebrity did not necessarily preclude Bollea from the right to privacy, especially since he did not know of the recording. Thiel knew that Gawker had become brash and overconfident in its many legal victories, and likely wouldn't properly prepare itself for a right-to-privacy suit. His team soon contacted Bollea and offered to fund his case against Gawker. Bollea, feeling powerless against this bullying media machine, was grateful for the help and did not want to ask questions—all the better, since Thiel wanted no one to find out about his involvement.

Several years passed as the case developed, and Thiel's

team found various other suits to support in the meantime. This included a workers' strike by Gawker's unpaid interns, which spoiled the company's image and resulted in a huge payout to these employees, and on top this, a scandal over one of its bloggers lending sexual favours for positive video game reviews. Both caused valuable advertisers to pull their accounts, costing the company millions of dollars in revenue. Thiel's private support allowed these scandalous and expensive issues to grow, with the effect of making Gawker's Nick Denton feel like attacks were coming from many sides all at once. The combined public outrage and legal liabilities became such a problem for Gawker that Denton was forced to reprimand several of his bloggers for their careless escapades. But new crises inevitably arose after these same bloggers continued to write libellous posts, sometimes even openly bragging on the website about their confidence in winning the Bollea case. Gawker's internal system of ranking and paying its bloggers according to the page views their pieces generated only incentivised more and more outrageous content—integrity and accuracy became less important than getting the biggest scoop first. Denton could hardly control this system—it was the very mechanism that earned the bulk of Gawker's revenues, and it was moving faster than ever before.

Throughout these crises, Denton remained blasé about the Bollea case. Gawker had fought off such cases before, and they believed Bollea had limited financial resources. Surely he was running low on funds by now? They could draw the case out until he ran out of resources and force him to accept a face-saving financial settlement on their terms. Not only that, but all the other crises facing Gawker distracted Denton—he didn't have time to look into a case that he saw as open-and-shut.

Back in 2013, during the case's first major depositions, the blogger who had posted the sex tape openly expressed contempt, even bewilderment that the case could proceed that far, and by now his colleagues' attitudes had barely changed—they felt untouchable.

But then, in 2016, Bollea gained a ruling that allowed him to sue Gawker for $100,000,000 in damages, and *Bollea v. Gawker* would go before a jury in Florida, Bollea's home state. This came as a surprising blow to Gawker. Why hadn't their lawyers been able to shut down the suit? Denton felt confused about Bollea's insistence on pursuing what he saw as a lost cause, doubling down in his belief that he didn't owe the washed-up wrestling star a penny. But he could not ignore the feelings of caution he had developed in the years of growing scandals. On the eve of the court case, Gawker's lawyers offered Bollea a settlement of $10,000,000, one tenth of the proposed damages, without the promise of a public apology. Bollea turned the offer down without hesitation, having gained a renewed fervour to win the case once and for all.

As soon as the trial began, Gawker found itself on the ropes. This case would be nothing like the First Amendment cases it had so arrogantly blown away in metropolitan New York. In the small-sized Florida courtroom, Bollea's team came prepared with printed visuals and well-practised technical displays. In one example, it showed all the gory details of "That Type of Girl Deserves It," a Gawker-published sex tape of a young woman that the website had refused to take down, in spite of her emotional protests. Gawker's lawyers had seemingly not bothered to prepare a coherent case, with evidence not displaying correctly on the courtroom's ancient AV system. Confident Gawker journalists smirked on the witness stand, acting as if the case was one big joke.

But worse, they had failed to recognise the significance of the court case being held in Florida. The jury, all salt-of-the-earth Floridians, revered their local heroes. When Gawker's lawyers and journalists tried to defend their snarky headlines and sex tapes of private individuals behind abstract notions of free speech, all the jury saw was a bunch of arrogant, dismissive city people dragging their beloved hero's name through the mud and trying to get away with it scot-free.

The jury ruled all the case's counts in Bollea's favour, awarding him $140,000,000 in damages. Bollea cried as they read out the result, his long-fought battle so strongly vindicated by his local community and his pride finally restored. The ruling forced Denton to shut Gawker down and declare bankruptcy, selling off his company's assets piece by piece. The powerful media empire now lay in ruins, with little time for Denton to understand what had caused such a precipitous downfall.

Behind the scenes, far away in California, Thiel watched on with a quiet satisfaction. He had brilliantly outmanoeuvred his foe, leading it towards its own utter destruction.

INTERPRETATION

Peter Thiel had good reason to feel angry. Gawker had publicly humiliated him, and it seemed like he had no method of recourse. So many others in the same situation had tried and failed to take the media empire head-on, getting caught up in ugly legal battles that emptied their wallets and soiled their reputations. But Thiel was far more strategic in his approach. After years of experience leading and investing in successful companies, he had learned that rationality and an objective perspective always worked better than succumbing to emotions. By investing in a wide range of *others'* lawsuits against Gawker, each stronger than his own due to nuances in American law, Thiel could help less wealthy people gain some legal representation. But perhaps more important to his overall goal, this would enable Thiel to attack his enemy on multiple fronts. This not only disoriented and disturbed Gawker's owner Nick Denton, it also distracted him from paying attention to the most important fight: Terry Bollea's.

Thiel and his team knew that Gawker had become confident in its ability to win legal battles. Even though the company had made many powerful enemies, it continued to embarrass people for the sake of page views. Desperate to win status and prestige within the company's publications, Gawker's bloggers sought more and more scandalous headlines. This system of incentives drove the machine faster than Denton could keep track, each new smear campaign providing fresh material for Bollea's lawsuit. None of Gawker's team took the lawsuit seriously, imagining that Bollea was merely making some last-ditch attempt to regain some of his former glory. Gawker saw Bollea as a washed-up star, and looked down upon the jurors who would rule on the case. They threw disgracefully low settlement offers at him, not realising the affront this would cause. Rather than seeing the situation objectively as Thiel had so brilliantly done from the start, Gawker saw it as an irritation to shoo away, and acted with genuine bewilderment when it persisted. Rather than being dazzled by their arguments on free speech as Gawker's lawyers expected, the local jurors thought, "Who the hell do these city people think they are?" In its hubris, Gawker acted with petulance at every opportunity, completely failing to recognise the critical importance of winning the jury's hearts and minds. Thiel lured Gawker right into the jaws of a deadly ambush, and the Florida jury punished them for their arrogance.

Enemies like Gawker are more common in life than you

might think. Unable to control their base emotions, they easily fall for tricks and ruses, particularly those which seem to confirm their pre-existing biases. Gawker saw the Bollea case as yet another angry celebrity who, if made to wait for long enough, would give up or run out of resources. They did not understand Bollea's determination to win the case, nor that behind him stood a similarly determined backer with near limitless resources. Gawker failed to see the situation objectively due to their own delusions, their stubborn refusal to treat the case as legitimate enough to warrant their proper attention. Thiel successfully doubled this effect by distracting them with a series of pinprick attacks on all sides —the unpaid interns, and the multiple scandals about its journalistic ethics. It virtually guaranteed that his foe would have neither the inclination nor the energy to give the Bollea case its proper attention.

If a boss or a co-worker has made you feel angry or resentful, stop this emotion from taking complete hold of you. Like Thiel, take a step back and assess the situation as a grand campaign. Measure the enemy's strengths and weaknesses—for Gawker, its strengths lay in its massive following and its First Amendment protection, while its weaknesses lay in its proclivity to cause expensive scandals and make dangerous enemies. Stop getting emotional about their behaviour and instead observe what they're trying to do—in particular, you must identify what they most respond to, what activates *their* emotions, what gets *them* to act without objective thought. Rather than being constantly tyrannised by their aggressive behaviour, you channel it to serve your own purposes. You take the front foot and gain control of the situation, a strategic position you should seek at all times. As Thiel showed, sometimes you can do this without ever showing your form, instead creating a widely dispersed smokescreen that distracts them, heightening their sense of tension and making them lose all sense of rational proportion. Creating an asymmetry of rationality between you and the enemy is always far more effective than any asymmetry in outer strength.

KEYS TO SOCIAL INTELLIGENCE

In modern workplaces there is often a colleague who gets his or her way through sheer aggression. Such anxiety-inducing individuals cause resentment and even unrest after joining an environment that used to be stable. They come full of new ideas and try to change all the existing procedures, while putting pressure on people to deliver results at a faster pace than they're used to. To managers, such staff seem like a dream come true—they work hard, they're proactive, and for a short while they appear to get everyone working more efficiently. But it doesn't take a student of Social Intelligence to spot the hidden, negative effects of such abrasive colleagues. What at first appears like heightened productivity soon turns into a decline in communication, resistance to procedures that are cheap and easy for managers to monitor but difficult for workers to use, and a gradual destruction in quality output as the most skilled workers correctly decide to leave for less oppressive environments. As a student of Social Intelligence you understand that such aggressive types are a toxic influence on organisations.

How can we deal with such types? In earlier chapters we have explored several approaches: becoming unfightable, by assuming the application of a polite, friendly, and formless front to confuse and nullify an attacker's blows; and becoming a dangerous, aggressive defender in your own right, by developing a strong reputation for competence and reciprocity, unafraid to launch effective counter-attacks when necessary. In this chapter, we will extend our application of Social Intelligence to the strategic realm by exploring the art of the baited ambush, a technique used since the dawn of organised warfare. If an enemy was strong but acted out of impulse, then a general would lure an enticing piece of bait, perhaps exposing some small portion of their force. The enemy, unable to resist, charges headlong at the bait only to expose themselves on a weak salient. The defending general lets loose his hidden forces, ambushing the impulsive foe from all sides, usually a complete annihilation if the ambushing forces are strong enough, and enough terrified surprise is induced in the aggressor's heart. You can see the strong parallels in this pattern with the fate that Gawker faced after wandering blithely into a trap of their own.

In 714 BC, the ancient Chinese kingdom of Jung invaded the neighbouring kingdom of Cheng. The Duke of Cheng had an army constituted mainly of horsed chariots, and offered small, pinprick attacks against the invaders. These chariot forces were fast and mobile, but could not hold their own in pitched battles against the Jung infantry. Though Cheng's guerrilla-like defence was effective at first, it now seemed that these invaders were only getting angrier and fiercer, making wild charges and wiping out many of the defenders. To the Duke of Cheng, the Jung army were just a rabble of barbarians, but he nevertheless felt nervous at the path of destruction they were causing. An advisor told the duke that since the Jung were frustrated and eager for a battle, they should send a small force to provoke the invaders and then flee into a shallow ravine. The Cheng men appearing cornered, the overconfident Jung would surely charge in, ripe for a flank attack by a hidden Cheng force. The duke agreed, and the plan prevailed, as a meagre Cheng infantry force destroyed the trapped and terrified

Jung men. Learning of this decisive battle, all other invading barbarian contingents fled from Cheng with great haste.

The baited ambush is one of our oldest tricks, yet it continues to work to this day. That is because we humans have a natural tendency to focus on the details at the expense of the wider picture. We get caught into thought patterns that consume our minds, sometimes distorting our picture of reality. When we finally see something that seems to confirm our biases, we leap after it in hot pursuit, like a hungry hunter-gatherer on the search for a juicy meal. Unfortunately, the simple and predictable prey that our ancestors hunted are no longer par for the course—instead, we live in a complex social world with hidden dynamics that seem confusing and contradictory from the outside. When our same hunter-gatherer brains rush us into a thoughtless charge at our ostensible prey, we now face humiliation and social ostracism. One rash snap at your boss can get you fired, and perhaps all it took to provoke you was some small injury to your ego. This readiness of ours to expose ourselves to injury is the reason why the baited ambush is, and always will be, a horribly effective technique for teaching brash opponents a lesson.

This technique's results vary with the type of opponent you are facing. A mature, stoic, and strategic opponent is worst suited, since they are unlikely to rise to your bait and will likely see through your intentions straight away, and then plot a counter-move now that you have so foolishly exposed yourself. Instead, you must seek those who are most easily riled up, who operate in a near constant state of tension, and possess an unusually high degree of orderliness. This person expects the world to fit into their narrow set of ideals, and will furiously work to correct any observed perturbations before you're likely to even register them. Such individuals are useful in organisations, because they keep on top of their tasks and are rarely caught napping. But their low threshold for disgust is also their biggest weakness. They believe that everything at work should only be about productivity, imagining a sterile environment devoid of chaos. But reality constantly impedes such fantasies. Overcome with deep emotion when reality doesn't conform to their expectations, they act out in ways that often irritate others, even making enemies in the long term. Reality is constantly changing and chaotic, manifesting in ways that no human can predict or contain. It is not reasonable to expect all events—particularly those caused by human beings—to conform to some abstract management paradigm that has only been proven to work in a few select cases.

It is natural to feel powerless when this type tries to bully you into following their idealistic fantasies. Say you have been doing your job for years and have become quite efficient at doing it. But this person demands that you follow some new paradigm, not from any experience, but from a purely theoretical source. When you express your concerns, citing your long experience, they will show the latent aggression they try so hard to hide, citing the logic behind their suggestion, accusing you of being obtuse and fighting progress. This can be quite a frightening experience if you're not used to conflict. They claim to want what's best for the company, so shouldn't you swallow your gut instincts and do what they say?

Understand that while you should give time to the new ideas people propose, you do not have to accept suggestions that go against your experience. Over the course of your career, you will develop a keen sense of what works in your field and what doesn't, so never allow someone inexperienced in your field to pummel you with rigorous—and completely abstract—logic. Although your intuitive grasp of your field might be hard to elaborate in words, particularly when under attack from a fast talker, know that this intuitive understanding is something very real. There is nothing productive in letting yourself become blown about by those with no practical experience in your field.

It is always best to explain your opinions through practically grounded examples and results, but sometimes this is not enough for aggressive idealisers. They will continue to fight for their cause, perhaps out of sheer stubbornness or a bruised ego. In such situations, you must never allow resentment or anxiety to cloud your mind. They will only guide you into snap reactions that make you (and consequently your ideas) look ridiculous, making it easier for the aggressors to discredit anything you might later come up with. Instead, realise that as the defender, you have a great deal of untapped invisible power at your disposal. By politely yet firmly declining a colleague's ideas, thoroughly taking it apart point-by-point, you are retaining a professional business-minded manner in a way that will infuriate the aggressive idealiser. They are used to inducing anger and other chaotic emotions in others through their quick thinking, but are ill-prepared for calm counter-attacks delivered with a smile. Your total reversal of their bullying tactics will catch them off guard, and your refusal to accept their demands will make them rant and rave to the boss. Unimpressed with these blind tirades about you, an experienced professional who explains their points politely and thoroughly, the boss gives the aggressor a verbal thrashing of his own. Not only that, the rest of the team will see their behaviour and turn away from them, making them isolated and devoid of allies. You will have completely outmanoeuvred a bully with little more than a polite manner and a calm trust in your results-oriented and time-tested ideas.

This tactic is not to be reserved only for the aggressive idealiser—it works on one and all, but particularly those prone to hammering their ideas through by force. Most people naturally avoid conflict, and the aggressor often gets used to receiving no resistance at all, further emboldening them while growing more fragile themselves. They expect easy victories and, as described in previous chapters, you can surprise a bully with a firm counter-strike that upsets their balance, making them leave you alone. But sometimes it is wise to reverse this policy, instead making yourself look simple, even rather stupid. Ask questions that make you seem a little slow without damaging your professional reputation too much, and express glowing awe at things that are rather base and simplistic. This alone will make you seem less threatening and earn you some unexpected friends from the group, particularly the more insecure types prone to envy. The bullies, however, will see you as a ripe target for exploitation, and this is something you want—see it as bringing them out of the woodwork. As you goad them into further attacks through the façade of happy-go-lucky politeness you show, your aggressor will look even more terrible for attacking someone seemingly so helpless, and you'll be surprised at how quickly your friends will ride in to your defence. A friendly, harmless front will double the effect of the baited ambush—a kind of passive force multiplier.

Napoleon used this same passive force multiplier in his rise to dominance over most of Europe. In November 1805, the newly crowned emperor had recently wiped out the Austrian army in the Ulm Campaign through a series of brilliant flanking manoeuvres, capturing the prized city of Vienna. But the Austrians had recently secured reinforcements from Russia, who were now on their way. Desperate to defeat the Third Coalition once and for all, Napoleon moved his forces north to the strategically valuable Pratzen Heights and then suddenly retreated. Then, Russian delegates sent to meet him were most shocked to see an anxious Napoleon making suggestions of a negotiated peace. To the Allies, this behaviour seemed bizarre, most unlike Napoleon's usual confidence. Why had he suddenly changed his tone? Why would he abandon such a strong defensive position? The only explanation for the emperor's erratic behaviour was that the long month of battles in the Ulm Campaign had taken a severe toll on his Grande Armée (this was in fact true, as Napoleon's army was exhausted and near mutiny) and his political position in France, where the people clamoured for peace.

The Allies had seen enough: they had a distinct numerical advantage, this seemed to be their best opportunity at stopping the French conqueror and, more importantly, that the remaining European monarchies could defeat this Corsican upstart, and so they charged forward to meet the remaining French forces massed near the town of Austerlitz in the modern-day Czech Republic.

As they got closer, they realised that Napoleon had appeared to leave his right flank weak, a juicy target they could not help but exploit—and they advanced right into the trap. To their horror, two more French corps led by Marshals Davout and Soult viciously attacked the Allies' rear that now lay exposed. The surprise attack destroyed the bulk of the Allied army, and the rest fled in an embarrassing rout. By presenting a weak front, Napoleon had lured a desperate, angry foe into a deadly trap with the prospect of an easy battle. To this day we rightly consider the Battle of Austerlitz one of the most masterful victories of modern history, and it shows the overtly forceful application of this chapter.

The baited ambush has also become a valued tool in the less overtly aggressive world of politics and social activism. In his 1971 book *Rules for Radicals*, Saul D. Alinsky explains that grassroots campaigners can exert authority over the establishment by goading them into overreactions. Alinsky cites various examples from recent American history, particularly the civil rights movement of the late 1950s and early 1960s. Black Americans wanted to change the practice of segregation throughout the South, but direct violence against law enforcement and the community would have been suicidal, and only confirmed existing prejudices. Instead, anti-segregation campaigners focused their efforts on peaceful resistance, such as Rosa Parks boarding a segregated bus and sitting in the rows marked "whites only."

These peaceful protests provoked a violent reaction from police and counter-protesters, all of which were famously photographed, recorded, and displayed for all to see on the nation's media. Americans opened the newspaper and switched on the television news to see the police setting vicious attack dogs on innocent black women and white lynch-mobs proudly standing above the charred, mutilated remains of their murdered victims. Horrified by what they saw, the American people demanded firm political and legal action to bring segregation and other race-based laws to an end, leading to a series of new federal laws expressly forbidding any form of racial discrimination in housing, education, or voting rights. The leaders of the civil rights movement achieved their goals by provoking a reaction that would show how they were the innocent victims of a brutal establishment.

Alinsky distils this strategy of provocation into his book's central maxim: "The action is in the reaction." Let us unpack this maxim and express it more explicitly with the following: The power you exert over others with the baited ambush lies precisely in the rash behaviour that you provoke through the use of passive resistance. The wider community observes all of this, horrified at the rash—often violent—response, and the clamour for change becomes stronger as the aggressors isolate themselves.

What makes this seem different from the overtly forceful

side, as demonstrated by Napoleon in the Battle of Austerlitz, is that the wider community's clamour for change is the "ambush." But as a Socially Intelligent Warrior, you understand that in the social realm, this passive form of violence exerted in the form of isolating the foe *is a precise analogue of the overtly violent move*. Ostracised and removed from the social group, the fooled aggressor has no choice but to either swallow his pride and repent his sins or "starve" in the wilderness—for our ancestors, this was literally the case. Wielding your sword in this manner, when called for, in a temporary and defensive posture, *improves* your own social standing within the group while eliminating an anxiety-inducing enemy force. It is the very height of Social Intelligence.

> I guess a man is the only kind of varmint who sets his own trap, baits it, and then steps in it.
>
> — JOHN STEINBECK

REVERSAL

Never fall into the trap of believing that you are the only person who knows how to use the baited ambush tactic—it is one of the oldest tricks in the book. The modern world is full of passive aggressors who are masters at pulling you down into their own games with emotional tricks. Try your new passive power strategies on these types, and you'll find yourself in a whirlpool of your own making. Remember that this chapter is about baiting *rash* enemies, not those with a penchant for strategy. It is always better to assume a posture of forthrightness first in any interaction, only pulling your gloves off when the circumstances call for such measures. There is nothing strategic about picking your victims indiscriminately, or activating a reaction you can't handle or control. Be careful with pushing the emotional buttons of the wrong person, someone strongly established with a wide power base—in such cases it is better to bow, retreat to the shadows, and plan a more subversive approach.

14

STRATEGIES FOR SOCIAL WARFARE

*A*lthough we try our best to build relationships and develop positive attitudes in the groups we lead, there are times when it is necessary to go to war. There are several indirect strategies you can use on your enemy, each one tested by centuries of human conflict: constrict his lifeline, cloud his vision with contradictory signals, and isolate him from his support base. These approaches yield horribly effective results, without the need for costly frontal assaults that only hurt you in the long run. Never go to war for its own sake; see the martial stance as a temporary posture to assume when your enemies have given you no choice. Do not shrink from smiting the enemy if he fails to show good faith and threatens everything you hold dear. Never fall victim to the softening, seductive encouragements for pacifism, lest you fall victim to one of these strategies yourself—there is nothing safer than possessing the will to put up a stout fight.

THE ART OF SOCIAL WAR

So far in this section we have described the need for indirectness in the social realm, and how we can use it to keep enemies at bay or trick them into rash attacks. As narrated in Chapter 11, Zhou Enlai used his charming personal manner and political mastery to fight enemies in the most oblique manner possible, all while gaining great popularity with the Chinese people. In Chapter 12, we saw how Robert E. Lee kept a series of larger and better-supplied Union forces at bay with aggressive counterattacks. Chapter 13 showed how the investor Peter Thiel tamed his emotions and stepped back to orchestrate a grand campaign against his foe, baiting the wild media publication company Gawker into rash mistakes that it paid for with its own existence. In each case, a master strategist saw beyond the simple act of fighting frontally, using their understanding of human nature to survive and even thrive.

Having grounded ourselves in the arts of indirection, we will now turn our attention to the specifics of warfare in the social realm. Far from being a contradiction in terms, anyone who works in a modern office setting can recognise the similarities to the old aristocratic court, with its intrigues providing endless daily stress and anxiety for people who just want to get on with their work. We support our leaders in creating the Ideal Team State (described in Chapter 8), but we must nevertheless hold a deep understanding of the moves required to keep ourselves alive should the need for them arise. To the young and inexperienced student of Social Intelligence, the modern workplace is both frightening and subversive. This chapter will arm you with a set of specific methods tested across countless human conflicts. It will also reveal the kind of moves that others may try to use on you, and the historical examples will help you to recognise the common behaviour patterns that such warlike aggressors will show. Take heart in the knowledge that any time you are threatened by a bullying colleague or enemy, you have a playbook filled with schemes that are as easy to learn as they are brutally effective.

Constrict the enemy's lifeline. Many people who like to study historical battles often pay most attention to the wonderful encircling manoeuvres of Napoleon or the flank attacks of Robert E. Lee. They focus on the dramatic crescendo of the fight between two competitors, completely ignoring the grim realities of waging a war. But this is the clearest mark of an armchair general. Real-life military leaders are far more concerned about the timely and efficient upkeep of their troops—the logistical supply line. Just as there is no good in advancing your army into a region where they can't get food, water, or other supplies, there is no sense in engaging in a costly battle with a colleague if you have bigger problems to worry about, like your job being at risk or your car breaking down. On the whole these issues are a lot more urgent, and if they become too much, then you decide to conserve your energy, retreat from petty battles at work, and reassess your priorities.

This natural hierarchy of priorities gives us a devilishly effective weapon to use against others. If we're engaged in a fight with a particularly toxic foe and all other bridge-building tactics have failed, then befriending someone they trust or depend upon can dampen their resolve. If you're fighting on a larger scale, with a competing company who threatens your market share, then converting their most valued customers and employees over to your side both weakens their foundations while strengthening yours. Other-wise, if they depend upon some key asset or resource, then cutting off their access to it can provide a swift and deadly blow that knocks them out of the fight without any need for costly battles. All of these tactics conform to the same core pattern: striking whatever the enemy most relies upon and, if possible, making use of it yourself. As well as severely restricting a very real part of the enemy's lifeline, damaging his ability to live, let alone fight, you also make him slowly realise that you're the type of foe who studies for an enemy's weaknesses and isn't afraid to strike at them. If your enemy is an aggressive bully, then the cold rationality you show by using this strategy will frighten him to death.

If you're not sure what the enemy covets, then strike different parts and see what he defends the most fiercely. During the Second World War, the Allies knew that the Nazi leader Adolf Hitler feared invasions via the resource-rich Balkans to the south, and Norway to the north, and losing these key entry points to Europe could spell disaster for the already thinly spread Axis armies. Strategic bombing campaigns and a series of fake invasion plans "leaked" by the Allies across these regions confirmed Hitler's fears, and he dispersed many thousands of troops across wide stretches of territory, moving them away from critical battles in the Soviet Union and elsewhere. Both Winston Churchill and Dwight D. Eisenhower also knew Hitler to be a paranoid leader, often known to rejoice when his suspicions were proven true. A proud, paranoid enemy is always ripe for this strategy— the mere suggestion of a threat to a piece of his soft underbelly will cause him unbearable anxiety.

Cloud the enemy's vision with unclear and contradictory signals. Just as we watch our enemies for clues of their intentions and future behaviour, they are also watching us. If we're too clumsy in our actions, blabbing our intentions to anyone who'll listen, we'll only enable these enemies to accurately predict our own future plans. To fight the shrewd and focused with such a careless attitude is no better than suicide. Present your enemies with a confusing front that betrays no clear future action, and they will be forced to disperse their forces in order to cover all of the possible scenarios, none of which appear like the obvious route. When you do strike a part of your enemy's line, they will be so thinly spread that your advance will be easy, and the enemy leadership doubly afraid of your ability to reach out and attack from the murky fog of war. An unclear front created by the use of various contradictory signals will grant you as many options as you desire.

Continuing our example from the Second World War, the Allied plans for their European invasion involved sending the Axis powers a series of contradictory signals, in order to maximise the effectiveness of the Normandy landings of June 1944. Hitler, now doubly paranoid after multiple assassination attempts from his high command, mistrusted even his most able officers. The Allies were able to exploit the Führer's arrogance and paranoia with a mass deception campaign, codenamed Operation Fortitude, that made him believe an invasion would occur at the Pas de Calais rather than at Normandy. The crossing to Calais would be the shortest possible route from the English coast, and numerous pieces of intelligence gathered from German spies seemed to confirm this would be case. One officer, whom they deeply distrusted, reported that an invasion of Normandy was imminent, likely occurring on 6 June. To Hitler and his high command, this seemed like proof that the invasion would occur on any day *except* 6 June, and in any other place, when in fact they were staring at the truth. Reports came in of the Allied forces' second-in-command Bernard Montgomery being sighted far away in Gibraltar, which made the idea of an imminent invasion seem even less likely (secretly the man was actually a deliberate lookalike of Montgomery). Another captured German officer was moved past the real invasion force massing in the county of Sussex, but deliberately misinformed that he was moving through the south-east county of Kent, a highly likely place to spring an invasion of Calais.

Although Allied troops faced stiff resistance across the Normandy beaches when the invasion finally occurred, particularly the Americans at Omaha Beach, the combined invading force advanced miles into French territory within the first few days. A well-planned campaign of misdirection enabled the Allies to break into Hitler's Europe and change the course of the war.

Just as the Allies weaved a blend of fact and fiction into their deception campaign, you must not be too obvious in your mixed signals. We humans have evolved to spot small perturbations and ignore the background noise, and so a sufficient amount of dull, mundane reality is necessary in the signals you give off. When presented with a front that seems both contradictory and with no obvious slant, your enemies will have no clue what you'll do next. There is a temptation to spin elaborate yarns, but these only come from a place of ego and self-absorption—never forget that the primary goal is to *misdirect* your enemies, not impress them. The most successful poker players often use a bland, unreadable face that the other competitors can't interpret, since a typically emotional response to a great hand of cards will ring alarm bells and put everyone on their guard. Mislead people with your intentions, be vague about your plans, and you will face anxious, mentally exhausted enemies who are forced to account for a hundred different options—it is the height of strategy.

Open an inner front. As described in earlier chapters, a group's leader often faces more opposition from inside her own camp than from her ostensible competitors outside it. Deliberately fomenting such dissent and tumult, often through infiltration, sabotage, or targeted propaganda, is known in military circles as opening an inner front. Creating a line of conflict that actually lies inside the enemy's structure creates all sort of annoying problems that gradually corrupt his operational effectiveness to the point where his efforts become completely unmanageable. When you understand that a toxic employee placed at an appropriate position in your enemy's team will do far more damage over the long run than any frontal assault, you will be able to employ this strategy to its greatest extent.

It does not matter what scale you're fighting on: if large, you can plant people in the enemy's organisation to encourage resentment with their leadership among the rank and file; if person-to-person, then identify their strongest allies and exploit those relationships to your advantage. By gaining a foothold into the enemy's camp, you gain not only the deep knowledge of their inner workings that all generals crave, you also gain a form of remote control over his future operations.

Isolate the enemy and make them feel surrounded. In the late 1960s when Mao Zedong began to suspect his defence minister Lin Biao of launching a coup, he didn't make a frontal attack on the man who by then had built a large power base for himself in the Chinese military. Instead, Mao began to purge and discredit Lin's closest allies both inside the party and the Chinese armed forces. Sensing that he might be next, and anxious that his position as Mao's successor might be in jeopardy, Lin tried to launch his own takeover of the party, but the widespread fear that Mao had created with his purges meant he had few allies left for such a coup to be successful. Zhou Enlai saw this rift unfold and attempted to mend the relationship between Mao and Lin, but it was no use. In 1971, Lin mysteriously died in a plane crash, and all remaining military officials close to Lin were dismissed from duty and ordered to submit self-criticisms, or disappeared entirely. The Chinese government has kept the true details around Lin's disappearance secret ever since, with foreign observers widely suspecting that Mao had planned the whole thing all along.

No one wants to feel isolated. When we see the people we trust turn their backs on us, we panic and undertake some rash action that makes our isolation even worse. As problems close in on us, seemingly from all sides, we have no one to call for help or rely upon, and the experience is as terrifying as it is futile. Generals across the ages have learned to exploit this fact to their advantage by using especially mobile troops to draw pieces of the enemy army out of the line, surround them, and then attack from every direction. With interpersonal battles, you can isolate your enemy by doing as Mao did, either souring relationships with his allies or outright getting rid of anyone close to him. You can also discredit them directly, though make sure you don't telegraph your true intentions too clearly. Remember that disunity is the key; you want to make sure that his friends are so disinclined through resentment, or fearful of being associated with someone so unpopular, that no one will come to his aid. When done right, the enemy often hastens his own downfall just like Lin Biao did before his disappearance, launching desperate efforts to regain their lost strength. This strategy is best done gradually, and without the enemy knowing you're behind it, because then they feel paranoid, perhaps even that their isolation is their fault. It is perhaps the darkest strategy of the five, but it will save you a lot of energy and enable you to destroy the enemy without any apparent responsibility.

Act boldly and strike suddenly with *shih*. Thousands of years ago the Chinese strategist Sun-Tzu described a concept called *shih*, which approximately means "readiness." He argued that before a key battle, a commander should have his force prepared to the maximal extent, and the enemy's resolves weakened to a similarly maximal extent. All the variables prepared in the commander's favour, and potential energy at its highest, the battle may be won in as swift and easy a manner possible. A good way to think of *shih* is when an archer's bow is stretched tight after years of practice, when a sprinter is poised in the "set" position before the starting gun fires, or when a story is about to reveal the great twist after hours of subtle yet pervasive foreshadowing. In all of these cases the peak of potential energy is reached after much time has been spent in focused preparation.

When you finally strike, it will be with such overwhelming force and effective planning that the enemy will have no choice but to retreat or surrender. Facing such an enemy as you, striking so hard and with such suddenness, will also terrify him about what you might do next, and an emotional enemy is always preferable. Like a thunder strike you smite the enemy anywhere at any time, at the point he least wants to defend. The initiative lies firmly on your side, where it always should be.

* * *

AVOID GRACELESS FRONTAL ATTACKS

In 1789, it seemed like France and the recently independent United States of America were destined to become perfect sister states. The French faithfully followed American example when they drafted the Declaration of the Rights of Man and of the Citizen, a document that was influenced heavily by the doctrine of natural rights, holding that all men are created equally and therefore deserve equal protection before the law. But as time passed, their paths diverged. To the French, the American model began to seem less relevant:

They had not had to deal with an absolute monarch, nor a powerful church and system of aristocratic privilege. In 1792, the French radical Maximilien Robespierre declared, "America's example, as an argument for our success, is worthless, because the circumstances are different." But Robespierre's view didn't represent that of every French revolutionary. The centre-left Gironde party's leader, Jacques-Pierre Brissot, still felt a strong bond with the Americans in spite of radicals like Robespierre, whom he mistrusted. Brissot worried that the same radicalisation was spreading in his own party. His party's members, collectively known as the Girondins, were getting out of control.

Most Americans, for their part, embraced France's blossoming democracy. Since it followed in America's footsteps, the French Revolution validated their struggle to become an independent republic, and they looked on with great pride. But as leaders like Robespierre rose to prominence and became more extreme in their rhetoric, Americans began to split in their opinions of the new nation being formed across the sea. For one thing, the Americans were having their own arguments about the path their republican system should take, and by 1792 two groups had emerged: the Federalists, led by John Adams and Alexander Hamilton, who believed in strong central government and a natural hierarchy; and the Democratic-Republicans, whose leader Thomas Jefferson mistrusted the English model of constitutional aristocracy and hoped America would move in parallel with France instead.

In 1793 the Girondins, responsible for France's foreign affairs, sent an emissary named Edmond-Charles Genêt into the middle of this political divide. Genêt's goals were simple: persuade the Americans to pay their debts from the American Revolution—which could not have succeeded without France's help—and to gain an official reiteration of their alliance. In the spring, France had just gone to war with Spain and Great Britain, and the prospect of American support was certainly valuable. The Girondins' leading members also hoped, in secret, to spark revolution in the territories surrounding America, specifically the Spanish colonies of Florida and Louisiana and the British colony of Canada to the north.

As soon as he landed, Genêt began working towards all of these goals. He gained promises of help for the French war effort from the governor of South Carolina and the French consul, and began a speaking tour as he travelled northwards up the East Coast. In every town he visited, Democratic-Republican societies and pro-French crowds greeted him with jubilant enthusiasm, a representative of the revolution that followed in America's footsteps. Genêt believed that in America, like France, the common man in the street could direct the country's politics, and decided to continue stirring up wild revolutionary support with anti-Federalist rhetoric. The split in American politics became even wider and angrier everywhere this firebrand diplomat went.

When he reached Philadelphia to meet with President George Washington and his cabinet, he assumed that he had arrived with a great deal of political capital after proving how much the American people seemed to want more extreme revolutionary change. To his great surprise, however, Washington rebuffed not only France's request for debt repayment but also any renegotiation of a commercial treaty, never mind a restatement of their old alliance. Alexander Hamilton and Thomas Jefferson joined in warning Genêt of his insensitivity to the divides in American politics.

Growing frustrated with his inability to gain any concessions from the Americans, Genêt decided to take a more underhanded approach. He tried to hire American adventurers to start an armed revolution in New Orleans to seize it back from the Spanish and make it into an independent republic, and then privately armed a group of American privateers to help him wage war against the British in the name of France. Genêt made angry public threats to Washington himself, saying that he would lead the American people in murdering the founding president if he didn't get the agreements he was after.

Genêt's comments angered the president and exasperated Thomas Jefferson, who up until this point had repeatedly tried to smooth things over with the upstart diplomat. Unfortunately, more bad news followed for Genêt. Many refugee planters had recently emigrated to America from the French colony of Saint-Domingue after having their slave property removed by the French parliament, and they took the opportunity to remind American slave owners like Washington and Jefferson that the French Revolution fomented disorder wherever it spread.

His days as a diplomat numbered, and any idea of a French-American deal now completely off the table, Genêt attempted one last bold move. He ordered the same French fleet that had brought over the Saint-Domingue planter refugees to attack the British at Halifax, a Nova Scotia trading post. Sick and tired of Genêt's rhetoric, the fleet commanders ignored him and simply sailed home to France. Far from tending to a blossoming relationship between two young sister republics, Genêt had completely ruined any chance of talks, and only confirmed the low international reputation of revolutionary France.

INTERPRETATION

George Washington privately kept tabs on Edmond-Charles Genêt throughout the diplomat's stay in America, and he wasn't impressed. In forming their plans for Genêt's visit, intended as a kind of self-serving political campaign, the French had completely failed to consider the delicate strategic position of the United States. France was at war with Britain and Spain, and America did not have the friendliest history with either country to say the least. But Washington did not want to pick sides and risk another war so soon after their own revolution against the British. Knowing that the French firebrand might ask for some kind of military aid, Washington issued a formal proclamation of neutrality as soon as Genêt landed. As he saw it, the French Revolution spread a messy combination of war and explosive division, two things he definitely didn't need. When Genêt saw the intense reactions to his arrival from ordinary Americans, he assumed that they, like the French people, could be whipped up into a powerful revolutionary fervour. But by threatening Washington himself, whom the American people greatly loved and respected, he turned the anger he'd created back on himself. He ruined relations between France and America with a series of foolish gambles based on little more than a hunch, ensuring that the French forces back home would have to face the Spanish and British alone and with less resources.

The pattern of events around the Genêt episode are typical whenever self-absorbed people try to enter a delicate situation with little regard for the subtle interests of others. They fail to realise how much they offend with their utter disregard for others' sentiments and feelings, only trying harder when their blunt tactics fail to work. Believing so much in their abstract theories, they assume that they can simply batter away at resistance with forceful logic, not understanding that the other party does not like being lectured at, and finds such treatment incredibly patronising. What did Genêt think he was doing when he attempted to undermine the fragile American stability with calls for revolution? Social warfare is a subtle game that requires deep awareness of the other players. You can't simply go around led by your pride alone, hoping that you can win your competitors over with dazzling rhetoric—no one is impressed, and people only deal with you as much as you can benefit them. Genêt made revolutionary France look like an embarrassment, too obsessed with their chaotic ideals to seriously work on the world stage.

How much more effective would Genêt's campaign have been if he had suppressed his personal feelings and instead played to American concerns, encouraging conciliation between the Federalists and Democratic-Republicans? Washington, Jefferson, and Hamilton would likely have been far more receptive to such an approach, perhaps securing the deals that France needed in the long term, and providing the onlooking world with a calmer, more rational impression than they expected. When you enter any situation where there are competing interests and you need to gain some concessions, consider all the interests involved. Subsume your ego and its impulses, and refuse to give into the temptation to blurt out your raw unvarnished thoughts. Think about the long term instead. What can you get from your adversaries that would help your people? Rather than shut down negotiations and go straight into war mode just because you can't compromise, build a relationship. An adversary that sees you as a friend, regardless of your true intentions, will be much more apt to help you than a patronising bore like Genêt.

LEAD YOUR PREY INTO A TRAP

In the summer of 1099, against all expectations, the forces that made it to the Middle East in the name of Christendom captured the ancient city of Jerusalem. Dozens of Christian émigrés made their way to the new Christian kingdom in the following decades, and many among them—including their leaders—realised that the new lives that they had started were much better than what they had left behind in Europe. The warmer climate was definitely a plus, although the excitement of a new life in conquered lands gave deep meaning to settlers and crusaders alike.

But survivors of the First Crusade soon discovered that in order to survive, they would need to learn to coexist with the Muslim and Jewish inhabitants. The crusader leaders, for their part, weren't much interested in maintaining a good relationship with the Muslim world, often undermining the kind of peace deals that a wise, forward-thinking leader might want to secure. By 1187, several uneasy truces had been gained with Muslim leaders including the great warrior-poet Saladin, but the peace was fragile. After much restraint on his part, Saladin had no choice but to declare jihad on the crusading Christians when they broke yet another treaty.

The Christian leaders were in a state of complete disarray. Raymond of Tripoli abandoned his fellow crusader states to join Saladin, only to renege on *that* deal and rejoin the other Christian leaders, but the disintegration of unity in their ranks was obvious. Desperate for solutions, they all dragged themselves to the city of Acre. The Christian leadership removed to the north of the region, Saladin surrounded his forces around Tiberias, Raymond's home city, taking his family as hostages. Then, Saladin simply waited.

Raymond sensed that this was a ruse of some kind, perhaps intended to draw the crusading soldiers into a trap. But he could not convince his fellow Christian leaders, all of whom decided to recapture Tiberias immediately for the honour of Christendom. On 3 July 1187, an army of 20,000 Christian men started their journey through eastern Galilee.

While many young knights rode out eagerly in search of their own crusader glory, Raymond went with great reluctance. Not only were they walking right into a trap, the other Christian leaders had insisted upon bringing a relic of the true cross, allegedly a piece of the wooden cross that Christ himself had died upon. Many among the ranks believed that the relic's presence would surely grant them God's grace in the battle to come.

The Christian army set out in the morning, and they reached the hills of Hattin right at the peak of the day's sunshine. They were thirsty for water, but Saladin had foreseen this and ordered his men to block the springs in the surrounding area. He also sent out bands of fast-moving cavalry to harass the Christian army and then flee in retreat, luring the already tired soldiers to run after them in pursuit. By the time they met the bulk of Saladin's army in the evening, the Christian army was exhausted and demoralised. Bloody fighting continued through the night, and it was a disaster for Raymond's troops. Those who hadn't collapsed from exhaustion or thirst were easily routed by Saladin's fast cavalry, all while the Christian leaders squabbled over tactics. To cap off their masterful victory, Saladin's forces seized the relic of the true cross, dragged it through mud in the streets of Damascus, and it was never seen again.

INTERPRETATION

After he had defeated such a significant portion of the Christian forces in the Middle East, Saladin easily conquered the other crusader kingdoms. Jerusalem fell only two months after the Battle of Hattin, and rather than execute or enslave the surrendering forces as most of his contemporaries would have done, Saladin allowed most of the vanquished crusaders to go free. Saladin was a master of generalship and human nature, and likely saw the advantages in letting the Christian presence meekly disperse instead of providing them with an excuse to gather strength and fight another day. He recognised the power that Hattin and the capture of Jerusalem held for the Muslim world, using it to further unify its many warring factions under his rule.

Richard the Lionheart would attempt a siege to recapture Jerusalem from Saladin in 1191, but it was no use. To Richard's surprise, Saladin consistently offered a remarkable degree of courtesy to the returning crusaders, and the mutual respect between the two leaders took on an almost mythic quality in the following centuries. Saladin and Richard did finally reach a treaty of their own after years of fighting that would allow Christian pilgrims to travel freely to the Holy Lands, but both sides knew that the results of Hattin could not be undone. It was a true turning point in medieval history.

The Battle of Hattin and its aftermath shows Saladin to be a model of Social Intelligence for a number of clear reasons. First was his timing: After years of infighting and tenuous treaties, he knew that the Christian leaders were at the peak of disunity. An enemy force without clear leadership, whose senior members squabble over petty details, is so clouded with emotion and resentment that it can never effectively stay aware of the real threats unfolding before them. Saladin, on the other hand, had spent the years of peace building up his support base among the disparate Muslim tribes, and by 1187 had amassed an army to rival that of the crusaders. Second was his trap: Knowing that the Christian leaders were all assembled in the northern city of Acre, Saladin captured the relatively minor city of Tiberias. Although it was small, it had great emotional and strategic significance: namely the link with Raymond of Tripoli, and the fact that the route from Acre to Tiberias spanned a line right across the desert from the sea, offering ripe opportunities for flanking manoeuvres. As we learned in the previous chapter, it is easy to bait a rash enemy into a foolish attack, and Saladin understood this better than anyone at the time.

Whenever an opponent gains some small victory over you and then takes that as an excuse to become proud and obnoxious about it, it is easy to respond by becoming emotional—there is both the crushing sense of defeat and the victor's unbearable insensitivity. In these situations, stillness is the key. Realise, as Saladin did in the face of a spirited Crusader threat, that your enemy's victory is only temporary and likely represents nothing more than a tenuous foothold. Rather than get angry about their pride and arrogance, *use* that against them. Lure them into a trap and once they're isolated, pounce. But don't let that same pride infect you when you get in a shot of your own—always remain conciliatory after a victory. Not only will you look like a wise, generous leader, you'll also provide the enemy with no ostensible front to fight against. Like the crusaders who had so proudly marched into the Holy Land and left it with little more than a sigh, it will be hard for your enemy to argue with such a resounding series of effective blows.

IRRATIONALITY: THE TRUE ENEMY

In the summer of 1956, US president Dwight D. Eisenhower could no longer ignore the crisis growing in Egypt. Fresh from his first presidential election in June, Gamal Abdel Nasser seemed bent on upsetting his American counterpart. Nasser officially recognised the communist Chinese regime under Mao Zedong, and publicly suggested asking the Soviet Union to fund the Aswan Dam project if American finance terms were unsatisfactory. Likely irritated by the upstart president's rhetoric, Eisenhower called Nasser's bluff, reneging on America's offer to finance the dam. Acting fast, Nasser responded with the announcement that his government would nationalise the British-owned Suez Canal Company, using the revenues to fund the Aswan Dam themselves.

The British were not impressed. Prime Minister Anthony Eden could not tolerate Nasser's threats to a British-owned company, and began advocating for a military strike in retaliation. Although Eisenhower understood Eden's protests, a military strike was exactly what Nasser wanted, and he would have none of it. A Western attack would give Nasser the justification he needed to continue his anti-imperialist rhetoric and solidify his status as a hero to the Egyptian people. Eisenhower instead sponsored a series of international conferences to cool down the situation and find a compromise solution. Although Eden appeared to pay lip service to the diplomatic talks, the British secretly began conspiring with the French and Israelis to overthrow Nasser and remove the upstart entirely.

The British were sure they could pull off their plan, but they needed to tread carefully. No part of the operation could fail. They had more than enough support from the French, who burned with resentment at Nasser after he had publicly supported the ongoing Algerian rebellion, and the Israelis were afraid that Nasser was building up an army in preparation for a ground war—for them, a pre-emptive strike was necessary to assert their military dominance over the region. The three countries planned to launch their assault in October 1956: Israel would advance south to seize the Sinai Peninsula, and then the British and French would demand that Israel and Egypt withdraw their forces from the area surrounding the Suez Canal. If Egypt refused, which seemed likely, then the British and French forces would seize control of the canal for themselves. The plan seemed foolproof, and they could finally shut up the Egyptian upstart once and for all.

The attack proceeded as planned. But neither Eden nor the French or Israelis had informed Eisenhower of their plan before the operation, and he reacted with public anger as the world watched these strange events unfold. Both US and Soviet diplomats condemned the attack in the United Nations—a rare sight near the height of the Cold War—and Eisenhower banned all oil exports to Europe until the British and French called off the attack. He also threatened to support UN sanctions against Israel for its own part in the plan. Facing such measures, the British, French, and Israelis had no choice but to withdraw, leaving a furious Eden humiliated and disgraced in the eyes of the international community. He would resign just two months after the end of the Suez Canal operation, and Nasser ruled Egypt for another fourteen years.

INTERPRETATION

Forcing British withdrawal from Egypt brought no great pleasure to Dwight D. Eisenhower. The situation in Egypt was tense, and the British had played right into Nasser's hands. He could not fail to act against a crisis that was at risk of sparking a major conflict a mere decade after the Second World War had ended. But this rapid erosion of British influence in the Middle East would allow the Soviet Union to expand its own influence in the region, and his blocking of Eden's intervention did not reassure countries at risk of a Soviet invasion. Eisenhower later tried to counter this unfolding dynamic by pressuring the Egyptians into joining an anti-Soviet diplomatic alliance, but this only further solidified the view that imperialist nations were trying to exert their will over the Middle East.

Nasser played the British like a fiddle, and got nearly everything he was after. Anti-communist sentiment was at its height during the Eisenhower administration, so his recognition of communist China and the Soviet finance talks were bound to rile up the Americans and heighten the stakes. By threatening to nationalise the Suez Canal Company, he was provoking the British and the West as a whole. Could a new Middle Eastern regime challenge the might of the former imperialist powers? Either way the crisis went, Nasser couldn't lose: if the British didn't act, then he'd be seen by the Egyptian people as a hero reclaiming a part of their territory for themselves; and if the British *did* act, then all of Nasser's rhetoric about imperialist threats would be proven right.

Nasser also knew that baiting Britain into attacking against Eisenhower's wishes would force a rift between America and the European powers. Rather than working together to encourage Egypt into a mature solution, they squabbled and Nasser became a hero. Britain was still holding onto its identity as a global power, even though it had shed many of its colonies in the decade since the Second World War—a small blow to their pride would be enough to provoke an attack, but still be insignificant enough to make the furious Eden look ridiculous once forced to end the crisis. The British completely miscalculated the situation and paid for it with a long-lasting blow to their international reputation.

Political types of Nasser's calibre are rare, but they often use the same tactics to get what they want from you. Although they clamour about moral issues to anyone who'll listen, they really couldn't care less. Anyone who invokes the moral argument, noisily painting you as some kind of brutish aggressor, is actually trying to draw that very behaviour out of you through provocation. As described in Chapter 13, opponents like Nasser *want* you to fight, because it allows them to spin a narrative where they are David facing you, the bullying Goliath. With the Suez Crisis, it allowed Nasser to rule unchallenged for over a decade afterwards, and helped to spark a burning resentment against the West that has lasted to the present day throughout the Middle East.

As a Socially Intelligent Warrior you must never give upstarts like Nasser the political capital they desire, never rising to their bait. Always take the high road when possible, offering olive branches and calling the baiter's bluff until they reveal their true intentions. By refusing to play their game you affirm yourself on the territory that *you* decide, refusing them the advantage they crave. How much better would it have been if Eden had swallowed his pride and joined Eisenhower in finding a compromise, with the threat of economic sanctions on Egypt? It is much wiser to make a justifiable threat only after you both make genuine attempts to mend the relationship, than to succumb to ego as the British did in the Suez Crisis. Wounded pride has ended more careers than we can ever count.

DESTROY THE ENEMY'S HOME

In late 1864, matters were more serious than ever for the Confederacy. The Union general William T. Sherman had successfully invaded Georgia and taken the key city of Atlanta. General Joseph E. Johnston had practically laid the path for Sherman, retreating to the city in the face of repeated flanking manoeuvres. President Jefferson Davis, tired of Johnston's timidity, replaced him with John Bell Hood. Hood had earned a reputation for aggression and bravery and seemed the right man to repel the Union invaders. His priority was moving the war out of Georgia, home to much of the South's railroads and cotton plantations. Davis approved Hood's plan to threaten Union supply lines to the north in Chattanooga, hoping this would distract Sherman and enable the South to reclaim crucial territory it had long lost.

Sherman followed Hood for a short while, but refused to play to his strategy. Both he and his friend Ulysses S. Grant, now the Union Army's commanding general, believed that the South would buckle only if the North could decisively break their capacity to wage warfare. Sherman had all of an undefended Georgia ahead of him, and a tight, battle-hardened force at his disposal. Working on Grant's orders, he made a plan of his own to march from Atlanta all the way through to Savannah on the coast, destroying key infrastructure and capturing slave property as they went. Sherman's goal was not only to pulverise the South's war industries but also to demoralise the civilian population. His army would need to move fast and disconnected from any supply lines, foraging and living off the land as both he and Grant had done in their recent successful campaigns in the American west. But if Sherman's plan to march from Atlanta to the sea could work, it would be decisive not only for the Union war effort, but it would also likely secure Abraham Lincoln's presidential re-election soon after.

Meanwhile, Hood's campaigns to the north-west of Sherman were complete disasters. He launched one frontal assault after another on Union forces throughout October and November, losing 6,000 men, twelve generals, and fifty-four regimental commanders. The Union general John M. Schofield blew through Hood's ill-considered attack and easily moved towards Nashville, another key city lost for the Confederacy. The magnitude of Hood's failure to mount a northern distraction campaign only gave Sherman more freedom in his March to the Sea. He met little resistance, averaging ten miles a day, reaching Savannah by Christmas.

On the way, Sherman showed Grant's strategy of exhaustion in full force, consuming or destroying millions of dollars' worth of agricultural and industrial goods. Sherman's men destroyed 300 miles of railroads, using fire to break and twist rails, leaving them wrapped around tree trunks. Since the Southern economy relied heavily upon slave labour, Sherman also liberated up to 10,000 slaves by one officer's estimate. The North rejoiced as news of the extensive damage caused by Sherman's army came in.

Although Robert E. Lee's army still fought on in northern Virginia, Sherman's March to the Sea virtually ended the war in the Deep South, breaking both the Confederacy's industries and its will to fight. It was a true turning point in the American Civil War. After he had captured the key port of Savannah, Sherman wrote a letter to Abraham Lincoln offering him the city as a Christmas gift. Lincoln, delighted with the good news and grateful for the general's hard-won victories, wrote back:

> Many, many thanks for your Christmas gift—the capture of Savannah. When you were leaving Atlanta for the Atlantic coast, I was anxious, if not fearful; but feeling that you were the better judge, and remembering that "nothing risked, nothing gained" I did not interfere. Now, the undertaking being a success, the honor is all yours; for I believe none of us went farther than to acquiesce. And taking the work of Gen. Thomas into the count, as it should be taken, it is indeed a great success. Not only does it afford the obvious and immediate military advantage; but, in showing to the world that your army could be divided, putting the stronger part to an important new service, and yet leaving enough to vanquish the old opposing force of the whole— Hood's army—it brings those who sat in darkness, to see a great light. But what next? I suppose it will be safer if I

leave Gen. Grant and yourself to decide. Please make my grateful acknowledgements to your whole army, officers and men.

INTERPRETATION

Sherman would continue his campaign of property destruction on through to South Carolina, where his army captured the city of Charleston. Conquering the city that had birthed secession was of great symbolic importance to Sherman's troops and the wider United States and reflects the true impact of his March to the Sea. While Sherman's campaign caused millions of dollars in damages to Southern infrastructure, he and Grant knew that the psychological impact would be far more profound. A Union army moving freely about the territory, destroying property and emancipating thousands of slaves, caused great panic and tumult among the civilians living in Georgia.

Sherman's destruction of civilian property and infrastructure is seen today as the beginning of "total war," a military conflict where the scope extends from the battlefield to every part of the opponent's home territory. The American Civil War ended soon after Sherman's campaigns in the South because he struck forcefully at its agriculture, its core means of production, and dulled its collective will to fight in a short space of time.

If you can strike the enemy in his home, then you have dealt him a great blow and also made a display of great power. You can reach into his territory at will, threatening his support base and even his way of life. Southern industry and culture depended heavily on agriculture, which depended on slave labour—at the outset of the war, the South had fewer industrial workers than the North had factories. Sherman's March to the Sea struck at every one of these core dependencies, including the railroads, which had allowed Confederate troops and supplies to move quickly across Southern terrain. This both worsened all the South's disadvantages *and* nullified all of its key advantages: the very essence of any exhaustion strategy.

Like Sherman, you must let go of any emotions you might have about your enemy and rationally assess his strengths and weaknesses. What does he completely depend upon? What, if removed, would most damage his ability to wage war? In the social realm, this can often mean support from key allies in a group, or some source of funding and resources. Work out a way to cut him off from these assets for good, and you will save a lot of time and effort in your campaign. Striking alone will do an effective job by itself, because it sends the message that you know what he needs and that you're willing to take it away.

THE OUTSTRETCHED BOW

In March 1971, Indira Gandhi and her Indian National Congress party won a landslide victory in the Indian general election. This came as a huge relief to Gandhi, after suffering from bitter internal party divisions for the previous two years. But even though she had regained many seats from her rival Morarji Desai, Gandhi could not rest on her laurels. On 26 March, media correspondents began reporting on a genocide in East Pakistan.

After Great Britain had granted India its independence in 1947, they split the former colony along religious lines, with Muslim Pakistan bordering India to the west and east. The 1,000-mile split between the territories caused endless tensions and administrative headaches, and now the Pakistani military had begun a crackdown on the eastern wing to suppress its growing calls for secession and independence. Gandhi watched as 10,000,000 people fled into her country across the eastern Indian border with Pakistan, and as further reports came in of mass murder and rape of the Bengali people, she could not stand idly by.

In April, Gandhi asked the Indian Army if they were ready for open war with Pakistan, and their leaders declined. The summer monsoon season would make a ground conflict almost impossible to supply, and their tanks were in the middle of being refitted with modern equipment. The prime minister was under huge pressure to act soon, but accepted her army's assessment and decided to wait until the time was right.

By November, war seemed inevitable. Pakistan ignored repeated warnings from the Soviet Union of a potential invasion by India, and its eastern wing's campaign of mass killings grew worse than ever, having killed over 1,000,000 Bengali people since March. Thousands of people marched in Lahore, Pakistan's western capital, led by conservative politicians calling for a military campaign to crush India for what they saw as their betrayal in encouraging East Pakistan's independence. In response, Gandhi only waited, continuing to build up the military's strength on the eastern border.

In December, the perfect time for a military strike seemed to have arrived. The ground was now drier in the east, opening up the terrain for fast ground movements, and snow had fallen heavily on the Himalayan passes, blocking the possibility of any flanking manoeuvre from the north. On 3 December, Pakistani air fighters launched a pre-emptive strike on the city of Agra in north-west India. Gandhi announced to the Indian people that very evening that Pakistan's air strike was a clear declaration of war against India.

After months of training, supplying, and waiting, her

army was prepared, and the air force poised to strike—now she could open the floodgates. The morning after her broadcast, Gandhi ordered a massive coordinated invasion by ground, sea, and air on every front surrounding East Pakistan, supported by Bengali resistance groups in the Pakistani interior. Dacca, the largest city in the region, fell on 16 December, and the East Pakistan military command surrendered the following day. Gandhi's forces had won a decisive victory in just thirteen days, putting a stop to the Bengali genocide. Replacing the disintegrated eastern wing of Pakistan, the independent country of Bangladesh was born.

INTERPRETATION

Indira Gandhi's invasion of East Pakistan is a perfectly executed example of Sun-Tzu's principle of *shih*. Had Gandhi listened to the impulsive men in her cabinet and struck in April when the circumstances were unsuitable, India's invasion would have likely failed. She had survived a coup attempt in her own party just two years before her re-election in March 1971, and the calls for action from her cabinet and the public were only getting louder. Fortunately for her and the Bengali people in what is now Bangladesh, she knew it was much better to take her time and wait for the situation to mature to her favour. Gandhi allowed the military to refit its tanks with modern armour and weapons, and gradually massed an army of 500,000 soldiers deployed at strategic points all up and down the eastern border.

On 3 December, the combined Indian armed forces came at the East Pakistan military with such overwhelming force and numerical superiority, and so suddenly, that the defenders had no choice but to surrender after less than a fortnight of fighting. Not only was the Indo-Pakistani War of

1971 one of the shortest in history, it was also one of the least bloody: India lost less than 1 per cent of its 675,000-strong invasion force, and Pakistan just over 10 per cent of its 365,000.

When you face an enemy that is both aggressive and brutal, try to suppress any feelings of resentment or indignation at their actions. Follow Indira Gandhi's example and rationally assess what you can do to stand up to the bully, including whether a fight would be necessary at all. If a fight seems winnable in the not-too-distant future, then ignore all impulsive calls to strike immediately and instead wait. Build your forces up and prepare as much as possible. Achieve *shih*, the state of maximal potential energy, and pounce only when the time is right. Your goal, like the Indian armed forces in December 1971, is to strike with overwhelming force in a perfectly coordinated manner—you can't do that if you succumb to rage and strike impulsively before you're ready, as the British did in the 1956 Suez Crisis. Know when to bow and retreat to the shadows when you're weak, even if such a state is temporary. Make time your friend, since gradual preparation can defeat any enemy. As the popular saying goes, "Don't get mad; get even."

REVERSAL

In all cases, you should first seek to build relationships and mend any rifts where possible. As explained to a great length throughout this book, such an approach will be the most rewarding one in the long term for both you and your wider community. However, there can be no substitute for preparedness in case you find yourself under attack. There are always aggressive types, and they will not hold the same group-positive ideals. Do not entertain naïve beliefs that disarming yourself against such threats is somehow moral—it isn't. There is nothing safer than competence; no better security than a watchful eye and a trained mind. For this reason, there can be no reversal to the art of social warfare. Anyone who tries to convince you otherwise is attempting to practise the most deceitful kind of domination possible.

15

SAFAVID PERSIA AND THE OTTOMAN EMPIRE

DISRUPT THE ENEMY GROUP'S UNITY BY EXPLOITING ITS INTERNAL DIVISIONS

T*he ultimate form of social warfare is the disruption of the unity that binds an enemy group. Identify their natural lines of division, and then stoke that division, encouraging either side to go blind with anger and resentment at each other. They will be so preoccupied with their inner squabbles that they will be ill-prepared for the true threat: you. Use propaganda, misinformation, and sudden, targeted attacks to exploit your enemy's latent prejudices. Likewise, you must take measures to protect your own group from such attacks. Build a group whose mythology is so strong that it can withstand any attempts at disruption, and emerge even stronger than before.*

THE GREAT DISRUPTION

By the end of the sixteenth century, several developments all began to peak in Europe. The Protestant Reformation had firmly taken hold in England and the Germanic states, and gold flowed in from the New World. Religious differences had caused the European kingdoms to tighten into clearly defined nation-states for the first time, and with gold burning holes in their pockets, the competition for new colonies, resources, and further wealth would be fierce. As the Renaissance drew to a close, a wide range of scientific developments coincided perfectly with a spirit of excitement for adventure and sea exploration.

In the Americas and sub-Saharan Africa, European colonists faced isolated groups of indigenous peoples, vulnerable to bacteria and infections to which the city-dwelling English and Spanish had developed strong immunities. The Europeans' superior weaponry easily dispatched those few who survived, and they were able to make indigenous peoples such as the Iroquois dependent on a steady supply of horses, guns, and alcohol, all destroying their ages-old native cultures.

In other places, however, Europeans met civilisations that had progressed into organised, wealthy societies. The Islamic heartland, in particular, had long since flourished into a rich tapestry of kingdoms, each with its own unique culture and national identity. Of particular importance to the Europeans were their large, bustling cities which dominated the Islamic world's trade. Europeans had already developed a complex history with Muslims, and they were now bumping up against the Muslim world just as the great Islamic empires were thriving in both power and cultural brilliance. Although odd flashes of violence had occurred since the end of the Crusades, the two worlds had blossomed independent of one another. By now, both sides were ripe for trade.

In 1598 two Englishmen, Robert and Anthony Shirley, found their way to Persia, the lands occupied by modern-day Iran. Shah Abbas, the greatest monarch of the Safavid dynasty, received an interesting proposition from the two Westerners: For a decent price, they would sell him European firearms and cannon, and provide the technical support to integrate these into his army. Not only would the shah's army grow in power, these men were offering their ongoing services. Perhaps they could advise on Western military strategies, or even help him dominate his outlying tribes with gunpowder weapons. Safavid Persia lagged behind its neighbours in military technology, and these Englishmen offered a quick solution. The shah accepted and appointed the Shirley brothers as commanders in his army.

Right around the same time, something odd was happening in the Ottoman Empire to Persia's north, in modern-day Turkey. The Ottomans had brushed up against Christian Europe repeatedly over the centuries, and most saw the edge of their territory as the border between the Islamic and European worlds. But plenty of Christians and Jews lived in the Ottoman Empire, and more continued to move there over the next century. The Ottoman Empire had almost become defined by its constant growth and wars with surrounding states, but for 100 years it had not faced a single major conflict. Now at its peak, and with no wars to wage, pressures began showing in the empire's interior.

Powerful state-sanctioned guilds controlled all manufacturing across the empire, and could only employ a limited number of people. Many men who would normally fight in the empire's vast armies ended up unemployed. Worse, the supply of captured Slavic and Hungarian peoples the empire used for its janissary ranks was also drying up. Janissaries were a caste of elite soldiers, normally forbidden from marrying and producing heirs of their own, to keep the ranks fresh with new blood. But now the expansion had stopped, and the janissary ranks were dying out, these elite Western soldiers began to breed and keep high-ranking positions in the empire for their children. Dullards with rich and socially elite parents now filled positions that had once been taken by low-born experts who had shown talent from an early age.

It was not until 1683, after many decades of internal softening, that the Ottoman made one last stab into Europe. By September, an invading force of 140,000 Ottoman troops had besieged the great imperial city of Vienna for two months. Faced with this existential threat, the European powers responded with great vigour. The Polish-Lithuanian Commonwealth and the Holy Roman Empire joined forces to win a decisive victory against the Ottomans, despite the invaders' superior numbers. The Battle of Vienna marked a turning point in history, when the Ottoman Empire ceased to be a realistic threat to Christian Europe. As Hungary and the Balkans returned to European rule, the Ottoman army trudged home to resentfully lick its wounds.

Not long after their failed siege of Vienna, the Ottomans poured whatever resources they had left into a military bulwark, fearing a counter-attack from their neighbours. But to their surprise, the government had only an exhausted supply of resources to work with. Where had all of their natural raw materials gone? Western traders had come and bought up most of the country's supply of raw materials— wool, metals, timber, to name a few—in the time that the Grand Vizier's army had been away in Europe. Because of the empire's firmly inbuilt guilds, Westerners could not trade in manufactured goods like shoes or furniture, and so instead they brought heaps of gold from the New World. Ottoman traders happily sold their stocks of raw materials to the Westerners in exchange for something truly valuable and were perhaps equally happy to undermine the snobbish guilds that had dominated Ottoman commerce for so long.

Government attempts to outlaw the sale of raw goods to outsiders made the situation even worse by creating a vicious and dominant black market. As criminal dealers took huge amounts of gold in exchange for the now-illegal goods, they bribed government officials to look the other way. Soon, corrupt officials filled every part of the Ottoman government. A huge amount of cash flowed into the Ottoman Empire's economy, just as its guilds' manufacturing output was declining, and inflation skyrocketed prices for ordinary citizens. Families and communities could no longer eat and suffered constant threats from spates of crime that the government could barely control. Over time, the Ottoman Empire became a corrupt, sickened machine bloated with gold that only flowed from criminals into the pockets of over-paid officials.

While this was happening, Safavid Persia suffered a similar unravelling process. Shah Abbas's deal with the Shirley brothers—among other deals with European military advisors—had helped to secure the Persian Empire's supremacy among its neighbours. But this only caused the Safavid dynasty to rest on its laurels, and a dynastic rot began to set in. Princes raised in luxury became idle and lazy, relying on the military to maintain order. Every time a successor to the throne died, a vicious power struggle erupted, and rulership of the great empire became more about raw military power than wisdom or legitimacy.

But a deeper division became clearer as Safavid Persia became less cohesive. The first Safavid kings had forged a distinctly Persian Islam by declaring Shi'ism the state religion. This only alienated a small Sunni minority at first, but as the throne weakened, these bordering states began rebelling and agitating for reform. An elite class of Shi'i religious scholars—the *ulama*—surrounded the throne, claiming that Safavid kings could only rule by their express approval. The *ulama* had strong ties both to the urban peasantry and middle class, but the choice for Persian kings was far from clear. None of them wanted to cede ultimate authority to the *ulama* ayatollahs, even though this would earn them popular legitimacy and stability in the long run.

Travelling European Christians offered the Safavid monarchy their own solution: bypass the ayatollahs entirely, and build up large, European-style armies under their command. They agreed, and European Christian military advisers helped to clamp down on the powerful Muslim scholarly class. As succession struggles became fiercer towards the end of the eighteenth century, contending factions hired their own European military advisors, each resorting to cruel new tactics to dominate the others. The crises came to a head when, in the 1780s, a set of tribes broke away and tore Persia into parts.

In 1789 a new Qajar dynasty came down from the Azerbaijani mountains, took control of the Persian throne, and ruled the empire with an iron first for 131 years. The national armies were still a mix of Europeans and Persians, the *ulama* were still permanently at odds with the throne, and the Qajar kings bullied anyone around them. A far cry from the proud, apex societies they had once been centuries before, Persia and the Ottoman Empire had become corrupt, impotent puppets of the European powers.

INTERPRETATION

There is nothing to suggest that Western influence on these two Islamic empires was in any way planned, or even deliberate in most cases. If you were an ordinary trader, struggling to feed yourself due to an oppressive system that favours elite guilds, and someone new comes asking to buy all of your wares in exchange for gold in bulk, are you going to say no? Most people would gladly accept such an offer. If you were a Hungarian janissary in the Ottoman military, and you suddenly gained the opportunity to marry and have your own children, would you try to guarantee the best education and government postings for them? You probably would. If you were a Safavid king with bloodthirsty enemies to the east, and a scheming court filled with nobles and rival families vying for power, would you accept the offer of advice and military aid from eager Westerners? Most would.

It is easy to blame the West for the unravelling that Persia and the Ottoman Empire suffered between 1500 and 1800, and it would be partly true. But complex systems—particularly those made up of competing factions—rarely require much interference to spiral into chaos. European travellers wreaked havoc on the indigenous peoples of the Americas, and they would likely have made the same choices had the Middle East been just as small and isolated. But it wasn't. European traders arrived with pockets full of gold, and met locals eager to sell their goods, and governments eager to gain a military advantage over their enemies. There isn't a "they" to blame, because the corruption that followed was slow, gradual, and the result of countless individuals acting in their own self-interest.

Fortunately for us, this story gives us a clear set of lessons for making even a great empire fall. It is not a fast process, but the effects scale based on the group's size, and its current degree of unity. A large group will take longer to unravel than a smaller one, but it is also likely to have developed more lines of internal division. For the Persians, the Shi'i and Sunni groups clearly defined these lines. All it took was the combination of a weak king, and the temptation presented by European military advisors offering their services. In the Ottoman Empire's case, the empire merely needed to stop growing so fast, since all of its society depended on the constant industry that war provided. Unemployment, spiralling inflation, and tumult soon followed.

You will find that enemy groups—particularly those with

short-sighted leaders—are eager to accept offers that satisfy their self-interest, even if those things exacerbate internal tensions and are destructive in the long run. As with all strategies in the social realm, this one requires subtlety of the highest order, and a deep knowledge of the enemy group. What are its main lines of division? Every group has them, no matter how well they approximate the Ideal Team State (described in Chapter 8). Undermining their group unity is of the highest importance, and the most effective ways to achieve this are through actions that invoke mutual resentment, fear, and mistrust. Ottoman traders resentful of powerful guilds were happy to accept European gold, splitting apart two classes that could have worked together to build a more stable and cohesive economy. Persian nobles were consumed by their need to dominate their opposing factions with European military aid when they should have sought ways to mend the rifts between Shi'is and Sunnis. In each case, external actors were all too happy to exploit internal tensions for personal gain.

By 1850, Europeans dominated every part of the Islamic world. They either lived in these countries as an upper class, or controlled the flow of resources, dictating the policies of these countries and even creating institutions barred from the local peoples whose daily lives they controlled. The European powers had done this without a shot being fired— in fact, few at the time showed any awareness of how they had done it. They had achieved this complete domination of the Islamic world through the subtlest forms of manipulation: turning uneasy neighbours into bitter enemies, without either realising who was to blame.

The Middle East has since thrown off the yoke of European domination, but the scars and resentments towards the West still show to this day. Put this pragmatic, amoral strategy to your own use, and you will achieve similar control over others. This method is perhaps the darkest application of Social Intelligence we can muster, and it causes incalculable human suffering. But it is undeniably effective for those patient and unscrupulous enough to wield it.

KEYS TO SOCIAL INTELLIGENCE

In modern times we like to think of ourselves as largely unified, with an open, globalist perspective. We believe, against the evidence, that other groups have our best interests at heart, often criticising pragmatic policies as selfish, even immoral. But we stand today with the same brains as our tribal predecessors, and our tendencies for self-interest and groupthink are more alive than ever. When compared to the millions of years of tribal life that we lived through, our present system of large economies joined internationally is narrow and recent. It doesn't even qualify as a recent age, or even as "history"—it's little more than a wafer-thin sliver of the human biography.

It is useless to deny that part of ourselves that craves group identity. This does not mean we have to feed these natural instincts of tribal mistrust; we merely have to stay conscious of them. Like all parts of our base human nature, they are ancient and more powerful than we care to admit. If we repress these tribal instincts, they will manifest in ugly ways. Recent years have seen the rise of so-called "identity politics," a well-intentioned concept designed to address inequalities, which in reality has only caused starker divides along ethnic and gender lines. Again, the answer is not to ignore our impulses, but to accept them as a fact with which we must deal. To fail in this pursuit is to stay divided and vulnerable to external control.

If we can stay conscious of these mistrustful factional urges, we can recognise when they're being used against us.

Imagine if the Persians and Ottomans had kept this awareness when Europeans worked to disrupt their fragile societies—history could have turned out very differently. When politicians try to stoke resentment in a minority group, they are only doing so for their own self-interest. In the age of online social media, publishers have learned that the most viral content—and thus most likely to generate page view earnings—triggers an anger response, often writing headlines with a shameless bias to one side of the argument, mixing opinion and news. We must spread the awareness that a perverse set of business incentives is driving our society further apart each day and making our pleasure-seeking brains dependent on yet more outrageous content.

More than ever the Socially Intelligent Warrior must stay wary of such attacks on group unity, and be ready to use the strategy herself if the situation arises. When applied sufficiently, the content supplied in this book's earlier chapters should provide a strong bulwark from targeted attacks—groups are at their most cohesive when led by an honest and responsible person, with a culture that emphasises competence, reciprocity, and learning. As Winston Churchill said, "When there is no enemy within, the enemies outside cannot hurt you." But when you face a tyrannical enemy that gives no quarter, rejecting all offers of reconciliation, you must use the "divide-and-conquer" strategy used by great military leaders like Napoleon: attack the group's joints, divide it into smaller parts, and then crush them all one by one. (The military term for this strategy is to defeat the enemy "in detail.") Although many examples of divide and conquer are available from the annals of history, it is just as devastating when applied to groups and larger societies.

In the Berlin Conference of 1884, Germany gained the colonies of Rwanda and neighbouring Burundi. Otto von Bismarck, the German chancellor, had organised the conference to settle once and for all the "Scramble for Africa," and the European powers divided up Africa amongst themselves. Bismarck was less concerned about building a large overseas empire than the British—he was far more interested in consolidating Germany's power in Europe—but still wanted to make the most of Germany's resource-rich holdings in Africa. The Germans thus ruled Rwanda primarily through its monarchy, placing members of the dominant Tutsi minority in key positions of power. They believed the Tutsi ethnic group to have migrated from Ethiopia, and that they were therefore racially superior to the Hutu majority. The Tutsi king welcomed Germany's help in strengthening his rule, particularly the small force of colonial troops.

During the First World War, Belgium seized control of Rwanda from Germany, and things largely carried on as they had done since the late 1800s. But a decade after the war had ended, the Belgian colonists took a more direct form of control over their conquered lands, formally issuing identity cards to the Tutsi and Hutu groups, organising them by race. Subjects with long noses were assigned cards designating them as Tutsi, and those with broad noses were identified instead as Hutus. Rwandan society had always been fractured, but a Hutu who had gathered enough social status and economic success could gain equal status to a Tutsi. Now, under Belgian colonial rule, all chance of social mobility disappeared. Most Hutus came to resemble a peasant class while a small elite class of Tutsis thrived.

After the Second World War, Hutus began to enjoy more freedoms, as political forces clamoured for an end to the socioeconomic divide that had ravaged and humiliated their country. The Tutsi responded with their own clamours for independence, claiming they were entitled to run their own country separate from the Hutus. The growing crisis came to a head in the early 1960s when the desperate Belgian colonists abruptly replaced all Tutsi administrators with Hutus, and finally granted the country its independence—but now it was an overwhelmingly Hutu republic, and Tutsis were suddenly a targeted group in the country they had once dominated. Hundreds of thousands of Tutsis fled to neighbouring Uganda. A group of these refugees, led by Paul Kagame, formed an army that became battle-ready by 1990. In October of that year, Kagame's force invaded, starting a bloody civil war that lasted for three years. But for many on both sides, the resulting peace was not enough. On the 6 April 1994, the Hutu president and vice-president were both assassinated in a single attack, and genocidal killings began the next day. Soldiers and police killed anyone they perceived as Tutsis. By the end of July, they had killed 1,000,000 innocent people—Tutsis and Hutus alike—and raped 500,000 women.

Looking back over the century of inter-group violence that culminated in the Rwandan Genocide of 1994, the horrible scale of the damage possible with the divide-and-conquer strategy is obvious. Belgium enacted racially divisive policies on its Rwandan subjects, and the result was a country plagued with resentment and anger. Oppressed Hutus, barred for so long from any recognition or real participation, felt the need to exact brutal revenge on their Tutsi rivals as soon as they gained power in the early 1960s. Rather than allow tensions to simmer down gradually, the Belgians acquiesced to the demands of Hutu populist politicians, shamefully abandoning the mess that they had helped to create.

Whenever an aggressor intentionally uses the divide-and-conquer strategy in the social realm or the workplace, they are trying to achieve two things: undermine each faction's authority, and make both of them depend upon him. With Belgian Rwanda, both the Tutsis and Hutus were so distracted by anger and resentment that they missed countless opportunities for reconciliation and growth together as a nation independent of Belgian control. Creating a rivalry— or worsening an existing one—allows the true aggressor to act as an intermediary between the warring factions, extracting power and benefits from either side in return for their loyalty. It is in the aggressor's interest not to fight a single, strong, and united force, but a series of small, weak, and distracted ones. Worse still, people rarely notice what is really happening until the damage is already done, and the effects can take years to fix. It is just another form of control.

We can also put this strategy to powerful use when on the defensive against a number of allied aggressors. This is easiest when facing three or more allies; in general, the more joints to break and relationships to sour, the better. Although they may seem united on the surface, there is always some pain point between them. Try to pick out the ally that is likely to gain the short end of the stick in the alliance, and point that out to them. If two of them are from the same department, then isolate the third, because the other two are more likely to stay allied. Look for the most junior ally, or the most insecure and paranoid. Remember: Just because they are allied, it does not mean your foes are perfect friends. Every human relationship comes with baggage and resentments, and when your position is under threat, it's your job to find out what those are and twist the screw. The most effective way is to push emotional buttons, never engaging their rational faculties, because they will be least likely to control their reactions and do something that spoils the alliance for good. Such a Machiavellian approach might seem a contradiction of Social Intelligence, but this is war, and if you are to survive, sometimes you must be ruthless.

When you are the victim of a two-way alliance, it's often more difficult to get one of them to change sides. In the first place, two people or groups working together are likely to have stronger bonds. In the second place, if they defeat you, then the division of spoils is simple: cut two ways. However, the way that two- or three-way alliances usually work, events usually transpire to make one ally dominate over the others. If things are going in that direction, point it out to the weaker ally, but ensure you have evidence to back this up, or they'll see through you—if your survival odds are slim, then fabricate the evidence. Play to the weaker ally's suspicions and be specific. An effective way to rupture an alliance in this way is to talk about a private deal with one of the allies, and pass on the evidence of his double-dealing to the other ally. It rarely fails to produce a serious argument, giving you time to recover and gain your strength.

It is also possible to use the divide-and-conquer strategy to isolate a strong foe, weakening his base of support. When Ethiopia was under attack by the Italians in 1935, times were desperate. The recently crowned emperor Haile Selassie ruled a country that badly needed a modernised army. His people were happy to protect their homeland and put up a stout fight against the Italians, but it was no use. The fast-moving Italian tanks and troop transports ensured an easy victory, and they annexed Ethiopia into their existing African colonial holdings. Rather than get emotional or act rashly, Selassie appealed to the League of Nations in 1936. He stood tall and proud, delivering his appeal in his native tongue, not English or French. Italian delegates hurled insults and curses at Selassie, who did not react, but carried on speaking in a humble yet dignified manner. For the onlooking international community, this was yet more proof of the vulgarity and barbarism that characterised the fascist dictator Benito Mussolini's rule. Here was a solemn, gentle-speaking monarch who resembled a leader of any of the European powers, upsetting their usual misconception of a primitive tribal king. The League was ineffective and did not immediately come to Ethiopia's aid, but it joined Selassie in condemning Italy's use of chemical weapons, and Mussolini's empire became isolated. When the Allies finally liberated Ethiopia in the Second World War, Selassie was restored to power, his empire mostly intact and his power consolidated.

It is possible to reaffirm control over a series of groups whose loyalties are uncertain with a subtle application of this manoeuvre. US president Franklin D. Roosevelt was the absolute master of this. At the height of his New Deal programme, aimed to kick-start the depressed American economy, Roosevelt set up dozens of government agencies to enact and enforce his new policies. But past presidents had suffered from a kind of dependency on government departments, and Roosevelt hated being ganged up on. So he reversed the dynamic entirely by making these new agencies depend on him instead. In each department, he generally set up two leading groups with overlapping responsibility. Because neither one had all the power, and both were so busy defending their own interests, they completely relied on White House support. By creating agencies with intentionally fractured structures, he made himself the benefactor and ally of all the opposing factions. He minimised the possibility for bureaucratic aggrandisement, ensuring that civil servants focused on their jobs and made his New Deal programme a success.

By rearranging your group's subdivisions in this way, you shift the incentives so that each team depends on your approval and support. But be careful with this strategy, particularly when there is no reason to feel hostile. Remember that Roosevelt was a notorious control freak who needed to feel powerful at all times. When pushing his New Deal policies through, he was facing a large, bumbling bureaucracy that had every intention of opposing his sweeping changes. While splitting his departments gave

Roosevelt more control over them during his presidency, these departments later engaged in endless infighting, refusing to share information in an effort to gain supremacy over the others. He needed to use such serious measures, otherwise his presidency would have been a failure, and America might not have been able to recover as quickly as it did before the Second World War, when its unparalleled industrial capacity proved invaluable in defeating the Axis powers.

In a less serious situation, dividing up your forces in such a way will only make you seem insecure and tyrannical, and in the long run your junior leaders will come to resent you and and perhaps wrest your power away—the opposite of what you want. As narrated in Chapter 10, Ed Catmull and his leadership team built Pixar so that everyone felt empowered in their capacities, and given ownership of their projects. This produced far better results than if Catmull had created a chain of dependence out of an insecure need to feel in control. He was wiser, and Pixar became the fountain of creativity we know it for today.

An important part of the group disruption strategy is ensuring that you stay at the centre. Notice in each of the stories narrated so far, each player stood at the centre of the dispute, forcing all the divided factions to work with them. This can mean holding the literal central location, which the Austrian Empire exploited to great effect in the Napoleonic Wars. As battles raged between France and the other European powers, Austria was comparatively weak, but its position in the centre of the continent gave it great influence. Klemens von Metternich, Austria's foreign minister and later its head of government, did not bind his country into long-lasting entanglements. He knew that while military alliances seemed like good news on paper, they actually often gave one fewer options in the long run. Instead, Metternich built relationships with all the major powers on both sides. Austria was beholden to no one, and European leaders often sought their favour in breaking disputes and stalemates—an eminently powerful position.

When it came to Napoleon himself, Metternich didn't form an explicit military alliance with the great general, because he favoured stability, and in his eyes the French Revolution had left nothing but chaos and destruction in its wake. His approach was to form an emotional bond with Le Petit Corporal instead, by arranging for him to marry the Austrian archduke's daughter. When Austria and Russia pounced after his failed invasion of 1812, they caught Napoleon completely off-guard, since he had expected his royal marriage to count for something. All along, Metternich had been playing him and his rivals like a fiddle. Even after the Napoleonic Wars, Metternich continued to play with alliances, ensuring Austria's stability and influence in European affairs. He barred Russia from invading the Balkans and held a tight control over Prussian expansion.

Although these efforts proved counterproductive in the long-run, it ensured that Austria stayed relevant and strong over much of the nineteenth century. Whenever you face a pack of wolves, as Metternich did, do not bow to feelings of fear or panic just because they are strong in numbers. They want you on the back foot, unwilling to take the initiative out of fear. People—especially those who gather allies just to look tough and gang up on the weak—are more cowardly than you think. By staying steady and holding the central position, perhaps through some important position, you inevitably split the enemy alliance and force them to expose the joints binding them together. But more importantly, take back the initiative and strike early if you can. If you fail to act and allow such a strong and unified alliance to advance with full momentum, you'll be overwhelmed. Find their mutual disagreements, the sore points that make them emotional, and aggravate them with all your subtlety and cunning. You not only blunt their momentum, discouraging them from their aggressive attack, you also make them fearful, divided, and easier to pick off in detail. Particularly evil opponents will make you feel bad for doing this, but have no shame. Putting such a stout defence up against a strong alliance of bullies will empower you and inject new confidence into your cause. It is the most cunning application of strategy for the Socially Intelligent Warrior.

> When a startup fails, we often imagine it succumbing to predatory rivals in a competitive ecosystem. But every company is also its own ecosystem, and factional strife makes it vulnerable to outside threats. Internal conflict is like an autoimmune disease: the technical cause of death may be pneumonia, but the real cause remains hidden from plain view.
>
> — PETER THIEL

REVERSAL

Be careful when breaking alliances and double-crossing your foes that you don't earn a negative reputation. A reputation is nearly impossible to break once it has been established, and it will hold you back from developing positive relationships—the very opposite result we want to achieve by developing Social Intelligence. If you sense you are under a reputation attack, perhaps an application of the divide-and-conquer rule from an aggressor, always make a show of pointing out this behaviour to others. This reverses the dynamic back onto the aggressor, isolating them instead.

Astute readers will notice that this also proves an obvious

pitfall in the divide-and-conquer strategy, in that if you face a Socially Intelligent Warrior with an awareness for such dirty tricks, they will ferret you out and rightly punish you. Mitigate the possibility of such isolation by building strong alliances based on more than mere self-interest. Rather than being broken by trivial propaganda and muck-raking, such attacks actually strengthen your bonds and enable you to fight together as a team. Always remember: True Social Intelligence is your ultimate sword and shield.

AUTHOR'S NOTE

Thank you for reading my book. I sincerely appreciate the time you've put into reading through to the end. But our journey together has only just begun. By applying what you have read and developing true Social Intelligence, you can make your working life less stressful and more productive.

As a faithful reader, you're also entitled to a special gift I've put together. If you would like to receive an exclusive guide describing how I wrote this book, then please visit socialintelligencebook.com, or just send me an email at jon@socialintelligencebook.com.

I always love hearing from my readers. If you have applied Social Intelligence to your workplace and found positive benefits, then let me know via email or social media. Hearing that you have made your workplace better will have made this whole project worthwhile.

Jonathan Baldie, August 2019

ALSO BY JONATHAN BALDIE

The 24 Laws of Storytelling: A Practical Handbook for Great Storytellers

www.ingramcontent.com/pod-product-compliance
Lightning Source LLC
Chambersburg PA
CBHW022052210326
41519CB00054B/317